Betty Crocker

Baking
for
Today

WILEY

Wiley Publishing, Inc.

Library of Congress Cataloging-in-Publication Data:

Betty Crocker baking for today : always in style, always gold medal.
    p. cm.
Includes index.
ISBN 0-7645-7613-5 (hardcover : alk. paper)
ISBN 0-7645-8997-0 (custom edition)
1. Baking. I. Title: Baking for today. II. Crocker, Betty.
TX763.B48 2005
641.8'15--dc22
                        2004011941

Manufactured in the United States of America

10 9 8 7 6 5 4 3

General Mills, Inc.

Director, Book and Online Publishing: Kim Walter

Manager, Book Publishing: Lois L. Tlusty

Editor: Cheri Olerud

Recipe Development and Testing: Betty Crocker Kitchens

Food Styling: Betty Crocker Kitchens

Photography: General Mills Photo Studios

Wiley Publishing, Inc.

Publisher: Natalie Chapman

Executive Editor: Anne Ficklen

Editor: Kristi Hart

Production Director: Diana Cisek

Cover Design: Jeff Faust

Interior Design and Layout: Mauna Eichner and Lee Fukui

Photography Art Direction: Becky Landes

Manufacturing Manager: Kevin Watt

 For consistent baking results, the Betty Crocker Kitchens recommend Gold Medal® Flour.

Find more great ideas and
shop for name-brand housewares at
BettyCrocker.com

DEAR FRIENDS,

Heard the news? Gold Medal, the award-winning flour that has been around for over a century, is turning 125 years old! Our celebration includes this endearing collection of the 150 best, all-time classic and fresh, new recipes of the last 125 years.

It all started in 1880 when Washburn Crosby received the esteemed Gold Medal award—Gold Medal flour was born. Since then, Gold Medal flour has made history happen numerous times. Included in this cookbook are historical highlights about especially notable recipes and memorable milestones.

The consistent, high-quality baking results and treasury of recipes that Gold Medal brought to home bakers more than a century ago are still relevant to baking today. In fact, imagine the inviting aroma and delicious flavor of fresh-from the-oven homemade bread or a warm batch of your favorite melt-in-your-mouth cookies—is there anything better? Home baking connects you to family and friends and allows you to share your love of baking with others.

So go ahead, let Gold Medal, the same flour that won the award 125 years ago, along with this wonderful collection of time-treasured classic and soon-to-become favorites transform your kitchen into the heart of your home.

Warmly,

Betty Crocker

Contents

At the Heart of the Kitchen

Home-baked breads, cakes, cookies and muffins are something to treasure—a gift that warms the heart. Baked goodies provide a rich, rewarding accomplishment, where many traditions, recipes and good times are captured and passed down from one generation to another. Let the inviting aromas and delicious flavors of home baking connect you to others, and share your love of baking with your family, neighbors and friends.

The Best Flour for all Bakers

There are different types of scratch bakers. In this cookbook, there are recipes that appeal to all of them: **enthusiastic novices**, very eager to learn; **experienced bakers** who love to bake, enjoy a new recipe challenge and bake for others; **weekend bakers** who take time on the weekend to fully engage in the art (and science) of baking; **artisan bread bakers** who heartily love the satisfaction of bread baking; **heritage bakers** who are inspired by old-fashioned recipes and the history that goes with them; **cookie bakers**, who just love to bake and share cookies and make the family's favorites over and over.

You'll also find it very rewarding to include your **little bakers** whenever you get out your bag of Gold Medal® flour. Let them have fun in the kitchen while you share your love of baking with them. Learning to bake and cook is a lifelong skill, enhances children's self-esteem and gives them a fulfilling sense of accomplishment. You'll find a whole chapter of recipes that kids will love to dig into; so go ahead, get out the flour and baking pans and bake up a storm! Besides enjoying tasty foods and good times, you'll also create cherished moments and fond memories sure to last a lifetime.

The Gold Medal Promise

Gold Medal, the flour that won a gold medal award for excellence in 1880, promises the same superior flour today. Gold Medal flour is made from the highest quality wheat harvested in the heart of America, the Midwest. All the recipes in this cookbook have been kitchen-tested in the Betty Crocker Kitchens to consistently perform to their highest standards and to ensure the same foolproof results in your home kitchen. Today, Gold Medal is still the country's premier flour, perfect for any baking occasion.

Timeless and Timely

In this cookbook, you'll find timeless **classic** recipes, some that were as popular a century ago as they are today. Gingerbread, Pound Cake, Lemon Squares, Chocolate Crinkles and other classic favorites are just a few of these gems. You'll also find timely new recipes that appeal to the trends and tastes of today, like Chocolate-Raspberry Triangles, Quick Chocolate Chip Strips, Currant Scones and Almond Biscotti. Each recipe includes a timely tip called "Baking for Today" to help you make successful substitutions, give your finished baked goods a special look, store and reheat your goodies or suggest a simple way to make the recipe easier or quicker. History lovers will find "timeless" information on the heritage of flour and milling and interesting facts about the recipe and evolution of baking.

It All Starts with a Kernel

Wheat is the world's most important food crop. Hundreds of millions of people throughout the world depend on foods made from the kernels of the wheat plant.

To produce wheat flour, millers grind the wheat kernels into a fine powder called flour. The endosperm, the inside part of the kernel, is present in all flours. The bran, the outer coating of the kernel, and wheat germ, however, are present only in whole wheat flour. They give flour a distinct flavor, texture and color. Wheat germ, the sprouting section of the seed, contains some fat that can cause the flour to become rancid and limits the storage life of whole wheat flour.

The Gold Medal Family of Flour

Gold Medal flour is milled from a combination of hard and soft wheats. Hard wheat is higher in protein and gluten, which provide structure to baked products, especially yeast breads. Soft wheat is lower in protein, forms a weaker gluten structure and results in a more tender product; it's well suited for cakes, pastries and biscuits. By combining the two types of flours, Gold Medal all-purpose flour is the ideal flour for all types of baking.

ALL-PURPOSE FLOUR is suitable for all types of baking; the recipes in this cookbook were developed to use all-purpose flour. Small amounts of bleaching agents are used to whiten the flour and improve baking results. If using all-purpose flour in recipes calling for self-rising flour, add 1 1/2 teaspoons baking powder and 1/2 teaspoon salt for each cup of flour.

UNBLEACHED FLOUR is all-purpose flour without bleaching agents. You can use unbleached flour interchangeably in all recipes calling for all-purpose flour. Because it is not as white as all-purpose flour, breads and other white baked goods will have a creamy color.

SELF-RISING FLOUR is all-purpose flour with baking powder and salt added. The biscuit recipes in this cookbook have been tested with self-rising flour and include information on how to substitute it for the all-purpose flour. Using recipes that are specifically tested and developed with self-rising flour ensures success.

BETTER FOR BREAD™ FLOUR is made from a special blend of wheats higher in protein than the wheats used in all-purpose flour. Protein produces gluten, which gives structure to baked goods made with yeast. Better for Bread flour is excellent for yeast breads and is ideal in automatic bread machines, but you can also use it for quick breads

WHEAT KERNEL

A kernel of wheat is a storehouse of nutrients because it contains significant amounts of protein, complex carbohydrates, B vitamins and iron. A kernel is made up of three parts: the **bran** (outer part), the **endosperm** (inside white part) and the **wheat germ** (embryo).

Endosperm
• Provides energy
• Carbohydrates, protein

Bran
• "Outer shell" protects seed
• Fiber, B vitamins, trace minerals

Germ
• Nourishment for the seed
• Antioxidants, vitamin E, fiber, B vitamins

and cookies. Unbleached Better for Bread flour is also available.

BETTER FOR BREAD™ WHEAT BLEND FLOUR is a specially formulated 100-percent hard wheat and wheat bran flour. The hard wheat provides the gluten structure needed for bread baking, and the wheat bran gives the texture, taste and appearance of wheat bread. If you bake whole wheat bread often, this is the flour for you. It produces loaves that are higher in volume and lighter in texture than those made with 100 percent whole wheat flour. Better for Bread wheat blend can be substituted cup for cup in recipes calling for all-purpose, whole wheat and bread flours.

WHOLE WHEAT FLOUR is a whole-grain flour milled from the complete wheat kernel (bran, germ and endosperm), giving it a wheat flavor and appearance. Whole wheat flour produces great breads, quick breads, cakes, cookies and pie crusts. It should not be sifted because sifting will cause it to lose the flavorful, nutritious particles. A few recipes in this cookbook call specifically for whole wheat flour, but if you would like to use it in place of all-purpose flour, just substitute whole wheat flour for half of the all-purpose flour in a recipe.

GOLD MEDAL WONDRA® is a quick-mixing all-purpose flour that is milled into granules so it pours freely and mixes instantly in liquid. Wondra flour makes great gravies, sauces, popovers and batters and can be substituted cup for cup in recipes calling for all-purpose flour. Some doughs will look and feel different from those made with all-purpose flour, but the result will be the same. If the dough seems dry at first, work it with your hands until it holds together.

Flour and Fat in Baking Q&A

We've gathered the answers to some of the most frequently asked flour and fat baking questions to help you bake successfully in your kitchen.

Q. How should I measure flour?

A. Spoon flour without sifting into a dry-ingredient measuring cup and level it with a straight-edged knife or spatula. Do not pack or tap into the cup because it will make the flour too heavy and cause you to overmeasure. All flours are sifted many times during milling, so there's no need to sift.

Q. How should I store flour?

A. All flours purchased in paper bags should be stored in airtight canisters in a cool, dry place. Gold Medal flour purchased in the resealable zip-top plastic bag can be stored right in the plastic bag in a cool, dry place.

Q. How long can I keep flour?

A. Gold Medal all-purpose, unbleached, Better for Bread and Wondra flours should be used within eighteen months if stored at room temperature. Self-rising flour should be used within nine months because the baking powder and soda will lose their strength. Whole wheat and wheat blend flours become rancid sooner, so they should be used within six to eight months. If flour is kept over an extended time, it is recommended that it be stored in a moisture-proof, vapor-proof bag or container in the refrigerator or freezer up to one year. Bring flour to room temperature before using.

Q. Is flour affected by humidity?

A. Flour does pick up and lose moisture over a period of time, and humidity will cause flour to absorb moisture. Yeast bread recipes often give a range of the amount of flour (for example, 3 1/2 to 4 cups). Start with the lower amount and gradually add more flour as needed. You may find that doughs and batters are more sticky, soft or fluid if the humidity is high. You can add small amounts of additional flour to make the dough or batter easier to work with. As a general guideline, during cold, dry weather, you'll often need less flour when making a dough, and in hot, humid weather, you'll need a bit more.

Q. Can flours be substituted cup for cup?

A. For most recipes, Gold Medal all-purpose, Better for Bread, unbleached, wheat blend and Wondra flours can be substituted cup for cup. You can substitute whole wheat flour for half of the all-purpose flour. When substituting all-purpose flour for cake flour, decrease the flour by 2 tablespoons per cup. However, substituting all-purpose flour isn't recommended for delicate cakes such as angel food, chiffon and sponge cakes unless the cake has been tested with all-purpose flour.

Q. Can I use margarine or butter-margarine blends in place of butter for baking?

A. Margarine can be substituted for butter, so recipes in this cookbook call for butter or margarine. If margarine doesn't give a satisfactory result, only butter is listed as an ingredient. Use only margarines sold in the stick form for baking. Margarines sold in a tub have air and water added so the amount of fat has been reduced. Butter-margarine blends sold in sticks can be used for baking. However, the blends sold in tubs shouldn't be used because the added air and water change the finished baked goods.

High Altitude Baking

The decrease in air pressure at higher altitudes changes the way foods cook and bake. Considerations that affect baking at high altitude include:

- Gases expand more from the leavening

- Liquids boil at a lower temperature
- Liquids evaporate more quickly

In baked goods, these changes translate into longer bake times, collapse of structure, drier finished products and possible overbrowning. Yeast bread dough rises more rapidly and can easily overrise, so it requires shorter rising times. In general, biscuits, cookies and muffins require the fewest modifications.

Common high altitude adjustments from the sea level recipe include one or more of the following:

- Increased oven temperature
- Increased amount of flour
- Increased amount of liquid
- Decreased amount of leavening
- Decreased amount of sugar
- Decreased amount of oil or fat
- Larger pan
- Longer bake time

There are no hard and fast rules to follow when baking at high altitude. Changes to recipes depend upon the type of food you are baking and the proportion of ingredients. All of the recipes in this book have been tested and adjusted for baking at high altitude, and each tells you if changes are needed for high altitude baking.

Ready, Set, Bake

If you're familiar with baking, you know that although baking is an art, it's also a science. Like any science, it's important to be accurate and consistent, particularly when it comes to measuring—and not all ingredients are measured the same way.

Measuring Ingredients

BUTTER: The markings on the paper or foil wrapper of a stick of butter show tablespoon and cup markings; you can use a sharp knife to cut off the amount you need. Or instead, measure by pressing it firmly into a dry measuring cup with a spoon or rubber spatula, then leveling off the excess with a straight-edged knife or spatula.

SHORTENING: Measure by pressing it firmly into a dry-ingredient measuring cup with a spoon or rubber spatula, then leveling off the excess with a straight-edged knife or spatula. You can also buy shortening in sticks and measure it using the measurements on the paper or foil wrapper.

SUGAR: Spoon granulated and powdered sugar into a dry-ingredient measuring cup and level off. Press brown sugar firmly into a dry-ingredient measuring cup so it holds the shape of the cup when it is removed.

LIQUIDS: Use a clear glass or clear plastic liquid-ingredient measuring cup set on a level surface. To read the amount, bend down so your eye is level with the markings on the cup. You can also buy new angled measuring cups that let you read the measurement quickly without bending, making it easier to quickly tell how much liquid is in the cup. When measuring a liquid in a measuring spoon, fill the spoon only to the top.

SPICES AND DRIED HERBS: Lightly fill the measuring spoon just to the top. A *dash* or *pinch* is less than 1/8 teaspoon, which is the smallest amount you can measure accurately using standard measuring spoons. However, there are specialty measuring spoons that include 1/8 and 1/16 measurements.

The Scoop on Bakeware

There are many types of baking equipment, and the materials can make a big difference in the success of your baked goods. In general:

- SHINY BAKEWARE reflects heat, slowing the browning, and is recommended by the Betty Crocker Kitchens for baking cookies, bars and cakes. Shiny bakeware, including aluminum, tin and stainless steel, will give you tender, light brown crusts and softer cookies that spread slightly more.

- DARK AND DULL-FINISH BAKEWARE absorbs more heat, so baked goods brown more quickly and evenly. Manufacturers of dark bakeware may recommend reducing the oven temperature by 25°F for some baked items to compensate for this. Dull-finish, including dull aluminum, tin and glass, is recommended for baking pies and breads. Pie crusts will evenly brown on the bottom as well as on top. Breads brown evenly and have a crisper crust.

- BLACK STEEL PANS give breads a crisp, dark crust and are often used for French bread and breadsticks to give them their distinctive crunch. Black steel popover pans are the best because the popovers will have a crisp, evenly browned crust.

- SILICONE PANS, the newest in bakeware, are also recommended by the Betty Crocker Kitchens. Soft and flexible, they are available in many fun colors and shapes such as round cake pans, fluted tube cake pans, muffin pans, mini loaf pans and more. They give even browning, can withstand extreme heat and are safe for the dishwasher, microwave and freezer. Because the pans are flexible, place them on a cookie sheet to easily remove from the oven. Use hot pads when moving pans from the cookie sheet to the cooling rack. Spray pans with cooking spray before the batter or dough is added so the baked food doesn't stick. Baked foods easily pop out after cooling by pushing on the bottom of the pan. Silicone bakeware is available in retail stores nationwide and in the Betty Crocker Catalog at www.BettyCrocker.com.

Essential Baking Equipment

Having the right baking utensils and equipment helps make baking enjoyable. Here are both some essential baking items and some fun-to-have items to help make your baking experience successful:

Measuring

Chef's or cook's knife

Glass or clear plastic measuring cups (for liquid ingredients)

Graduated nesting measuring cups (for dry ingredients)

Graduated measuring spoons

Small rubber spatula

Straight-edge metal spatula

Mixing

Electric mixer

Flatware forks, teaspoons and tablespoons

Hand beater

Large rubber spatula

Mixing bowls (set of three)

Spoons (wooden and plastic)

Wire whisk

Baking

13 x 9-inch rectangular baking pan

8- and 9-inch round and square baking pans

Fluted tube cake pan

Cake tester or toothpicks

Cookie and biscuit cutters

Cookie sheet(s)

Loaf pans

Muffin pan

Pancake turner

Pastry brush

Pie plate

Popover pan

Pot holders

Rolling pin

Timer

Wire cooling rack(s)

Fun-to-Have Baking Equipment

There are many new **timely** as well as **timeless** kitchen gadgets that are fun to have for baking and serving your baked treats. For the latest in kitchen and baking gadgets, shop your favorite kitchen equipment store or buy on the Internet.

ANGLED LIQUID MEASURING CUP has a unique angled rim inside the cup so you can quickly and accurately read the measurement without bending down to see it.

CAKE CUTTER AND SERVER takes the guesswork out of cutting and serving cake and dessert. The three-sided blade cuts down through the cake or dessert, and the two handles gently squeeze together to lift the serving piece. It is available in a V shape for round cakes and rectangular shape for square or rectangular cakes.

CERAMIC BAKING STONE is heated in a hot oven before bread or pizza dough is placed on it. The ceramic holds the heat so breads are crustier on the outside and pizza crust is crisper on the bottom.

COFFEE GRINDER for grinding whole spices. Be sure to use the grinder only for spices and not also for coffee.

COOKIE DOUGH OR ICE-CREAM SCOOP with a spring action to make uniform-sized cookies that will bake evenly. (See page 19 for more information.) A larger scoop also works well for filling muffin cups and individual tart pans.

COOKIE DROPPER looks like a pancake turner with a nylon "pusher" to push uniformly sized portions of cookie dough onto the cookie sheet. Cleans easily.

COOKING TORCH is a small butane torch that can be used to caramelize sugar, melt cheese or add more browning to tops of meringues.

JUMBO COOKIE SPATULA has a wide, flexible blade with a beveled edge that easily slides under baked cookies. Can also be used for turning pancakes.

KITCHEN SCISSORS for cutting up dried fruits and fresh herbs and trimming edge of unbaked pie pastry before fluting.

MARBLE PASTRY BOARD is excellent for doughs because the board stays cool and does not absorb fat or moisture. This helps prevent dough from becoming warm and sticky during kneading, shaping or rolling.

MINI-CHOPPER can be electric or manual. Used to chop nuts, dried fruits and fresh herbs.

NONSKID MIXING BOWL has a rubber ring inserted in the bottom of the bowl to help keep it from moving.

Offset spatula (or spreader) has a metal blade with a bend in it. It is great for spreading batters evenly in a pan and for frosting cakes and bars in the pan.

Parchment paper is a heavy paper that is resistant to grease and moisture and is great for lining baking pans and cookie sheets. It also makes disposable decorating bags.

Pastry blender has five or six sturdy U-shaped wires that are attached to a wooden handle. It is used to quickly and easily cut fat into flour and other dry mixtures.

Pastry cloth is a large canvas cloth used for rolling delicate cookie and pastry doughs. Flour is rubbed into the cloth to make it a nonstick surface. Rolling pin stockinets are available that slip over the rolling pin; flour is rubbed into the stockinet. Both the cloth and stockinet must be thoroughly washed before storing because they can become rancid due to the fat in the dough. Check kitchen stores for round boards with a removable, elasticized linen pastry cloth marked with circles for various crust dimensions.

Pastry scraper is a wide metal blade with a rolled handle used to scrape dough and excess flour from the kneading and rolling surface. Also good for lifting and moving chopped ingredients from a cutting board to a bowl or pan.

Silicone baking mat is a flexible, nonstick liner that fits on a cookie sheet. It eliminates the need for greasing and is easy to clean. It is excellent for delicate cookies that you don't want to brown on the bottom or edges. For regular cookies, the bake time may be a little longer than when using just a cookie sheet.

Silicone pot holders are innovative because they are very flexible, have raised spots for gripping, withstand very high temperatures and can be washed in hot, soapy water or the dishwasher. They also make 1 great trivet and can be used as a jar opener.

Specialty fluted tube cake pans are available in a variety of designs to create fun and interesting cakes. They are also available as mini-pans, which are great for individual servings.

Specialty muffin pans are available in mini and jumbo sizes and as muffin-top pans.

Springform pan has a removable bottom and spring-release side that is easy to remove from the baked item.

Tart pan is a round or rectangular pan, often with a removable bottom, that has scalloped decorative edges and is used to bake tarts. Tart pans are available in regular size, individual size (call tartlets) or mini size.

The Basics on Yeast Breads

Who can resist the aroma of fresh-baked bread? Its mouthwatering smell just says "home." Even if you're new to baking, it's an aroma you can easily bring into your home. Making yeast breads isn't hard; it just takes time for rising, and the results are well worth the wait.

Yeast Bread Ingredients

What does it take to make yeast bread? Flour, yeast, water, salt, sugar and, for some doughs, fat, are the most common bread ingredients. You'll also need a little time to mix the dough, knead it so it is smooth and let it rise. Kneading and shaping bread dough can be very relaxing, and of course, you also get to enjoy the results!

Flour: See page 7.

Yeast: Yeast is a living organism that converts its food to alcohol and carbon dioxide. It's the carbon dioxide bubbles that make dough rise. Yeast is very sensitive—too much heat will kill it, and cold will prevent it from growing. Check the expiration date on the yeast package before using it. If you're using quick active dry yeast, rising times may be shorter.

LIQUIDS: Water and milk are used most often. Water gives bread a crisper crust; milk provides a velvety texture and adds nutrients.

SALT: Salt is needed to control the growth of the yeast and to prevent the dough from rising too much, which can cause the bread to collapse.

SWEETENERS: Sugar, honey and molasses provide "food" for the yeast to help it grow, add flavor and help brown the crust. Artificial sweeteners aren't good for yeast baking because they won't "feed" the yeast.

FAT: Butter, margarine, shortening and vegetable oil make bread tender. Butter and margarine also add flavor.

Signature Bread Crusts

Just before baking, give your bread one of these professional finishing touches:

- For a **shiny crust,** brush the top of the bread with an egg or egg white beaten with a little water. If desired, sprinkle with poppy or sesame seed or oats.
- For a **softer, deep golden brown crust,** brush with softened butter or margarine.
- For a **crisp crust,** brush or spray lightly with water.
- For a **soft, tender crust,** brush with milk.

Bread Machine Tips

Enjoy the old-fashioned aroma and goodness of home-baked bread the fun and easy way: using an electric bread machine! Use these tips to help you make the best bread-machine bread.

- Read your bread machine manual from start to finish. Add ingredients in the order listed by the manufacturer.

- Measure ingredients with standard measuring cups and spoons. Even little variations can dramatically affect the finished loaf.

- Ingredients should be at room temperature, except for those normally stored in the refrigerator, like milk, sour cream and eggs.

- Use bread machine yeast because its finer granulation helps the yeast mix more thoroughly during mixing and kneading.

- Peek only during mixing and kneading. If you open the machine during rising or baking, the loaf can collapse.

- Be sure the yeast doesn't come in contact with liquid or wet ingredients when using the delay cycle. Don't use the delay cycle with recipes that use eggs, fresh dairy products (butter and margarine can be used), honey, meats or fresh fruits and vegetables because bacteria can grow while these ingredients stand in the bread machine for several hours.

- If you get the urge to experiment by changing the ingredients, make just one change at a time so you can see the result.

- Keep your bread machine away from drafts and areas of your house where heat and humidity fluctuate, and keep the area around your bread machine open for good ventilation.

FASTER DOUGH RISING

To help yeast dough rise a little faster, place the covered bowl on a wire rack over a bowl of very warm water. Or to let dough rise in the microwave, fill a measuring cup with water and microwave until the water boils; place the bowl of dough in the microwave with the steaming water.

Cutting Bread

After you've spent time baking fresh homemade bread, you'll want to know the easiest way to slice it.

- Place loaf on a cutting board. Slice with a serrated bread knife or an electric knife with a light sawing motion to avoid tearing bread. If bread is very fresh or still warm, turn it on its side to avoid squashing the top.

- Cut round loaves into wedges or slices.

- Add a kid-friendly touch by cutting slices into strips or cutting with cookie cutters into fun shapes.

The Basics on Quick Breads

Quick breads, including muffins, biscuits and scones, are quick and easy to make because they are leavened with baking powder or baking soda rather than with slower-acting yeast. To make sure your quick breads are the best they can be:

- Check the expiration date on your containers of baking powder and baking soda; it's best to use fresh ingredients because your quick breads will not rise properly if the baking powder or soda is old.

- Grease only the bottoms of the pans for muffins and quick breads so that the batter doesn't form a lip (overhanging or hard, dry edge) during baking. For some muffin recipes, however, you will have to grease the whole cup so the muffins won't stick, so be sure to follow the recipe. Better yet, use paper baking cups for easy cleanup.

- Mix according to each recipe's directions; some batters are mixed until smooth, others just until the ingredients are moistened. If mixed too much, the finished muffin or quick bread can become tough.

The Basics on Cakes

Any occasion can call for cake, from birthdays to weddings to just surprising the family with a homemade treat. There are almost as many cakes as there are occasions to celebrate with them.

Mixing Cakes

Cake recipes in this cookbook were tested with electric hand mixers. If using a heavy-duty stand mixer, follow the manufacturer's directions for the speed setting because overmixing the batter causes tunnels or a sunken center.

You can also mix cake batter by hand with a spoon. Stir the ingredients until they're well combined, then beat 150 strokes for each minute of beating time (3 minutes = 450 strokes). If a cake isn't beaten long enough, it will be lower in volume.

Baking Cakes

- Shiny metal pans are the best choice for baking cakes. They reflect heat away from the cake for a tender, light brown crust.

- Use the pan size recommended in the recipe. To determine the pan size, measure the length and width from *inside* edge to *inside* edge; not across the bottom of the pan. If the pan is too large, the cake will be flat and may overbake. If it is too small, the cake may bake over the edges and not get done in the center.

- Fill cake pans half full. To determine how much batter a specialty pan (such as heart-shaped) can hold, fill it with water, then measure the water. Use half that amount of batter. Make cupcakes with any extra batter.

- Bake cakes on an oven rack placed in the center of the oven.

- Cakes are done when a toothpick poked in the center comes out clean. Cool cakes completely on a wire rack away from drafts before frosting or cutting. Serve cakes warm only when the recipe suggests it.

Frosting Cakes

- Cool cakes completely before frosting them. On a hot cake, the frosting will become too soft or melt.

- Frosting should be soft enough to spread without running down the sides of the cake. If frosting is too stiff, it will pull and tear the cake surface, adding crumbs to the frosting. If frosting is too thin, add more powdered sugar, a couple of tablespoons at a time; if too thick, add a few drops of water or milk.

- Stick butter, margarine or butter blends are recommended for frostings. Tubs of margarine, whipped butter or butter blends contain more water and/or air and less fat, so frostings made with them are too soft.

- To frost easily, use a flexible metal spatula. Use a light touch to help prevent cake layers from sliding and squishing out the filling between layers.

Cutting Cakes

LAYER CAKES: Use a sharp, long, thin knife. If the frosting sticks to the knife, dip the knife in hot water and wipe with a damp paper towel after cutting each slice.

ANGEL FOOD, CHIFFON AND POUND CAKES: Use a long, serrated knife in a sawing motion, or use an electric knife.

Storing Cakes

- Cool unfrosted cakes completely before covering and storing to keep the top from becoming sticky.

- Store cakes with a creamy powdered sugar frosting at room temperature, loosely covered with foil, plastic wrap or waxed paper or in a "cake saver."

- During humid weather, refrigerate cakes with very moist ingredients, such as chopped apples, applesauce, shredded carrots or zucchini, banana or pumpkin. If stored at room temperature, mold can grow quickly.

- Store cakes with cream cheese frostings or whipped cream toppings or fillings in the refrigerator.

The Basics on Pies

Everyone loves pie, and baking great pies doesn't have to be hard. Even a beginning cook can make a blue-ribbon pie with just a little practice and these expert tips:

Easy-Does-It Mixing

- Use the fat called for in the recipe; shortening is the type of fat most often used and results in a flaky crust. Pastry and crusts contain enough fat that you don't have to grease pie plates.

- With a pastry blender or by pulling two table knives through ingredients in opposite directions, cut shortening into flour and salt until particles are the size of small peas.

- Mix only until all ingredients are worked in. If you overwork pastry dough, it can become tough.

- For easier rolling, after you've made the pastry dough and shaped it into a flattened round, wrap it tightly

DRIZZLE IT!

Making beautiful drizzles of glaze is easy. Drizzle glaze from the tip of a flatware teaspoon. Or pour the glaze into a resealable plastic food-storage bag; snip off a tiny corner and gently squeeze the bag, moving it back and forth over the top of the cake. Make the hole bigger if you want a thicker drizzle.

and refrigerate for at least 45 minutes or overnight. This helps the fat to solidify (for a flakier crust), the gluten to relax and the moisture to be absorbed evenly.

Rolling the Pastry

- With a floured rolling pin, roll the pastry on a lightly floured surface or pastry cloth into a circle that's two inches larger than the upside-down pie plate you are using.

- Roll the pastry from the center to the outside edge in all directions, lifting and turning pastry occasionally to keep it from sticking. To keep the edge from becoming too thin, use less pressure on the rolling pin as it approaches the edge. If the pastry begins to stick, rub more flour, a little at a time, on the rolling surface and rolling pin.

- Fold pastry into fourths, and place it in the pie plate with the point in the center of the plate. Unfold and gently ease into the plate, being careful not to stretch pastry, which would cause it to shrink when baked.

- Or instead of folding pastry, you can roll pastry loosely around the rolling pin and transfer to the pie plate. Unroll pastry and ease into plate.

Showstopping Top Crusts

- Spoon or pour the filling into the pastry-lined pie plate. Trim the bottom pastry so that it's only 1/2 inch wider than the pie plate.

- Roll out the top pastry, and cut small slits in it to allow steam to escape. Fold the pastry into fourths, or roll it around the rolling pin, then carefully place it over the filling; unfold to cover filling.

- Trim edge of top pastry to one inch; fold under and press lightly on rim of pie plate.

- Form a stand-up rim, pressing with fingers.

- You can add special touches to top crusts before baking. However, these pie crusts may brown more quickly. If this happens, put a sheet of foil loosely on top of the pie to slow the browning.

  - SHINY CRUST: Brush crust with milk.
  - SUGARY CRUST: Brush crust lightly with water; sprinkle with granulated sugar or white coarse sugar crystals (decorating sugar).
  - GLAZED CRUST: Brush crust lightly with a beaten egg or egg yolk mixed with a little water.

Baking Pies

- Choose a heat-resistant glass pie plate or a dull-finish aluminum pie pan; don't use a shiny pie pan because your pie will have a soggy bottom crust.

- The most common pie plate size is nine inches. The recipes in this cookbook were developed with nine-inch pie plates that hold about five cups of ingredients. We sometimes use up to eight cups of fruit for a

PASTRY CLOTH FOR ROLLING PASTRY

Using a pastry cloth and a rolling pin cover, called a stockinet, makes rolling pastry easy because the dough doesn't stick to the rolling surface or rolling pin. Use a lint-free kitchen towel if you don't have a pastry cloth.

Secure the pastry cloth or kitchen towel around a large cutting board (at least 12 x 12 inches) with masking tape. Or tape the cloth or towel securely to a flat working surface. Slip the stockinet on the rolling pin. Rub flour into both the cloth and the stockinet; this prevents sticking and working the flour into the pastry. Roll as directed above.

two-crust pie to give a full baked pie, and the fruit will cook down somewhat during baking.

- Pies are baked at high temperatures (375°F to 425°F) so that the rich pastry becomes flaky and golden brown and the filling cooks all the way through.

- To prevent the pie edge from getting too brown, cover it before baking with a strip of foil carefully folded over the edge or use an edge protector ring. Remove the foil 15 minutes before the end of the bake time so the edge browns.

- If the top crust is getting too brown and the pie isn't done, place a piece of foil on top of the pie to help prevent further browning.

Storing Pies

- Store pies that contain eggs, such as pumpkin and cream pies, in the refrigerator and use within three to five days.

- Fruit pies and pecan pies can be loosely covered and stored at room temperature up to three days.

Freezing Pies

Many pies can be frozen. Pecan and pumpkin pies need to be baked before freezing; fruit pies can be frozen unbaked or baked. Use these tips when freezing pies:

- Cream pies, custard pies and pies with meringue toppings can't be frozen because they break down and become watery.

- Cool baked pies completely before freezing. Place pies in the freezer uncovered. When completely frozen, wrap tightly in foil or place in a resealable plastic freezer bag.

- Freeze baked pies up to four months; unbaked pies up to three months.

- To heat *unbaked* pies: Unwrap and bake frozen pie at 475°F for 15 minutes; reduce oven temperature to 375°F and bake for 45 minutes longer or until center is bubbly.

- To heat *baked* pies: Unwrap and bake frozen pie at 325°F for 45 minutes or until thawed and warm.

The Basics on Cookies and Bars

Who doesn't love homemade cookies and bars? Not only are they easy to bake, they're also portable and fun to eat.

Mixing Cookies and Bars

- Use the stick form of butter or margarine for best results. Tubs of margarine, whipped butter or butter

MAKE A LATTICE TOP CRUST

Cut top pastry into strips about 1/2 inch wide. You can use a sharp knife or pastry cutting wheel to do this.

FOR A CLASSIC LATTICE, place 5 to 7 strips across filling in pie plate. Starting in center, weave cross-strips alternately over and under first strips to create lattice design. Trim ends of strips. Fold trimmed edge of bottom crust over ends of strips, forming a high stand-up rim; seal and flute.

FOR AN EASY LATTICE, place 5 to 7 strips across filling. Place cross-strips over tops of first strips instead of weaving them. Trim ends of strips. Fold trimmed edge of bottom crust over ends of strips, forming a high stand-up rim; seal and flute.

blends contain more water and/or air and less fat, so cookies made with them will be soft, puffy and tough and will dry out quickly.

- Most cookie and bar recipes call for softened butter or margarine. Perfectly softened butter should give gently to pressure (you should be able to leave a fingerprint and slight indentation on the butter), but it shouldn't be soft in appearance. Butter that is too soft or melted results in dough that is too soft, causing cookies to spread too much during baking. You can let butter soften at room temperature for 30 to 45 minutes, or soften it in the microwave.

- An electric mixer or a spoon can be used to mix dough for most cookie and bar recipes. Sugar, fats and liquid can easily be mixed together with an electric mixer. Flour and other dry ingredients should be mixed on very low speed or by hand to prevent overmixing, which can result in tougher cookies.

Selecting Cookie Sheets

Many types of cookie sheets are available, and choosing the right cookie sheet adds to your success when baking cookies. Having at least three or four cookie sheets to use is helpful. When one batch of cookies is finished baking, another is ready to go!

SHINY SMOOTH-SURFACE OR TEXTURED ALUMINUM COOKIE SHEETS are recommended for baking cookies. These sheets reflect heat, letting cookies bake evenly and brown properly. The recipes in this book were tested using shiny aluminum cookie sheets.

INSULATED COOKIE SHEETS help prevent cookies from turning too dark on the bottom and edges. Cookies on these sheets may take longer to bake, the bottoms will be light colored and the cookies may not brown as much overall. Cookies may be difficult to remove from these cookie sheets because the cookie bottom is more tender, so it helps to wait about one minute after removing cookies from the oven before taking them off the sheet.

NONSTICK AND DARK-SURFACE COOKIE SHEETS absorb heat. Cookies may be smaller in diameter and more rounded because the dough sets before it can spread for a nicely shaped cookie. The tops, and especially the bottoms, will be more browned, and the bottoms may be hard. Check cookies at the minimum bake time so they don't get too brown or burn.

Choosing Pans for Bars

- Shiny metal pans are recommended for baking bars. They reflect the heat away from the bars, preventing the crust from getting too brown and hard.

- Use the exact size of pan called for in a recipe. Bars baked in pans that are too big become hard and overcooked, and those baked in pans that are too small can be doughy in the center and hard on the edges.

- Pans can sometimes get scratched when bars are cut with a metal knife, so try using a plastic knife.

QUICK PAN CLEANUP!

Line baking pans with foil for super-quick cleanup and to help cut bars and brownies evenly. To line baking pans with foil, turn the pan upside down, tear off a piece of foil longer than the pan and shape the foil around the pan; remove foil. Flip the pan over and gently fit the shaped foil into the pan. When the bars are cool, just lift them out of the pan by the foil "handles," peel back the foil and cut the bars.

Baking Cookies and Bars

- Because cookies have a high fat-to-flour ratio, greasing cookie sheets is not usually necessary. Instead of greasing, try lining your cookie sheets with a silicone baking mat or cooking parchment paper. The cookies will not stick during baking, and the cleanup is easy.

- **Bake one test cookie** following the directions in the recipe to make any adjustments before baking a whole sheet of cookies. If the cookie spreads too much, add 1 to 2 tablespoons of flour to the dough, or refrigerate the dough 1 to 2 hours before baking. If it's too dry, add 1 to 2 tablespoons of milk to the dough.

- Use a spring-action cookie or ice-cream scoop to form cookie dough and make the cookies all the same size so they bake evenly.

- Scoop cookie dough onto completely cooled cookie sheets. Cookies will spread too much if put on a hot or warm cookie sheet.

- Bake cookies and bars on the middle oven rack. For even baking, baking one sheet at a time is recommended. To bake two sheets at once, position oven racks as close to the middle as possible, and switch the position of the sheets halfway through baking so cookies bake more evenly.

- Check cookies and bars at the minimum bake time listed in the recipe, and remove cookies from the cookie sheet and cool as directed.

- Remove cookies from a cookie sheet using a flat, thin turner. Cool on wire cooling racks.

- If cookies were left to cool too long on the cookie sheet and are difficult to remove without breaking them, here's what to do: Put the cookies back in the oven for 1 to 2 minutes to warm them, and they should come off the sheet easily.

- Cool bars and brownies in the pan on a wire rack.

Storing Cookies and Bars

To keep your fresh-baked cookies as fresh as possible:

- Store crisp cookies at room temperature in a loosely covered container.

- Store chewy and soft cookies at room temperature in resealable plastic food-storage bags or tightly covered container.

- Don't store crisp and chewy or soft cookies together in the same container because the crisp cookies will become soft.

- Let frosted or decorated cookies set or harden before storing; store them between layers of waxed paper, plastic wrap or foil.

- Freeze cookies and bars, tightly wrapped and labeled. Freeze unfrosted cookies up to twelve months and frosted cookies up to three months. Put delicate frosted or decorated cookies in single layers in freezer containers, and cover with waxed paper before adding another layer.

COOKIE SCOOPS

Spring-action cookie or ice-cream scoops are available in various sizes referred to by number; the larger the number, the smaller the scoop. Two scoop sizes good for cookies are the #70 scoop, which is equal to a level tablespoon, and the #16, which is equal to 1/4 cup. Because not all manufacturers' sizes are the same, measure the volume of the scoop with water first. Use the size of scoop that drops the amount of dough called for in a recipe.

SAVORY SWISS CHEESE TWIST

Best-Ever Yeast Breads

Potato Refrigerator Roll Dough

Classic

Mashed potatoes add flavor and moistness to these heritage American rolls and loaves. Long-ago country cooks used every single ingredient—even the water from cooking the potatoes was thought to add great flavor and important nutrients. You, too, can use the water from cooking your potatoes or sweet potatoes. Just let 1 1/2 cups of the water cool to 105°F to 115°F, and use it to dissolve the yeast.

Prep Time: 20 min; Start to Finish: 8 hr 20 min   **Yield will vary depending on type of rolls made.**

1 package regular active dry yeast (2 1/4 teaspoons)

1 1/2 cups warm water (105°F to 115°F)

2/3 cup sugar

1 1/2 teaspoons salt

2/3 cup butter or margarine, softened

2 eggs

1 cup lukewarm mashed potatoes*

7 to 7 1/2 cups Gold Medal all-purpose flour

1 cup lukewarm mashed cooked winter squash (1 medium) can be substituted for the mashed potatoes.

1 In large bowl, dissolve yeast in warm water. Add sugar, salt, butter, eggs, potatoes and 3 cups of the flour. Beat with electric mixer on low speed 1 minute, scraping bowl frequently. Beat on medium speed 1 minute, scraping bowl frequently. Stir in enough remaining flour to make dough easy to handle.

2 On lightly floured surface, knead dough about 5 minutes or until smooth and springy. Grease large bowl with shortening or spray with cooking spray. Place dough in bowl, turning dough to grease all sides. Cover bowl tightly; refrigerate at least 8 hours but no longer than 5 days.

3 Gently push fist into dough to deflate. Divide dough into 3 equal parts (2 parts if making bread loaves). Use dough to make rolls, loaves or buns as directed below.

Braided Dinner Rolls

1/3 recipe Potato Refrigerator Roll Dough (above)
1 egg
1 tablespoon water
3/4 teaspoon poppy seed
3/4 teaspoon sesame seed

Lightly grease cookie sheet with shortening or spray with cooking spray. Divide dough into 18 equal parts. Roll each part into 7-inch rope on lightly floured surface. Place groups of 3 ropes close together on cookie sheet. Braid ropes gently and loosely. Do not stretch. Pinch ends to fasten; tuck under securely. Cover and let rise in warm place 1 hour to 1 hour 30 minutes or until dough has doubled in size.

Heat oven to 375°F. In small bowl, beat egg and water slightly; brush over braids. Sprinkle each of 3 braids with 1/4 teaspoon poppy seed and each of remaining 3 braids with 1/4 teaspoon sesame seed. Bake about 15 minutes or until golden brown. 6 rolls.

High Altitude (3500 to 6500 feet): For two 9-inch loaves, bake at 375°F for 40 to 45 minutes.

1 Slice: Calories 160 (Calories from Fat 45); Fat 5g (Saturated 3g); Cholesterol 25mg; Sodium 150mg; Carbohydrate 26g (Dietary Fiber 1g); Protein 3g **Exchanges:** 1 Starch, 1 Other Carbohydrates, 1/2 Fat **Carbohydrate Choices:** 2

Bread Loaves: Grease bottom and sides of two 9 x 5-inch loaf pans with shortening or spray with cooking spray. Divide Potato Refrigerator Roll Dough in half. On lightly floured surface, roll each half into 18 x 9-inch rectangle. Roll up dough, beginning at 9-inch side. Press with thumbs to seal after each turn. Pinch edge of dough into roll to seal. Pinch each end of roll to seal. Fold ends under loaf. Place each loaf, seam side down, in pan. Brush loaves with softened butter or margarine. Cover and let rise in warm place about 2 hours or until dough has doubled in size. (Dough is ready if indentation remains when touched.)

Heat oven to 375°F. Place loaves on low oven rack so tops of pan are in center of oven. Pans should not touch each other or sides of oven. Bake 30 to 35 minutes or until loaves are deep golden brown and sound hollow when tapped. Remove from pans to wire rack. Brush with softened butter or margarine; cool. 2 loaves.

Casserole Rolls: Lightly grease bottom and side of 9-inch round pan with shortening or spray with cooking spray. Shape one-third of Potato Refrigerator Roll Dough into 36 balls (about 1 inch). Place in pan. Brush with softened butter or margarine. Cover and let rise in warm place 1 hour to 1 hour 30 minutes or until dough has doubled in size. Heat oven to 400°F. Bake 13 to 15 minutes or until light brown. 3 dozen rolls.

Cloverleaf Rolls: Grease 12 medium muffin cups with shortening or spray with cooking spray. Shape one-third of Potato Refrigerator Roll Dough into 36 balls (about 1 inch). Place 3 balls in each muffin cup. Brush with softened butter or margarine. Cover and let rise in warm place 1 hour to 1 hour 30 minutes or until dough has doubled in size. Heat oven to 400°F. Bake 13 to 15 minutes or until light brown. 1 dozen rolls.

Hamburger Buns: Grease cookie sheet with shortening or spray with cooking spray. Divide one-third of Potato Refrigerator Roll Dough into 12 equal parts. On lightly floured surface, shape each part into smooth ball with lightly greased fingers; flatten. Place about 1 inch apart on cookie sheet. Cover and let rise in warm place 1 hour to 1 hour 30 minutes or until dough has doubled in size. Heat oven to 400°F. Brush buns with softened butter or margarine; sprinkle with sesame seed or poppy seed. Bake 13 to 15 minutes or until golden brown. 1 dozen buns.

BAKING FOR TODAY

This recipe, developed more than seventy-five years ago, still has its place today because you always have dough on hand to shape and bake at any time.

POTATO REFRIGERATOR ROLL DOUGH

Country Crust Bread

Classic

The development of the milling industry by Washburn Crosby Company in the late 1800s was a major breakthrough in baking, as it guaranteed dependable results. Before that, everything was variable: the flour, the cup and spoon sizes, unregulated ovens and no leavening. Measurements were no more specific than "add a wine glass," "add a tea cup" or add a "lump" of an ingredient.

Prep Time: 20 min; Start to Finish: 3 hr 5 min	2 loaves (16 slices each)

2 packages regular active dry yeast (4 1/2 teaspoons)

2 cups warm water (105°F to 115°F)

1/2 cup sugar

2 teaspoons salt

2 eggs

1/4 cup vegetable oil

6 to 6 1/2 cups Gold Medal all-purpose flour

Additional vegetable oil

Butter or margarine, softened

1 In large bowl, dissolve yeast in warm water. Add sugar, salt, eggs, 1/4 cup oil and 3 cups of the flour. Beat with electric mixer on low speed 1 minute, scraping bowl frequently. Beat on medium speed 1 minute, scraping bowl frequently. Stir in enough remaining flour to make dough easy to handle.

2 On lightly floured surface, knead dough 8 to 10 minutes or until smooth and springy. Grease large bowl with shortening or spray with cooking spray. Place dough in bowl, turning dough to grease all sides. (At this point, dough can be refrigerated 3 to 4 days.) Cover and let rise in warm place about 1 hour until dough has doubled in size. Dough is ready if impression remains when touched.

3 Grease bottoms and sides of two 9 x 5-inch loaf pans or spray with cooking spray. Gently push fist into dough to deflate; divide in half. Roll each half into 18 x 9-inch rectangle. Roll dough up tightly, beginning at 9-inch side. Press with thumbs to seal after each turn. Pinch edge of dough into roll to seal. Pinch each end of roll to seal. Fold ends under loaf. Place seam side down in pan. Brush loaves with additional oil. Cover and let rise in warm place about 1 hour until dough has doubled in size.

4 Move oven rack to low position so that tops of pans will be in center of oven. Heat oven to 375°F. Bake 30 to 35 minutes or until loaves are deep golden brown and sound hollow when tapped. Remove from pans to wire rack. Brush loaves with butter; cool.

Cinnamon-Raisin Bread: Knead 1/2 cup raisins into each half of dough. After rolling dough into rectangles, brush with oil. In small bowl, mix 1/2 cup sugar and 1 tablespoon ground cinnamon; sprinkle each rectangle with half of the cinnamon-sugar.

Oatmeal Bread: Use 1/2 cup packed brown sugar instead of the granulated sugar. Stir 2 cups old-fashioned or quick-cooking oats into yeast-water mixture.

High Altitude (3500 to 6500 feet): No changes.

1 Slice: Calories 135 (Calories from Fat 25); Fat 3g (Saturated 1g); Cholesterol 15mg; Sodium 150mg; Carbohydrate 21g (Dietary Fiber 1g); Protein 3g
Exchanges: 1 1/2 Starch, 1/2 Fat
Carbohydrate Choices: 1 1/2

BAKING FOR TODAY

This bread, named for its old-fashioned flavor and texture, gains even more country charm when dusted with flour before baking. Want greater volume in your bread? Use Gold Medal Better for Bread flour in place of the all-purpose flour.

Honey–Whole Wheat Bread

Classic

A quote from a 1910 Gold Medal flour cookbook: "Bread can be no better than the flour from which it is made. Therefore, Gold Medal flour will eventually be used by all particular house-wives. It retains the virile strength of the original wheat." This led to the famous advertising campaign for Gold Medal flour, "Eventually . . . Why Not Now?"

Prep Time: 20 min; Start to Finish: 3 hr 15 min — 2 loaves (16 slices each)

2 packages regular or quick active dry yeast (4 1/2 teaspoons)

1/2 cup warm water (105°F to 115°F)

1/3 cup honey

1/4 cup butter or margarine, softened

2 teaspoons salt

1 3/4 cups warm water (105°F to 115°F)

3 cups Gold Medal whole wheat flour

3 to 4 cups Gold Medal all-purpose flour

Additional butter or margarine, softened

1 In large bowl, dissolve yeast in 1/2 cup warm water. Add honey, 1/4 cup butter, the salt, 1 3/4 cups warm water and the whole wheat flour. Beat with electric mixer on low speed 1 minute, scraping bowl frequently. Beat on medium speed 1 minute, scraping bowl frequently. Stir in enough all-purpose flour to make dough easy to handle.

2 On lightly floured surface, knead dough about 10 minutes or until smooth and springy. Grease large bowl with shortening or spray with cooking spray. Place dough in bowl, turning dough to grease all sides. Cover and let rise in warm place about 1 hour or until dough has doubled in size. Dough is ready if indentation remains when touched.

3 Grease bottoms and sides of two 9 x 5-inch or 8 x 4-inch loaf pans with shortening or spray with cooking spray. Gently push fist into dough to deflate; divide in half. Flatten each half with hands or rolling pin into 18 x 9-inch rectangle. Fold crosswise into thirds, overlapping the 2 sides. Roll dough up tightly, beginning at one of the open ends. Press with thumbs to seal after each turn. Pinch edge of dough into roll to seal. Pinch each end of roll to seal. Fold ends under loaf. Place seam side down in pan. Brush with additional butter; sprinkle with whole wheat flour or crushed oats if desired. Cover and let rise in warm place about 1 hour until dough has doubled in size.

4 Move oven rack to low position so that tops of pans will be in center of oven. Heat oven to 375°F. Bake 40 to 45 minutes or until loaves are deep golden brown and sound hollow when tapped. Remove from pans to wire rack; cool.

High Altitude (3500 to 6500 feet): Use two 9 x 5-inch loaf pans. Bake 42 to 47 minutes.

1 Slice: Calories 140 (Calories from Fat 20); Fat 2g (Saturated 1g); Cholesterol 5mg; Sodium 170mg; Carbohydrate 25g (Dietary Fiber 4g); Protein 5g **Exchanges:** 1 1/2 Starch, 1/2 Fat **Carbohydrate Choices:** 1 1/2

BAKING FOR TODAY

Combining all-purpose and whole wheat flours gives you more of a wheaty taste, without heaviness. Wheat flour is unique because it contains gluten-forming proteins that work with the water, yeast and kneading step to create a light, airy texture to bread. That's why kneading is so important to homemade bread.

HONEY-WHOLE WHEAT BREAD

Classic Sourdough Bread

Sourdough starter dates back to the American frontier, where every traveler carried a crock of sourdough starter for bread and flapjacks.

Prep: 30 min; Starter Stand: 4 to 5 days; Bread: 4 hr   2 loaves (16 slices each)

1 cup Sourdough Starter (below)

2 1/2 cups Gold Medal all-purpose flour or Better for Bread flour

2 cups warm water (105°F to 115°F)

3 3/4 to 4 1/4 cups Gold Medal all-purpose flour or Better for Bread flour

3 tablespoons sugar

1 teaspoon salt

3 tablespoons vegetable oil

1. In 3-quart glass bowl, mix Sourdough Starter, 2 1/2 cups flour and warm water with wooden spoon until smooth. Cover and let stand in warm, draft-free place 8 hours.

2. Add 3 3/4 cups flour, the sugar, salt and oil to bowl. Stir until dough is smooth and flour is absorbed. (Dough should be just firm enough to gather into ball. If necessary, add remaining 1/2 cup flour gradually, stirring until flour is absorbed.)

3. On heavily floured surface, knead dough about 10 minutes or until smooth and springy. Grease large bowl with shortening or spray with cooking spray. Place dough in bowl, turning to grease all sides. Cover and let rise in warm place about 1 hour 30 minutes or until dough has doubled in size.

4. Grease large cookie sheet with shortening or spray with cooking spray. Gently push fist into dough several times to remove air bubbles; divide in half. Shape each half into a round, slightly flat loaf. Do not tear dough by pulling. Place loaves on opposite corners on cookie sheet. Make three 1/4-inch-deep slashes in top of each loaf with sharp knife. Cover and let rise about 45 minutes or until dough has doubled in size.

5. Heat oven to 375°F. Brush loaves with cold water. Place in middle of oven. Bake 35 to 45 minutes, brushing occasionally with water, until loaves sound hollow when tapped. Remove from cookie sheet to wire rack. Cool completely, about 1 hour.

Sourdough Starter

1 teaspoon regular active dry yeast

1/4 cup warm water (105°F to 115°F)

3/4 cup milk

1 cup Gold Medal all-purpose flour

In 3-quart glass bowl, dissolve yeast in warm water. Stir in milk. Gradually stir in flour; beat until smooth. Cover with towel or cheesecloth; let stand in warm, draft-free place (80°F to 85°F) about 24 hours or until starter begins to ferment (bubbles will appear on surface of starter). If starter has not begun fermentation after 24 hours, discard and begin again. If fermentation has begun, stir well; cover tightly with plastic wrap and return to warm, draft-free place. Let starter stand 2 to 3 days or until foamy.

When foamy, stir well; pour into 1-quart crock or glass jar with tight-fitting cover. Refrigerate. Starter is ready when a clear liquid has risen to top. Stir before using. Use 1 cup starter in recipe. To remaining starter, add 3/4 cup milk and 3/4 cup flour. Store covered at room temperature about 12 hours or until bubbles appear; refrigerate.

Use starter regularly. If bread volume decreases, dissolve 1 teaspoon active dry yeast in 1/4 cup warm water. Stir in 1/2 cup milk, 3/4 cup flour and remaining starter.

BAKING FOR TODAY

Each time you make this delicious bread, it will have a bit more sourdough taste because the starter gains more flavor as it ages.

High Altitude (3500 to 6500 feet): No changes.

1 Slice: Calories 125 (Calories from Fat 20); Fat 2g (Saturated 0g); Cholesterol 0mg; Sodium 75mg; Carbohydrate 24g (Dietary Fiber 1g); Protein 3g
Exchanges: 1 Starch, 1/2 Other Carbohydrates, 1/2 Fat
Carbohydrate Choices: 1 1/2

Classic Dinner Rolls

Classic

3 1/2 to 3 3/4 cups Gold Medal all-purpose flour or Better for Bread flour

1/4 cup sugar

1/4 cup butter or margarine, softened

1 teaspoon salt

1 package regular or quick active dry yeast (2 1/4 teaspoons)

1/2 cup very warm water (120°F to 130°F)

1/2 cup very warm milk (scalded then cooled to 120°F to 130°F)*

1 egg

Additional butter or margarine, melted, if desired

*To scald milk, heat over medium heat until tiny bubbles form at the edge (do not boil).

1 In large bowl mix 2 cups of the flour, the sugar, 1/4 cup butter, salt and yeast. Add warm water, warm milk and egg. Beat with electric mixer on low speed 1 minute, scraping bowl frequently. Beat on medium speed 1 minute, scraping bowl frequently. Stir in enough remaining flour to make dough easy to handle.

2 On lightly floured surface, gently roll dough to coat. Knead about 5 minutes or until dough is smooth and springy. Grease large bowl with shortening or spray with cooking spray. Place dough in bowl, turning dough to grease all sides. Cover bowl loosely with plastic wrap and let rise in warm place about 1 hour or until dough has doubled in size. Dough is ready if indentation remains when touched.

3 Grease bottom and sides of 13 x 9-inch pan with shortening or spray with cooking spray. Gently push fist into dough to deflate. Divide dough into 15 equal parts. Shape each part into a ball; place in pan. Brush with melted butter. Cover loosely with plastic wrap and let rise in warm place about 30 minutes or until double.

4 Heat oven to 375°F. Bake 12 to 15 minutes or until golden brown. Serve warm or cool.

Bread Machine Dinner Rolls: Use 3 1/4 cups Better for Bread flour, 1/4 cup sugar, 2 tablespoons softened butter, 1 teaspoon salt, 3 teaspoons yeast, 1 cup room-temperature water and 1 egg; omit milk. Measuring carefully, place ingredients in bread machine pan in the order recommended by the manufacturer. Select Dough/Manual cycle; do not use Delay cycle. Remove dough from pan. Continue as directed in step 3 for shaping and rising (rising time may be shorter because dough will be warm when removed from bread machine). Bake as directed in step 4.

Do-Ahead Dinner Rolls: After placing rolls in pan, cover tightly with foil and refrigerate 4 to 24 hours. Before baking, remove from refrigerator; remove foil and cover loosely with plastic wrap. Let rise in warm place about 2 hours or until dough has doubled in size (if some rising has occurred in the refrigerator, rising time may be less than 2 hours). Bake as directed in step 4.

High Altitude (3500 to 6500 feet): Bake 18 to 21 minutes.

1 Roll: Calories 150 (Calories from Fat 35); Fat 4g (Saturated 2g); Cholesterol 25mg; Sodium 190mg; Carbohydrate 25g (Dietary Fiber 1g); Protein 4g
Exchanges: 1 1/2 Starch, 1/2 Fat
Carbohydrate Choices: 1 1/2

BAKING FOR TODAY

In early American times when families made their own bread, they baked often so they always had fresh bread and rolls. Now we can rely on our freezers to help us out. You can freeze these baked rolls for up to two months. To reheat, thaw rolls, then warm them, wrapped in foil, at 275°F for 10 minutes.

Easy Cheese Casserole Bread
Classic

1 package regular or quick active dry yeast (2 1/4 teaspoons)

1/2 cup warm water (105°F to 115°F)

1/2 cup lukewarm milk (scalded then cooled)*

2/3 cup butter or margarine, softened

2 eggs

1 teaspoon salt

3 cups Gold Medal all-purpose flour

1 cup shredded Swiss or Cheddar cheese (4 oz)

1/2 teaspoon pepper

Additional butter or margarine, softened

To scald milk, heat over medium heat until tiny bubbles form at the edge (do not boil).

1 In large bowl, dissolve yeast in warm water. Add milk, 2/3 cup butter, the eggs, salt and 1 cup of the flour. Beat with electric mixer on low speed 30 seconds, scraping bowl constantly. Beat on medium speed 2 minutes, scraping bowl occasionally. Stir in remaining flour, the cheese and pepper. Scrape batter from side of bowl.

2 Cover and let rise in warm place about 40 minutes or until dough has doubled in size. Batter is ready if indentation remains when touched with floured finger.

3 Grease bottom and side of 2-quart casserole with shortening or spray with cooking spray. Stir down batter by beating about 25 strokes. Spread evenly in casserole. Cover and let rise in warm place about 45 minutes or until dough has doubled in size.

4 Move oven rack to low position so that top of casserole will be in center of oven. Heat oven to 375°F. Bake 40 to 45 minutes or until loaf is brown and sounds hollow when tapped. Loosen side of bread from casserole; immediately remove from casserole to wire rack. Brush top of bread with additional butter; cool.

Onion-Dill Casserole Bread: Omit cheese and pepper. Stir in 1 small onion, finely chopped (1/4 cup), and 1 tablespoon dried dill weed with the second addition of flour. Before baking, brush top of loaf with butter and sprinkle with sesame seed or poppy seed.

BAKING FOR TODAY

The pebbled-surface appearance and coarse texture of batter bread is a little different from bread that's kneaded, but batter bread is equally as tasty. Because they do not require kneading, batter breads take less time to make than most home-baked breads. You can team this yummy bread with chicken, beef, soup or stew to make dinner special.

High Altitude (3500 to 6500 feet): For 2-quart round casserole, no changes.

1 Slice: Calories 125 (Calories from Fat 65); Fat 7g (Saturated 4g); Cholesterol 35mg; Sodium 150mg; Carbohydrate 12g (Dietary Fiber 0g); Protein 4g
Exchanges: 1 Starch, 1 Fat
Carbohydrate Choices: 1

EASY CHEESE CASSEROLE BREAD

Oatmeal and Wheat Batter Bread

2 loaves (16 slices each)

Cornmeal

4 1/2 to 4 3/4 cups Gold Medal all-purpose flour or Better for Bread flour

2 tablespoons sugar

1 teaspoon salt

1/4 teaspoon baking soda

2 packages regular or quick active dry yeast (4 1/2 teaspoons)

2 cups milk

1/2 cup water

1/2 cup Gold Medal whole wheat flour

1/2 cup wheat germ

1/2 cup quick-cooking oats

1 Grease bottoms and sides of two 8 x 4-inch loaf pans with shortening or spray with cooking spray; sprinkle with cornmeal.

2 In large bowl, mix 3 1/2 cups of the all-purpose flour, the sugar, salt, baking soda and yeast. In 1-quart saucepan, heat milk and water over medium heat, stirring occasionally, until very warm (120°F to 130°F). Add milk mixture to flour mixture. Beat with electric mixer on low speed until moistened. Beat on medium speed 3 minutes, scraping bowl occasionally.

3 Stir in whole wheat flour, wheat germ, oats and enough remaining all-purpose flour to make a stiff batter. Divide batter evenly between pans. Round tops of loaves by patting with floured hands. Sprinkle with cornmeal. Cover loosely with plastic wrap and let rise in warm place about 30 minutes or until batter is about 1 inch below tops of pans.

4 Heat oven to 400°F. Bake 20 to 25 minutes or until tops of loaves are light brown and loaves begin to pull away from sides of pans. Remove from pans to wire rack; cool.

Whole Wheat Batter Bread: Increase whole wheat flour to 2 cups. Omit wheat germ and oats. Stir in 1 cup raisins with the second addition of all-purpose flour.

BAKING FOR TODAY

Batter breads give you homemade goodness without kneading, and there is only one rising so they are quicker to make than most home-baked breads. This oat and wheat combination is truly delicious and also makes great toast!

High Altitude (3500 to 6500 feet): Bake about 30 minutes.

1 Slice: Calories 95 (Calories from Fat 10); Fat 1g (Saturated 0g); Cholesterol 0mg; Sodium 90mg; Carbohydrate 18g (Dietary Fiber 1g); Protein 3g
Exchanges: 1 Starch
Carbohydrate Choices: 1

French Bread

The year 1921 was important in America's—and flour's—history. Why? An avalanche of mail asking baking questions and requesting recipes led Washburn Crosby Company to create Betty Crocker as a pen name to answer consumers' letters. And the rest—as they say—is history!

Prep Time: 25 min; Start to Finish: 3 hr 30 min　　　　　　　　　　　　　　　　**2 loaves (12 slices each)**

3 to 3 1/2 cups Gold Medal all-purpose flour or Better for Bread flour

1 tablespoon sugar

1 teaspoon salt

1 package regular or quick active dry yeast (2 1/4 teaspoons)

1 cup very warm water (120°F to 130°F)

2 tablespoons vegetable oil

Cornmeal

1 egg white

1 tablespoon cold water

Poppy seed or sesame seed

1. In large bowl, mix 2 cups of the flour, the sugar, salt and yeast. Add warm water and oil. Beat with electric mixer on low speed 1 minute, scraping bowl frequently. Beat on medium speed 1 minute, scraping bowl frequently. Stir in enough remaining flour, 1/2 cup at a time, to make dough easy to handle (dough will be soft).

2. On lightly floured surface, knead dough about 5 minutes or until smooth and elastic. Grease large bowl with shortening or spray with cooking spray. Place dough in bowl, turning dough to grease all sides. Cover and let rise in warm place 1 hour 30 minutes to 2 hours or until dough has doubled in size. (Rising time is longer than times for traditional breads, which gives the typical French bread texture.) Dough is ready if indentation remains when touched.

3. Grease large cookie sheet with shortening or spray with cooking spray; sprinkle with cornmeal. Gently push fist into dough to deflate; divide in half. On lightly floured surface, roll each half into 15 x 8-inch rectangle. Roll dough up tightly, beginning at 15-inch side, to form a loaf. Pinch edge of dough into roll to seal. Roll gently back and forth to taper ends. Place both loaves on cookie sheet.

4. Cut 1/4-inch-deep slashes across tops of loaves at 2-inch intervals with sharp knife. Brush loaves with cold water. Let rise uncovered in warm place about 1 hour or until dough has doubled in size.

5. Heat oven to 375°F. In small bowl, mix egg white and 1 tablespoon cold water; brush over loaves. Sprinkle with poppy or sesame seed. Bake 25 to 30 minutes or until loaves are golden brown and sound hollow when tapped. Remove from cookie sheet to wire rack; cool.

Crusty Hard Rolls: Grease large cookie sheet with shortening or spray with cooking spray; sprinkle with cornmeal. After deflating dough, divide into 12 equal parts. Shape each part into a ball; place on cookie sheet. Brush rolls with cold water. Let rise uncovered about 1 hour or until dough has doubled in size. Heat oven to 425°F. In small bowl, mix egg white and 1 tablespoon cold water; brush over rolls. Sprinkle with poppy or sesame seed. Bake 15 to 20 minutes or until brown. 12 rolls.

High Altitude (3500 to 6500 feet): No changes.

1 Slice: Calories 70 (Calories from Fat 10); Fat 1g (Saturated 0g); Cholesterol 0mg; Sodium 100mg; Carbohydrate 13g (Dietary Fiber 1g); Protein 2g
Exchanges: 1 Starch
Carbohydrate Choices: 1

BAKING FOR TODAY

If you prefer a more crunchy crust to this delightful bread, spray the loaves with water right before baking and add a pan of water to the oven.

Overnight Caramel-Pecan Rolls

Classic

2 packages regular active dry yeast (4 1/2 teaspoons)

1/2 cup warm water (105°F to 115°F)

2 cups lukewarm milk (scalded then cooled)*

1/3 cup granulated sugar

1/3 cup vegetable oil or softened butter or margarine

3 teaspoons baking powder

2 teaspoons salt

1 egg

6 1/2 to 7 1/2 cups Gold Medal all-purpose flour

1 cup packed brown sugar

1/2 cup butter or margarine, softened

2 tablespoons light corn syrup

1 cup pecan halves

4 tablespoons butter or margarine, softened

1/2 cup granulated sugar

1 tablespoon plus 1 teaspoon ground cinnamon

To scald milk, heat over medium heat until tiny bubbles form at the edge (do not boil).

High Altitude (3500 to 6500 feet): Rising times may be slightly shorter. Heat oven to 375°F. Bake 25 to 30 minutes.

1 Roll: Calories 315 (Calories from Fat 115); Fat 13g (Saturated 5g); Cholesterol 25mg; Sodium 310mg; Carbohydrate 45g (Dietary Fiber 2g); Protein 5g
Exchanges: 2 Starch, 1 Other Carbohydrates, 2 Fat
Carbohydrate Choices: 3

1. In large bowl, dissolve yeast in warm water. Add milk, 1/3 cup sugar, the oil, baking powder, salt, egg and 3 cups of the flour. Beat with electric mixer on low speed 1 minute, scraping bowl frequently. Beat on medium speed 1 minute, scraping bowl frequently. Stir in enough remaining flour to make dough easy to handle.

2. On generously floured surface, knead dough 8 to 10 minutes or until smooth and springy. Grease large bowl with shortening or spray with cooking spray. Place dough in bowl, turning dough to grease all sides. Cover and let rise in warm place about 1 hour 30 minutes or until dough has doubled in size. Dough is ready if indentation remains when touched.

3. In 1-quart saucepan, heat brown sugar and 1/2 cup butter until melted; remove from heat. Stir in corn syrup. Divide mixture between two 13 x 9-inch pans. Sprinkle each with 1/2 cup pecan halves.

4. Gently push fist into dough to deflate; divide in half. Roll each half into 12 x 10-inch rectangle. Spread each rectangle with 2 tablespoons butter. In small bowl, mix 1/2 cup sugar and the cinnamon; sprinkle half of the cinnamon-sugar over each rectangle. Roll up dough, beginning at 12-inch side. Pinch edge of dough into roll to seal. Stretch roll to make even.

5. Cut each roll into 12 slices. Place slightly apart in pans. Wrap tightly with heavy-duty foil. Refrigerate at least 12 hours but no longer than 48 hours. (To bake immediately, do not wrap. Cover and let rise in warm place about 30 minutes or until dough has doubled in size. Bake as directed below.)

6. Heat oven to 350°F. Remove foil from pans. Bake 30 to 35 minutes or until golden. Immediately place large heatproof tray upside down onto pan; turn tray and pan over. Let pan remain 1 minute so caramel can drizzle over rolls; remove pan.

Overnight Cinnamon Rolls: Omit brown sugar, 1/2 cup butter or margarine, the corn syrup and pecans; omit step 3. Grease bottoms and sides of two 13 x 9-inch pans with shortening or spray with cooking spray. Roll, slice, refrigerate and bake as directed. Frost with Powdered Sugar Frosting: In small bowl, mix 1 cup powdered sugar, 1 tablespoon milk and 1/2 teaspoon vanilla with spoon until smooth and spreadable (frosts 1 batch of rolls).

BAKING FOR TODAY

This recipe is meant to be a two-day recipe, so it's a perfect do-ahead. You can make the dough and refrigerate overnight, then your family can wake up to the heavenly aroma and taste of fresh-baked caramel or cinnamon rolls.

OVERNIGHT CARAMEL-PECAN ROLLS

Garlic and Asiago Loaves

Prep Time: 20 min; Start to Finish: 2 hr 45 min **4 small loaves (6 slices each)**

3 tablespoons olive or vegetable oil

2 cloves garlic, finely chopped

5 to 5 1/2 cups Gold Medal Better for Bread flour

2 tablespoons sugar

1 1/2 teaspoons salt

2 packages regular or quick active dry yeast (4 1/2 teaspoons)

2 cups very warm water (120°F to 130°F)

3/4 cup shredded Asiago cheese (3 oz)

1 In 6-inch skillet, heat oil over medium heat. Cook garlic in oil, stirring frequently, until garlic just begins to brown. Remove from heat.

2 In large bowl, mix 2 cups of the flour, the sugar, salt and yeast. Add very warm water and garlic with oil. Beat with electric mixer on medium speed 3 minutes, scraping bowl occasionally. Stir in cheese and enough remaining flour to make dough easy to handle.

3 On lightly floured surface, knead dough 5 to 10 minutes or until dough is smooth and springy. Grease large bowl with shortening or spray with cooking spray. Place dough in bowl, turning dough to grease all sides. Cover bowl loosely with plastic wrap and let rise in warm place 1 hour to 1 hour 30 minutes or until dough has doubled in size.

4 Grease large cookie sheet with shortening or spray with cooking spray. Gently push fist into dough to deflate. Divide dough into fourths. Shape each into 6-inch round. Place each round with smooth side up on corner of cookie sheet. Cut 1/2-inch-deep slash in top of each round with serrated knife. Cover loosely with plastic wrap and let rise in warm place about 30 minutes or until dough has doubled in size.

5 Heat oven to 375°F. Remove plastic wrap. Bake 20 to 25 minutes or until golden brown. Remove from cookie sheet to wire rack; cool if desired.

BAKING FOR TODAY

Bread baking is very rewarding as everyone loves fresh bread. Another plus—this unusual bread isn't readily available—so making it yourself means you can have it any time you like.

High Altitude (3500 to 6500 feet): No changes.

1 Slice: Calories 125 (Calories from Fat 25); Fat 3g (Saturated 1g); Cholesterol 5mg; Sodium 180mg; Carbohydrate 21g (Dietary Fiber 1g); Protein 4g
Exchanges: 1 Starch, 1/2 Other Carbohydrates, 1/2 Fat
Carbohydrate Choices: 1 1/2

GARLIC AND ASIAGO LOAVES

Parmesan-Parsley Breadsticks

1 cup water

2 tablespoons butter or margarine, softened

2 1/2 cups Gold Medal Better for Bread flour

1/4 cup grated Parmesan cheese

2 teaspoons sugar

1 tablespoon parsley flakes

3/4 teaspoon salt

1 1/2 teaspoons bread machine yeast

1 egg, beaten

1 Measure carefully, placing all ingredients except egg in bread machine pan in the order recommended by the manufacturer.

2 Select Dough/Manual cycle. Do not use Delay cycle.

3 Remove dough from pan, using lightly floured hands; place on lightly floured surface. Cover dough and let rest 10 minutes.

4 Grease 2 large cookie sheets with shortening or spray with cooking spray. Divide dough into 12 parts, using floured hands. Roll each part into 8-inch rope. Place 1 inch apart on cookie sheets. Cover and let rise in warm place 15 to 20 minutes or until dough has almost doubled in size.

5 Heat oven to 375°F. Brush beaten egg over dough. Bake 15 to 20 minutes or until golden brown. Serve warm, or cool on wire rack.

BAKING FOR TODAY

Your home-baked bread-machine breads will have higher volume and well-formed loaves if you use Better for Bread flour instead of all-purpose flour. A special blend of hard wheats, bread flour is high in gluten, the type of protein that gives bread its structure.

If your dough is too sticky when you are forming the ropes, sprinkling a little flour over the rolling surface will be a big help.

High Altitude (3500 to 6500 feet): No changes.

1 Breadstick: Calories 140 (Calories from Fat 25); Fat 3g (Saturated 2g); Cholesterol 25mg; Sodium 210mg; Carbohydrate 23g (Dietary Fiber 1g); Protein 5g
Exchanges: 1 1/2 Starch, 1/2 Fat
Carbohydrate Choices: 1 1/2

Savory Swiss Cheese Twist

3/4 cup plus 1 tablespoon water

1 egg

2 tablespoons butter or margarine, softened

3 1/4 cups Gold Medal Better for Bread flour

2 tablespoons sugar

1 1/2 teaspoons salt

1 1/2 teaspoons bread machine yeast

Savory Filling (below)

1/3 cup shredded Swiss or mozzarella cheese

1 Measure carefully, placing all ingredients except Savory Filling and cheese in bread machine pan in the order recommended by the manufacturer.

2 Select Dough/Manual cycle. Do not use Delay cycle.

3 Remove dough from pan, using lightly floured hands; place on lightly floured surface. Cover dough and let rest 10 minutes.

4 Make Savory Filling. Grease large cookie sheet with shortening or spray with cooking spray. Roll dough into 15 x 10-inch rectangle. Spread filling over dough to within 1/2 inch of edges. Roll up dough, beginning at 15-inch side; pinch edge of dough into roll to seal.

5 Cut roll lengthwise in half. Place halves, filling sides up and side by side, on cookie sheet. Twist together gently and loosely; pinch edges to seal. Cover and let rise in warm place about 25 minutes or until dough has doubled in size. (Dough is ready if indentation remains when touched.)

6 Heat oven to 375°F. Bake 20 to 25 minutes or until golden brown; immediately sprinkle with cheese. Serve warm.

Savory Filling

1/2 cup shredded Swiss or mozzarella cheese (2 oz)

1/4 cup finely chopped red or green bell pepper

1 tablespoon chopped fresh cilantro

2 tablespoons chopped green onions (2 medium)

2 tablespoons mayonnaise or salad dressing

1/2 teaspoon ground cumin

In small bowl, mix all ingredients.

High Altitude (3500 to 6500 feet): No changes.

1 Slice: Calories 215 (Calories from Fat 65); Fat 7g (Saturated 3g); Cholesterol 30mg; Sodium 350mg; Carbohydrate 31g (Dietary Fiber 1g); Protein 7g **Exchanges:** 2 Starch, 1 Fat **Carbohydrate Choices:** 2

BAKING FOR TODAY

Creating this masterpiece with the help of your bread machine lets you spend less time in the kitchen. Be sure to use a sharp knife or scissors when cutting the roll lengthwise in half to prevent the knife from pulling on the filling.

Multigrain Loaf

	1 1/2-Pound (12 Slices)	2-Pound (16 Slices)
Water	1 1/4 cups	1 1/2 cups
Butter or margarine, softened	2 tablespoons	2 tablespoons
Gold Medal Better for Bread flour	1 1/3 cups	1 1/2 cups
Gold Medal whole wheat flour	1 1/3 cups	1 1/2 cups
7-grain or multigrain hot cereal (uncooked)	1 cup	1 1/4 cups
Unsalted sunflower nuts	1/3 cup	1/3 cup
Packed brown sugar	3 tablespoons	1/4 cup
Salt	1 1/4 teaspoons	1 1/2 teaspoons
Bread machine yeast	2 1/2 teaspoons	2 1/2 teaspoons

1 Make 1 1/2-pound recipe with bread machines that use 3 cups flour, or make 2-pound recipe with bread machines that use 4 cups flour.

2 Measure carefully, placing all ingredients in bread machine pan in the order recommended by the manufacturer.

3 Select Basic/White cycle. Use Medium or Light crust color. Remove baked bread from pan; cool on wire rack.

Note: The same amount of yeast is needed for both the 1 1/2-pound and 2-pound recipes.

BAKING FOR TODAY

You'll find 7-grain cereal in the hot-cereal section of your supermarket or at a natural foods or co-op store. The sunflower nuts add a natural, nutty flavor to this often-requested recipe.

High Altitude (3500 to 6500 feet): Not recommended.

1 Slice: Calories 175 (Calories from Fat 35); Fat 4g (Saturated 1g); Cholesterol 5mg; Sodium 230mg; Carbohydrate 30g (Dietary Fiber 3g); Protein 5g
Exchanges: 2 Starch, 1/2 Fat
Carbohydrate Choices: 2

Mediterranean Herbed Bread

Prep Time: 15 min; Start to Finish: About 3 hr 40 min

	1 1/2-Pound (12 Slices)	2-Pound (16 Slices)
Water	1 cup	1 cup plus 3 tablespoons
Butter or margarine, softened	1 tablespoon	1 tablespoon
Gold Medal Better for Bread flour	3 cups	4 cups
Sugar	2 tablespoons	2 tablespoons
Dry milk	1 tablespoon	1 tablespoon
Salt	1 1/2 teaspoons	1 3/4 teaspoons
Chopped fresh basil leaves	1 teaspoon	1 1/2 teaspoons
Chopped fresh oregano leaves	1 teaspoon	1 1/2 teaspoons
Chopped fresh thyme leaves	1 teaspoon	1 teaspoon
Bread machine yeast	2 1/4 teaspoons	2 1/4 teaspoons

1 Make 1 1/2-pound recipe with bread machines that use 3 cups flour, or make 2-pound recipe with bread machines that use 4 cups flour.

2 Measure carefully, placing all ingredients in bread machine pan in the order recommended by the manufacturer.

3 Select Basic/White cycle. Use Medium or Light crust color. Remove baked bread from pan; cool on wire rack.

Note: The same amount of yeast is needed for both the 1 1/2-pound and 2-pound recipes.

BAKING FOR TODAY

Fresh herbs give a wonderful flavor and aroma to this home-baked bread, but if you have only dried herbs, you can use 1/2 teaspoon each basil, oregano and thyme for the 1 1/2-pound recipe and 3/4 teaspoon each for the 2-pound recipe.

High Altitude (3500 to 6500 feet): No changes.

1 Slice: Calories 135 (Calories from Fat 10); Fat 1g (Saturated 1g); Cholesterol 0mg; Sodium 270mg; Carbohydrate 28g (Dietary Fiber 1g); Protein 4g
Exchanges: 1 Starch, 1 Other Carbohydrates
Carbohydrate Choices: 2

SOUR CREAM COFFEE CAKE

Chapter 2

Easy Breads, Biscuits and More

Danish Puff

Classic

In 1925, a new program for testing Gold Medal flour, called "Kitchen-tested," was developed at Washburn Crosby Company. Home economists tested the flour in typical baked products as the flour was produced and verified its quality before it was shipped for sale to consumers. Danish Puffs, a popular recipe since the early days of the Betty Crocker Kitchens, was one of the recipes used to test flour.

Prep Time: 25 min; Start to Finish: 2 hr **10 to 12 servings**

1/2 cup butter or margarine, softened

1 cup Gold Medal all-purpose flour

2 tablespoons water

1/2 cup butter or margarine

1 cup water

1 teaspoon almond extract

1 cup Gold Medal all-purpose flour

3 eggs

Powdered Sugar Glaze (below)

1/4 cup chopped nuts

1 Heat oven to 350°F. In small bowl, cut 1/2 cup butter into 1 cup flour, using pastry blender (or pulling 2 table knives through ingredients in opposite directions) until mixture looks like small peas. Sprinkle 2 tablespoons water over mixture; mix with fork. Round dough into a ball; divide in half. On ungreased cookie sheet, pat each half with hands into 12 x 3-inch strip. Strips should be about 3 inches apart.

2 In 1-quart saucepan, heat 1/2 cup butter and 1 cup water to a rolling boil. Remove from heat and quickly stir in almond extract and 1 cup flour. Stir vigorously over low heat about 1 minute or until mixture forms a ball. Remove from heat. Add eggs; beat with spoon until smooth. Divide in half; spread each half evenly over each strip.

3 Bake about 1 hour or until topping is crisp and golden brown. Cool completely on cookie sheet, about 30 minutes. Frost with Powdered Sugar Glaze; sprinkle generously with nuts.

Powdered Sugar Glaze

1 1/2 cups powdered sugar

2 tablespoons butter or margarine, softened

1 1/2 teaspoons vanilla

1 to 2 tablespoons warm water

In small bowl, mix all ingredients until smooth and spreadable.

High Altitude (3500 to 6500 feet): No changes.

1 Serving: Calories 395 (Calories from Fat 225); Fat 25g (Saturated 16g); Cholesterol 120mg; Sodium 160mg; Carbohydrate 38g (Dietary Fiber 1g); Protein 5g **Exchanges:** 2 Starch, 1/2 Other Carbohydrates, 4 1/2 Fat **Carbohydrate Choices:** 2 1/2

BAKING FOR TODAY

To cut the bake time to 30 minutes, you can make 2 dozen Individual Danish Puffs: Pat dough into 3-inch circles, using 1 1/2 teaspoons for each. Spread 1 1/2 tablespoons batter over each circle, extending it just beyond edge of circle (topping will shrink slightly when baked). Bake 30 minutes.

French Breakfast Puffs

Classic

Prep Time: 15 min; Start to Finish: 45 min   15 puffs

1 1/2 cups Gold Medal
all-purpose flour

1 1/2 teaspoons baking powder

1/2 teaspoon salt

1/4 teaspoon ground nutmeg

1/3 cup butter or margarine,
softened

1/2 cup sugar

1 egg

1/2 cup milk

1/2 cup sugar

1 teaspoon ground cinnamon

1/2 cup butter or margarine,
melted

1 Heat oven to 350°F. Grease 15 medium muffin cups with shortening or spray with cooking spray. In small bowl, mix flour, baking powder, salt and nutmeg. In medium bowl, mix 1/3 cup butter, 1/2 cup sugar and the egg with spoon. Stir in flour mixture alternately with milk. Fill muffin cups 2/3 full.

2 Bake 20 to 25 minutes or until golden brown. Meanwhile, in small bowl, mix 1/2 cup sugar and the cinnamon. Immediately after baking, roll puffs in melted butter, then in cinnamon-sugar. Serve warm.

French Breakfast Coffee Cake: Heat oven to 375°F. Grease bottom and sides of 9-inch square pan with shortening or spray with cooking spray. Spread batter in pan. Bake 20 to 25 minutes or until golden brown. Omit 1/2 cup sugar, 1 teaspoon cinnamon and 1/2 cup butter or margarine, melted. While hot, brush 2 tablespoons butter or margarine, melted, on coffee cake and sprinkle with mixture of 2 tablespoons sugar and 1/4 teaspoon ground cinnamon.

BAKING FOR TODAY

A very tender and light bread prepared in muffin pans, these breakfast puffs are great served any time but are at their best when warm. To reheat, warm in the microwave; for one puff, microwave on High for about 15 seconds.

High Altitude (3500 to 6500 feet): No changes.

1 Puff: Calories 195 (Calories from Fat 100); Fat 11g (Saturated 7g); Cholesterol 40mg; Sodium 200mg; Carbohydrate 23g (Dietary Fiber 0g); Protein 2g
Exchanges: 1 Starch, 1/2 Other Carbohydrates, 2 Fat
Carbohydrate Choices: 1 1/2

Buckwheat Pancakes

Classic

Buckwheat, a grain that was very popular in early America, harks back to a simpler time. It's usually paired with another flour to offset its robust flavor and give structure to the recipe.

1 egg

1/2 cup buckwheat flour

1/2 cup Gold Medal whole wheat flour

1 cup milk

1 tablespoon sugar

2 tablespoons vegetable oil

3 teaspoons baking powder

1/2 teaspoon salt

Whole bran or wheat germ, if desired

1 In medium bowl, beat egg with hand beater until fluffy. Beat in remaining ingredients except bran just until smooth.

2 Heat griddle or skillet over medium heat or to 375°F. (To test griddle, sprinkle with a few drops of water. If bubbles jump around, heat is just right.) Grease griddle with vegetable oil if necessary (or spray with cooking spray before heating).

3 For each pancake, pour about 3 tablespoons batter from cup or pitcher onto hot griddle. Cook pancakes until puffed and dry around edges. Sprinkle each pancake with 1 teaspoon bran. Turn and cook other sides until golden brown.

BAKING FOR TODAY

These pancakes, made from a combination of whole wheat and buckwheat flours, have long been a favorite. If you don't have whole wheat flour, you can use all-purpose instead.

High Altitude (3500 to 6500 feet): Use 2 1/4 teaspoons baking powder.

1 Pancake: Calories 95 (Calories from Fat 35); Fat 4g (Saturated 1g); Cholesterol 25mg; Sodium 280mg; Carbohydrate 12g (Dietary Fiber 1g); Protein 3g **Exchanges:** 1 Starch, 1/2 Fat **Carbohydrate Choices:** 1

Blueberry Pancakes

Prep Time: 15 min; Start to Finish: 25 min

9 pancakes (4 inch)

1 egg

1 cup Gold Medal whole wheat flour

1 cup buttermilk

1 tablespoon granulated or packed brown sugar

2 tablespoons vegetable oil

1 teaspoon baking powder

1/2 teaspoon baking soda

1/4 teaspoon salt

1/2 cup fresh or frozen (thawed and well drained) blueberries, raspberries or blackberries

1 In medium bowl, beat egg with hand beater until fluffy. Beat in remaining ingredients except berries just until smooth. Stir in berries. For thinner pancakes, stir in additional 1 to 2 tablespoons milk.

2 Heat griddle or skillet over medium heat or to 375°F. (To test griddle, sprinkle with a few drops of water. If bubbles jump around, heat is just right.) Grease griddle with vegetable oil if necessary (or spray with cooking spray before heating).

3 For each pancake, pour slightly less than 1/4 cup batter from cup or pitcher onto hot griddle. Cook pancake until bubbly on top and puffed and dry around edges. Turn and cook other side until golden brown.

BAKING FOR TODAY

If you don't keep whole wheat flour on hand, you can use Gold Medal all-purpose flour in place of the whole wheat to make traditional buttermilk pancakes; just leave out the berries.

High Altitude (3500 to 6500 feet): Use 1 1/4 cups buttermilk.

1 Pancake: Calories 100 (Calories from Fat 35); Fat 4g (Saturated 1g); Cholesterol 25mg; Sodium 220mg; Carbohydrate 13g (Dietary Fiber 2g); Protein 3g **Exchanges:** 1 Starch, 1/2 Fat **Carbohydrate Choices:** 1

Bacon-Buttermilk Waffles

3 eggs

1 1/2 cups Gold Medal all-purpose flour

1/2 cup butter or margarine, melted

1 1/2 cups buttermilk

2 teaspoons baking powder

1 teaspoon baking soda

1 teaspoon sugar

1/4 teaspoon salt

8 slices bacon, crisply cooked and crumbled (1/2 cup)

Maple or blueberry syrup, if desired

1 Heat waffle iron. (Waffle irons without a nonstick coating may need to be brushed with vegetable oil or sprayed with cooking spray before batter for each waffle is added.)

2 In large bowl, beat eggs with wire whisk or hand beater until fluffy. Beat in remaining ingredients except syrup just until blended.

3 Pour about 1/2 cup batter from cup or pitcher onto center of hot waffle iron. (Check manufacturer's directions for recommended amount of batter.) Close lid of waffle iron.

4 Bake about 5 minutes or until steaming stops. Carefully remove waffle. Repeat with remaining batter. Serve with syrup.

BAKING FOR TODAY

You can mix equal parts peanut butter and honey or maple syrup to make a tasty topper for these super waffles. Another easy topper: mix 1 cup plain yogurt with 1/4 cup of any flavor of preserves.

High Altitude (3500 to 6500 feet): Use 1 3/4 cups buttermilk.

1 Waffle: Calories 220 (Calories from Fat 125); Fat 14g (Saturated 8g); Cholesterol 95mg; Sodium 480mg; Carbohydrate 17g (Dietary Fiber 1g); Protein 7g
Exchanges: 1 Starch, 1/2 High-Fat Meat, 2 Fat
Carbohydrate Choices: 1

BACON-BUTTERMILK WAFFLES

Sour Cream Coffee Cake
Classic

Coffee cake, a sweet bread baked every week and usually served to guests with coffee or tea, used to be standard in American homes, but today, people rarely make a coffee cake every week. Still it's wonderful to bake it whenever you can, with or without the glaze—and treat friends and family to a "blast from the past" with this classic.

Prep Time: 20 min; Start to Finish: 1 hr 45 min — 16 servings

Cinnamon Filling or Almond Filling (below)

3 cups Gold Medal all-purpose flour or whole wheat flour

1 1/2 teaspoons baking powder

1 1/2 teaspoons baking soda

3/4 teaspoon salt

1 1/2 cups granulated sugar

3/4 cup butter or margarine, softened

1 1/2 teaspoons vanilla

3 eggs

1 1/2 cups sour cream

1/2 cup powdered sugar

1/4 teaspoon vanilla

1 to 2 teaspoons milk

1 Heat oven to 325°F. Grease bottom and side of 10 x 4-inch angel food cake pan (tube pan) or 12-cup fluted tube cake pan with shortening or spray with cooking spray. Make Cinnamon Filling or Almond Filling; set aside.

2 In small bowl, mix flour, baking powder, baking soda and salt. In large bowl, beat granulated sugar, butter, 1 1/2 teaspoons vanilla and eggs with electric mixer on medium speed 2 minutes, scraping bowl occasionally. Beat in flour mixture alternately with sour cream on low speed.

3 Spread 1/3 of the batter (about 2 cups) in pan; sprinkle with 1/3 of the filling (about 1/3 cup). Repeat twice.

4 Bake about 1 hour or until toothpick inserted near center comes out clean. Cool 20 minutes; remove from pan. In small bowl, mix remaining ingredients until smooth and thin enough to drizzle; drizzle over coffee cake.

Cinnamon Filling

1/2 cup packed brown sugar

1/2 cup finely chopped nuts

1 1/2 teaspoons ground cinnamon

In small bowl, mix all ingredients.

Almond Filling

1 package (3.5 oz) almond paste (or half of 7-oz package), cut into small pieces

1/2 cup powdered sugar

1/4 cup butter or margarine

1/2 cup sliced almonds

In 1-quart saucepan, cook almond paste, powdered sugar and butter over medium heat, stirring constantly, until smooth. Stir in almonds.

High Altitude (3500 to 6500 feet): Heat oven to 350°F. Use 3/4 teaspoon baking powder, 3/4 teaspoon baking soda, 1/2 teaspoon salt, 1/2 cup butter or margarine and 1 1/4 cups sour cream. Bake 1 hour to 1 hour 10 minutes.

1 Serving: Calories 335 (Calories from Fat 145); Fat 16g (Saturated 8g); Cholesterol 75mg; Sodium 360mg; Carbohydrate 48g (Dietary Fiber 1g); Protein 5g Exchanges: 2 Starch, 1 Other Carbohydrates, 3 Fat Carbohydrate Choices: 3

BAKING FOR TODAY

Why not try one of the new silicone pans for baking this country coffee cake? You can count on them for even browning of baked goods, quick cooling and easy removal. They also come in really fun colors, like red and blue.

Fruit Swirl Coffee Cake

Classic

This recipe has long been a favorite in the Betty Crocker Kitchens and was served for many years in the Betty Crocker Dining Room, a special dining room for employees and their guests where only the best, most-requested recipes were served.

Prep Time: 20 min; Start to Finish: 1 hr 5 min — 30 bars or 18 squares

1 1/2 cups granulated sugar

1 cup butter or margarine, softened

1 1/2 teaspoons baking powder

1 teaspoon vanilla

1 teaspoon almond extract

4 eggs

3 cups Gold Medal all-purpose flour

1 can (21 oz) cherry, apricot or blueberry pie filling

1 cup powdered sugar

1 to 2 tablespoons milk

1 Heat oven to 350°F. Generously grease bottom and sides of one 15 x 10 x 1-inch pan or two 9-inch square pans with shortening or spray with cooking spray.

2 In large bowl, beat granulated sugar, butter, baking powder, vanilla, almond extract and eggs with electric mixer on low speed 30 seconds, scraping bowl constantly. Beat on high speed 3 minutes, scraping bowl occasionally. Stir in flour.

3 Spread 2/3 of the batter in 15-inch pan, or spread 1/3 of the batter in each square pan. Spread pie filling over batter. Drop remaining batter by tablespoonfuls onto pie filling.

4 Bake about 45 minutes or until toothpick inserted near center comes out clean. Meanwhile, in small bowl, mix powdered sugar and milk until smooth and thin enough to drizzle. Drizzle glaze over warm coffee cake. For bars, cut cake in 15-inch pan into 6 rows by 5 rows; or for squares, cut cake in each square pan into 3 rows by 3 rows.

High Altitude (3500 to 6500 feet): Heat oven to 375°F. Generously grease two 9-inch square pans with shortening or spray with cooking spray. Use 1 1/4 cups granulated sugar and 1 teaspoon baking powder. Spread 1 1/2 cups batter in each pan; spread with pie filling. Continue as directed. Bake about 40 minutes.

1 Serving: Calories 185 (Calories from Fat 65); Fat 7g (Saturated 4g); Cholesterol 45mg; Sodium 75mg; Carbohydrate 28g (Dietary Fiber 1g); Protein 2g
Exchanges: 1 Starch, 1 Fruit, 1 Fat
Carbohydrate Choices: 2

BAKING FOR TODAY

You can make smaller Fruit Cake Tarts with this dough: Generously grease bottom and sides of 15 x 10 x 1-inch pan with shortening or spray with cooking spray. Spread all of the batter in pan. Lightly score batter into 24 squares. Drop about 1 tablespoon pie filling onto center of each square. Bake as directed. Sprinkle with powdered sugar. Cut into 24 squares.

Overnight Eggnog Streusel Coffee Cake

Prep Time: 20 min; Start to Finish: 9 hr, 20 min — 15 servings

Streusel Topping (below)

1 cup granulated sugar

1/2 cup butter or margarine, softened

1 cup eggnog

1 container (8 oz) sour cream

1 teaspoon rum extract

2 eggs

2 1/2 cups Gold Medal all-purpose flour

1 1/2 teaspoons baking powder

1/2 teaspoon baking soda

1/2 teaspoon salt

1/2 cup powdered sugar

1 to 2 tablespoons eggnog

1 Grease bottom only of 13 x 9-inch pan with shortening or spray with cooking spray. Make Streusel Topping; set aside.

2 In large bowl, beat granulated sugar and butter with electric mixer on medium speed, or mix with spoon. Beat in 1 cup eggnog, the sour cream, rum extract and eggs until blended. Stir in flour, baking powder, baking soda and salt. Spread in pan.

3 Sprinkle Streusel Topping over batter. Cover and refrigerate overnight.

4 Heat oven to 350°F. Uncover and bake 35 to 40 minutes or until toothpick inserted in center comes out clean. Cool 20 minutes.

5 In small bowl, mix powdered sugar and 1 to 2 tablespoons eggnog until smooth and thin enough to drizzle; drizzle over coffee cake. For servings, cut into 5 rows by 3 rows.

Streusel Topping

1/3 cup granulated sugar

1 tablespoon Gold Medal all-purpose flour

1 tablespoon butter or margarine, softened

1/2 teaspoon ground nutmeg

1/4 teaspoon ground cinnamon

In small bowl, mix all ingredients with fork until crumbly.

BAKING FOR TODAY

High Altitude (3500 to 6500 feet): Bake uncovered 45 to 50 minutes.

1 Serving: Calories 275 (Calories from Fat 100); Fat 11g (Saturated 7g); Cholesterol 70mg; Sodium 230mg; Carbohydrate 40g (Dietary Fiber 1g); Protein 4g **Exchanges:** 1 1/2 Starch, 1 Other Carbohydrates, 3 Fat **Carbohydrate Choices:** 2 1/2

The beauty of this festive make-ahead coffee cake is just that—it makes a great do-ahead, especially during the holidays when time is at a premium. Refrigerating overnight is a convenience, but you can also skip the refrigeration time and just bake the coffee cake as directed in Step 4. When eggnog is not in season, use half-and-half in both the batter and the glaze, adding 1/4 teaspoon ground nutmeg to the glaze.

Classic Cake Doughnuts

Early recipes and cookbooks often provided vague directions and ingredient quantities, such as "bake in a rather quick oven for 1/2 an hour." Today, our recipes give specific directions and ingredient amounts—there's no guesswork at all, and the recipe is a success every time.

Prep Time: 15 min; Start to Finish: 45 min — **2 dozen doughnuts**

Vegetable oil

3 1/3 cups Gold Medal all-purpose flour

1 cup granulated sugar

3/4 cup milk

3 teaspoons baking powder

1/2 teaspoon salt

1/2 teaspoon ground cinnamon

1/4 teaspoon ground nutmeg

2 tablespoons shortening

2 eggs

Chocolate Glaze (below), if desired

1. In deep fryer or 3-quart saucepan, heat 3 to 4 inches oil to 375°F.

2. In large bowl, beat 1 1/2 cups of the flour and the remaining ingredients except Chocolate Glaze with electric mixer on low speed 30 seconds, scraping bowl constantly. Beat on medium speed 2 minutes, scraping bowl occasionally. Stir in remaining flour.

3. On generously floured surface, roll dough lightly to coat. Gently roll to 3/8-inch thickness. Cut dough with floured 2 1/2-inch doughnut cutter.

4. Slide doughnuts into hot oil, using wide spatula. Turn doughnuts as they rise to the surface. Fry 2 to 3 minutes until golden brown on both sides. Remove from oil with long fork; do not prick doughnuts. Drain on paper towels; cool slightly. Serve doughnuts plain, spread cooled doughnuts with Chocolate Glaze or sprinkle with sugar.

Chocolate Glaze

2 1/2 cups powdered sugar

1 oz unsweetened baking chocolate, melted and cooled

1/2 teaspoon vanilla

1/4 cup milk

In medium bowl, mix powdered sugar, chocolate and vanilla. Gradually stir in milk until smooth and spreadable.

High Altitude (3500 to 6500 feet): Use 2 teaspoons baking powder. Heat oil to 360°F. Fry doughnuts 3 to 4 minutes.

1 Doughnut: Calories 195 (Calories from Fat 45); Fat 5g (Saturated 1g); Cholesterol 20mg; Sodium 120mg; Carbohydrate 35g (Dietary Fiber 1g); Protein 3g **Exchanges:** 1 Starch, 1 Other Carbohydrates, 1 Fat **Carbohydrate Choices:** 2

BAKING FOR TODAY

These old-fashioned doughnuts are perfect for dunking into your favorite hot beverage. If you'd like to try buttermilk doughnuts, you can substitute buttermilk for the milk, decrease baking powder to 2 teaspoons and add 1 teaspoon baking soda.

Classic Popovers

Winning the Gold Medal at the Millers' International Exhibition in 1880 was a great victory for Cadwallader Washburn. After winning the esteemed award, Washburn Crosby began selling "Gold Medal" flour. And, it's just as great today in these popovers.

Prep Time: 10 min; Start to Finish: 45 min | 6 popovers

2 eggs

1 cup Gold Medal all-purpose flour or Gold Medal Wondra quick-mixing flour

1 cup milk

1/2 teaspoon salt

1 Heat oven to 450°F. Generously grease 6-cup popover pan with shortening. Heat popover pan in oven 5 minutes.

2 Meanwhile, in medium bowl, beat eggs slightly with fork or wire whisk. Stir in flour, milk and salt with fork or wire whisk just until smooth (do not overbeat).

3 Fill cups about half full. Bake 20 minutes.

4 Reduce oven temperature to 325°F. Bake 10 to 15 minutes longer or until deep golden brown. Immediately remove from pan. Serve warm.

BAKING FOR TODAY

Prepare a double batch of popovers when you bake, and freeze the extras. Pierce each freshly baked popover with the point of a knife to let out the steam. Cool them on a wire rack, then wrap tightly and freeze. To reheat thawed popovers, cover loosely with foil and bake at 375°F for about 15 minutes or until warm.

High Altitude (3500 to 6500 feet): Use 1 cup plus 1 tablespoon flour.

1 Popover: Calories 125 (Calories from Fat 25); Fat 3g (Saturated 1g); Cholesterol 75mg; Sodium 240mg; Carbohydrate 18g (Dietary Fiber 1g); Protein 6g
Exchanges: 1 Starch, 1 Fat
Carbohydrate Choices: 1

POPOVERS

Steamed Brown Bread

Classic

An authentic dark bread made with cornmeal and flavored with molasses, this bread, also called Boston Brown Bread, was created in Colonial times. Originally, it often called for rye meal, which was readily available at the time. The combination of all-purpose and whole wheat flours creates extra flavor, and the steaming gives the bread its unique, characteristic texture.

Prep Time: 15 min; Start to Finish: 3 hr 20 min   **4 loaves (8 slices each)**

1 cup Gold Medal all-purpose flour

1 cup Gold Medal whole wheat flour

1 cup cornmeal

1 cup raisins

2 cups buttermilk

3/4 cup molasses

2 teaspoons baking soda

1 teaspoon salt

1 Remove labels from four 4 1/4 x 3-inch cans (15- to 16-oz vegetable cans). Grease cans or heatproof 7-inch tube mold with shortening or spray with cooking spray. In large bowl, beat all ingredients with electric mixer on low speed 30 seconds, scraping bowl constantly. Beat on medium speed 30 seconds, scraping bowl constantly.

2 Fill cans about 2/3 full. Cover tightly with foil. Place cans on rack in Dutch oven or steamer; pour boiling water into pan to level of rack. Cover pan.

3 Keep water boiling over low heat about 3 hours or until toothpick inserted in center comes out clean. (Add boiling water during steaming if necessary.) Immediately loosen sides of bread with metal spatula and unmold bread; cool on wire rack.

BAKING FOR TODAY

You can save time by making Baked Brown Bread: Heat oven to 325°F. Grease 2-quart casserole with shortening or spray with cooking spray. Pour batter into casserole. Bake uncovered about 1 hour or until toothpick inserted in center comes out clean.

High Altitude (3500 to 6500 feet): Use 1 teaspoon baking soda. In step 3, keep water boiling over medium-low heat.

1 Slice: Calories 90 (Calories from Fat 10); Fat 1g (Saturated 0g); Cholesterol 0mg; Sodium 170mg; Carbohydrate 19g (Dietary Fiber 1g); Protein 2g
Exchanges: 1 Starch
Carbohydrate Choices: 1

Banana Bread

Classic

1 1/4 cups sugar

1/2 cup butter or margarine, softened

2 eggs

1 1/2 cups mashed very ripe bananas (3 medium)

1/2 cup buttermilk

1 teaspoon vanilla

2 1/2 cups Gold Medal all-purpose flour

1 teaspoon baking soda

1 teaspoon salt

1 cup chopped nuts, if desired

1 Move oven rack to low position so that tops of pans will be in center of oven. Heat oven to 350°F. Grease bottoms only of two 8 x 4-inch loaf pans or one 9 x 5-inch loaf pan with shortening or spray with cooking spray.

2 In large bowl, mix sugar and butter. Stir in eggs until well blended. Stir in bananas, buttermilk and vanilla; beat until smooth. Stir in flour, baking soda and salt just until moistened. Stir in nuts. Divide batter evenly between pans.

3 Bake 8-inch loaves about 1 hour, 9-inch loaf about 1 hour 15 minutes, or until toothpick inserted in center comes out clean. Cool 10 minutes in pans on wire rack.

4 Loosen sides of loaves from pans; remove from pans and place top side up on wire rack. Cool completely, about 2 hours, before slicing. Wrap tightly and store at room temperature up to 4 days, or refrigerate up to 10 days.

Blueberry-Banana Bread: Omit nuts. Stir 1 cup fresh or frozen blueberries into batter.

BAKING FOR TODAY

Banana bread seems to have been around as long as ripe bananas and flour have been around, and many people have their own favorite recipe. This one is the favorite of the Betty Crocker Kitchens—with the addition of buttermilk, it makes a premium bread. For the best moistness and most flavor, be sure to use very ripe bananas.

High Altitude (3500 to 6500 feet): Bake 8-inch loaves about 1 hour 5 minutes, 9-inch loaf about 1 hour 20 minutes.

1 Slice: Calories 70 (Calories from Fat 20); Fat 2g (Saturated 1g); Cholesterol 15mg; Sodium 95mg; Carbohydrate 12g (Dietary Fiber 0g); Protein 1g
Exchanges: 1 Starch
Carbohydrate Choices: 1

Zucchini-Raisin-Nut Bread

Prep Time: 20 min; **Start to Finish:** 2 hr 30 min   2 loaves (16 slices each)

3 cups shredded zucchini
(2 to 3 medium)

1 1/2 cups sugar

2/3 cup vegetable oil

2 teaspoons vanilla

4 eggs

3 cups Gold Medal
all-purpose flour

1/2 cup coarsely chopped nuts

1/2 cup golden raisins

4 teaspoons baking powder

1 teaspoon salt

1 teaspoon ground cinnamon

1/2 teaspoon ground cloves

1 Heat oven to 350°F. Grease bottoms only of two 8 x 4-inch or 9 x 5-inch loaf pans with shortening or spray with cooking spray. In large bowl, mix zucchini, sugar, oil, vanilla and eggs. Stir in remaining ingredients. Pour into pans.

2 Bake 50 to 60 minutes or until toothpick inserted in center comes out clean. Cool 10 minutes. Loosen sides of loaves from pans; remove from pans to wire rack. Cool completely, about 1 hour, before slicing. Wrap tightly and store at room temperature up to 4 days, or refrigerate up to 1 week.

BAKING FOR TODAY

Cut your time in the kitchen by dividing and conquering this recipe with your family. You can shred the zucchini while one of the kids measures sugar, oil and vanilla. In a separate bowl, have another child or your spouse measure dry ingredients. Then mix everything together and bake. You'll be out of the kitchen in half the time!

High Altitude (3500 to 6500 feet): Heat oven to 375°F. Use 2 1/2 teaspoons baking powder. Bake 55 to 60 minutes.

1 Slice: Calories 155 (Calories from Fat 65); Fat 7g (Saturated 1g); Cholesterol 25mg; Sodium 145mg; Carbohydrate 21g (Dietary Fiber 1g); Protein 2g
Exchanges: 1 Starch, 1 Vegetable, 1 Fat
Carbohydrate Choices: 1 1/2

ZUCCHINI-RAISIN-NUT BREAD

Blueberry-Oat Bread

Classic

2/3 cup packed brown sugar

3/4 cup milk

1/2 cup vegetable oil

2 eggs

2 1/4 cups Gold Medal all-purpose flour

1 cup old-fashioned or quick-cooking oats

3 teaspoons baking powder

1 teaspoon ground cinnamon

1 teaspoon grated lemon peel

1 tablespoon lemon juice

1/4 teaspoon salt

1 cup fresh or frozen (thawed and drained) blueberries

1 Heat oven to 350°F. Grease bottom only of 8 x 4-inch or 9 x 5-inch loaf pan with shortening or spray with cooking spray.

2 In large bowl, mix brown sugar, milk, oil and eggs with spoon. Stir in remaining ingredients except blueberries; beat with spoon 30 seconds. Fold in blueberries. Pour into pan. Sprinkle with additional oats if desired.

3 Bake 55 to 65 minutes or until toothpick inserted in center comes out clean. Cool 10 minutes. Loosen sides of loaf from pan; remove from pan to wire rack. Cool completely, about 2 hours, before slicing. Wrap tightly and store at room temperature up to 4 days, or refrigerate up to 10 days.

BAKING FOR TODAY

Bake to your highest standard with the flour that has the highest quality, Gold Medal. With the delicious combination of all-purpose flour and oats in this berry bread, you'll be adding whole-grain goodness to your family's eating.

High Altitude (3500 to 6500 feet): Not recommended.

1 Slice: Calories 165 (Calories from Fat 65); Fat 7g (Saturated 1g); Cholesterol 20mg; Sodium 115mg; Carbohydrate 22g (Dietary Fiber 1g); Protein 3g
Exchanges: 1 Starch, 1/2 Fruit, 1 Fat
Carbohydrate Choices: 1 1/2

Luscious Lemon Loaf

Classic

1 3/4 cups Gold Medal all-purpose flour

1/2 teaspoon baking soda

1/4 teaspoon salt

1 cup granulated sugar

1/2 cup butter or margarine, softened

2 eggs

1/2 cup sour cream

2 tablespoons grated lemon peel

1/4 cup lemon juice

Lemon Glaze (below)

1 Heat oven to 325°F. Grease bottom only of 8 x 4-inch or 9 x 5-inch loaf pan with shortening or spray with cooking spray. In small bowl, mix flour, baking soda and salt; set aside. In large bowl, beat sugar and butter with electric mixer on medium speed, scraping bowl occasionally, until fluffy. Beat in eggs, sour cream, lemon peel and lemon juice until blended. Gradually beat in flour mixture until blended. Pour into pan.

2 Bake 55 to 65 minutes or until toothpick inserted in center comes out clean. Cool 10 minutes. Loosen sides of loaf from pan; remove from pan to wire rack. Cool completely, about 1 hour. Prepare Lemon Glaze. Drizzle over top of cake, allowing some to drizzle down sides.

Lemon Glaze

1/2 cup powdered sugar   1 to 2 tablespoons lemon juice

1 teaspoon grated lemon peel

In small bowl, mix all ingredients until smooth and thin enough to drizzle.

BAKING FOR TODAY

This luscious bread was developed to use lemon, but if you prefer lime, you can use lime juice and peel in the bread and in the glaze. Whatever you use, this citrus bread packs a power of flavor and perks up the everyday with a little pucker power.

High Altitude (3500 to 6500 feet): Heat oven to 350°F. Bake 1 hour to 1 hour 10 minutes.

1 Slice: Calories 260 (Calories from Fat 100); Fat 11g (Saturated 6g); Cholesterol 60mg; Sodium 170mg; Carbohydrate 37g (Dietary Fiber 1g); Protein 3g **Exchanges:** 1 Starch, 1 1/2 Other Carbohydrates, 2 Fat **Carbohydrate Choices:** 2 1/2

Pepper Jack Cheese Quick Bread

Prep Time: 15 min; Start to Finish: 1 hr 35 min

1 loaf (16 slices)

2 cups Gold Medal all-purpose flour

1 cup shredded Monterey Jack cheese with jalapeño peppers (4 oz)

1 teaspoon sugar

1 teaspoon baking powder

1/2 teaspoon baking soda

1/2 teaspoon salt

1 cup buttermilk

1/4 cup butter or margarine, melted

2 eggs, slightly beaten

1 Heat oven to 350°F. Lightly grease bottom only of 9 x 5-inch or 8 x 4-inch loaf pan with shortening or spray with cooking spray.

2 In medium bowl, mix flour, cheese, sugar, baking powder, baking soda and salt. Stir in remaining ingredients just until moistened (batter will be lumpy). Spread in pan.

3 Bake 35 to 45 minutes or until golden brown and toothpick inserted in center comes out clean. Cool 5 minutes; run knife around edges of pan to loosen. Remove from pan to wire rack. Cool 30 minutes before slicing.

BAKING FOR TODAY

This wonderful savory quick bread can be an easy addition to your supper. Serve it with any casserole, chili, soup or stew. You'll notice that buttermilk is used in many bread recipes—such as this one. That's because buttermilk is made with skim milk that's cultured, so it adds a great dairy flavor without too many extra calories.

High Altitude (3500 to 6500 feet): Bake 45 to 55 minutes.

1 Slice: Calories 125 (Calories from Fat 55); Fat 6g (Saturated 4g); Cholesterol 40mg; Sodium 220mg; Carbohydrate 13g (Dietary Fiber 0g); Protein 5g
Exchanges: 1 Starch, 1 Fat
Carbohydrate Choices: 1

PEPPER JACK CHEESE QUICK BREAD

Walnut, Bran and Plum Muffins

Prep Time: 20 min; **Start to Finish:** 35 min   12 muffins

1 1/4 cups Gold Medal all-purpose flour

1 cup bran flake cereal, crushed

1/4 cup packed brown sugar

2 teaspoons baking powder

1/2 teaspoon baking soda

1/4 teaspoon salt

1 egg, slightly beaten

1 cup buttermilk

1/2 cup vegetable oil

1 cup quartered orange-flavored or regular dried plums

1/2 cup coarsely chopped walnuts

1 tablespoon granulated sugar

1 Heat oven to 400°F. Grease 12 medium muffin cups with shortening, or line with paper baking cups and spray with cooking spray.

2 In large bowl, mix flour, cereal, brown sugar, baking powder, baking soda and salt. Stir in egg, buttermilk and oil just until moistened. Gently stir in plums and walnuts. Divide batter evenly among muffin cups. Sprinkle 1/4 teaspoon granulated sugar on each muffin.

3 Bake 13 to 15 minutes or until toothpick inserted in center comes out clean. Remove from pan to wire rack. Serve warm.

BAKING FOR TODAY

These tasty muffins are very moist, so they keep well. To store, place in a resealable plastic freezer bag or covered container and freeze. Thaw one for your breakfast or snack by warming it in the microwave on High for about 35 seconds.

High Altitude (3500 to 6500 feet): Use 1 teaspoon baking powder. Use paper baking cups. Bake 15 to 17 minutes.

1 Muffin: Calories 215 (Calories from Fat 115); Fat 13g (Saturated 2g); Cholesterol 20mg; Sodium 230mg; Carbohydrate 21g (Dietary Fiber 1g); Protein 4g **Exchanges:** 1 Starch, 1/2 Fruit, 2 1/2 Fat
Carbohydrate Choices: 1 1/2

Oatmeal-Cranberry Muffins

Native Americans in the Cape Cod area added cranberries and nuts to their corn breads, and taught the early settlers to cook with cranberries. Today we know how great cranberries taste in breads of all kinds, and use them commonly.

Prep Time: 15 min; Start to Finish: 35 min   12 muffins

1 cup buttermilk or sour milk

1 cup old-fashioned oats

1/3 cup butter or margarine, melted

1/2 cup packed brown sugar

2 teaspoons grated orange peel, if desired

1 egg

1/2 cup Gold Medal all-purpose flour

1/2 cup Gold Medal whole wheat flour

1 1/2 teaspoons baking powder

1 teaspoon salt

1 teaspoon ground cinnamon

1 cup fresh or frozen cranberries, chopped

1 Heat oven to 400°F. In small bowl, pour buttermilk over oats. Grease bottoms only of 12 medium muffin cups with shortening, or line with paper baking cups.

2 In large bowl, mix butter, brown sugar, orange peel and egg with spoon. Stir in flours, baking powder, salt and cinnamon just until flour is moistened. Stir in oat mixture; fold in cranberries. Fill muffin cups 3/4 full.

3 Bake 15 to 20 minutes or until golden brown. Immediately remove from pan to wire rack.

BAKING FOR TODAY

The combination of all-purpose and whole wheat flours gives this hearty muffin a homespun look and taste. Why is it called whole wheat flour? Because it contains the whole grain, including all parts of the kernel: bran, the outer shell; endosperm, the inner part; and wheat germ, the embryo where many nutrients are stored.

High Altitude (3500 to 6500 feet): Use 3/4 teaspoon baking powder and 1/4 teaspoon salt. Bake 20 to 25 minutes.

1 Muffin: Calories 170 (Calories from Fat 65); Fat 7g (Saturated 4g); Cholesterol 35mg; Sodium 320mg; Carbohydrate 23g (Dietary Fiber 2g); Protein 4g **Exchanges:** 1 Starch, 1/2 Fruit, 1 1/2 Fat
Carbohydrate Choices: 1 1/2

Sugar-Topped Raspberry Muffins

Prep Time: 20 min; Start to Finish: 45 min   12 muffins

2 cups Gold Medal
all-purpose flour

1/2 cup granulated sugar

3 teaspoons baking powder

1/4 teaspoon salt

1/4 teaspoon ground nutmeg

1 egg, beaten

1 cup milk

1/4 cup butter or margarine,
melted

2 teaspoons vanilla

1 cup fresh or frozen
raspberries

2 tablespoons white coarse
sugar crystals (decorating
sugar) or granulated sugar

1 Heat oven to 375°F. Grease 12 medium muffin cups with shortening, or line with paper baking cups.

2 In large bowl, mix flour, granulated sugar, baking powder, salt and nutmeg. Stir in egg, milk, butter and vanilla just until blended. Gently fold in raspberries. Divide batter among muffin cups, using 1/4 cup batter for each cup. Sprinkle sugar crystals over batter.

3 Bake 20 to 25 minutes or until toothpick inserted in center comes out clean. Remove from pan to wire rack.

BAKING FOR TODAY

Add a little sparkle to your baked goods by sprinkling a bit of sugar or even colored sugar over muffins or cookies before baking. If you prefer a streusel-topped muffin, just use the streusel from the Berry-Streusel Muffins on page 162.

High Altitude (3500 to 6500 feet): Use 1 1/2 teaspoons baking powder. Use paper baking cups.

1 Muffin: Calories 175 (Calories from Fat 45); Fat 5g (Saturated 3g); Cholesterol 30mg; Sodium 210mg; Carbohydrate 29g (Dietary Fiber 1g); Protein 3g **Exchanges:** 1 Starch, 1 Fruit, 1 Fat **Carbohydrate Choices:** 2

Classic Baking Powder Biscuits

1 3/4 cups Gold Medal all-purpose flour*

2 1/2 teaspoons baking powder

3/4 teaspoon salt

1/3 cup shortening

3/4 cup milk

If using Gold Medal self-rising flour, omit baking powder and salt.

1 Heat oven to 450°F. In medium bowl, mix flour, baking powder and salt. Cut in shortening, using pastry blender (or pulling 2 table knives through ingredients in opposite directions), until mixture looks like fine crumbs. Stir in just enough milk so dough leaves side of bowl and rounds up into a ball. (Too much milk makes dough sticky; not enough milk makes biscuits dry.)

2 On lightly floured surface, knead dough lightly 10 times. Roll or pat 1/2 inch thick. Cut with floured 2-inch biscuit cutter. Place on ungreased cookie sheet about 1 inch apart for crusty sides, touching for soft sides.

3 Bake 10 to 12 minutes or until golden brown. Immediately remove from cookie sheet. Serve warm.

Biscuit Sticks: Heat oven to 450°F. In 9-inch square pan, melt 1/3 cup butter or margarine in oven; remove from oven. Roll dough into 8-inch square. Cut dough in half; cut each half into eight 1-inch strips. Dip strips into butter, coating all sides. Arrange strips in 2 rows in pan. Sprinkle with garlic salt, sesame seed or poppy seed. Bake about 15 minutes or until golden brown. 16 sticks.

Buttermilk Biscuits: Decrease baking powder to 2 teaspoons. Add 1/4 teaspoon baking soda to dry ingredients. Substitute buttermilk for the milk.

Drop Biscuits: Grease cookie sheet with shortening or spray with cooking spray. Increase milk to 1 cup. Drop dough by 12 spoonfuls onto cookie sheet. (If desired, first drop dough into sesame seed; coat all sides.)

Sweet Potato Biscuits: In large bowl, mix 2 cups flour, 1/4 cup sugar, 2 1/2 teaspoons baking powder and 1 teaspoon salt. Cut in 1/2 cup shortening. In small bowl, mix 1 cup mashed cooked sweet potatoes or squash and 1/2 cup milk; stir into flour mixture until soft dough forms. Knead dough on generously floured surface. Roll or pat 3/4 inch thick. Place biscuits 1 inch apart on ungreased cookie sheet. Bake 12 to 15 minutes until light golden brown.

Whole Wheat Biscuits: Substitute Gold Medal whole wheat flour for the all-purpose flour.

High Altitude (3500 to 6500 feet): Use 1 1/4 teaspoons baking powder. Bake 11 to 13 minutes.

1 Biscuit: Calories 120 (Calories from Fat 55); Fat 6g (Saturated 2g); Cholesterol 0mg; Sodium 260mg; Carbohydrate 15g (Dietary Fiber 0g); Protein 2g **Exchanges:** 1 Starch, 1 Fat **Carbohydrate Choices:** 1

BAKING FOR TODAY

To freshen these tender biscuits, you can warm them in the microwave. Microwave 1 room-temperature biscuit 10 to 15 seconds, 2 biscuits 20 to 30 seconds or 6 biscuits 40 to 45 seconds. To heat frozen biscuits, microwave 1 biscuit 20 to 25 seconds, 2 biscuits 35 to 40 seconds or 6 biscuits 1 minute 45 seconds to 2 minutes.

Easy Cream Drop Biscuits

1 3/4 cups Gold Medal
all-purpose flour*

2 1/2 teaspoons baking powder

1/2 teaspoon salt

1 1/3 cups whipping (heavy)
cream

*If using Gold Medal
self-rising flour, omit baking
powder and salt.

1 Heat oven to 450°F. Grease cookie sheet with shortening or spray with cooking spray. In large bowl, mix flour, baking powder and salt. Stir in whipping cream just until blended and a dough forms. Add 1 to 2 tablespoons additional cream if dough is very thick.

2 Drop dough by 12 spoonfuls onto cookie sheet.

3 Bake 10 to 12 minutes or until bottoms are golden brown. Immediately remove from cookie sheet. Serve warm.

BAKING FOR TODAY

Sprinkle sesame or poppy seed over these delicious biscuits just before baking for a special touch.

High Altitude (3500 to 6500 feet): Grease large cookie sheet. Use 3/4 teaspoon baking powder and 1 cup whipping cream. Stir in 1/3 cup water with the whipping cream. Drop dough by 14 spoonfuls. Bake 11 to 13 minutes. Makes 14 biscuits.

1 Biscuit: Calories 140 (Calories from Fat 70); Fat 8g (Saturated 5g); Cholesterol 30mg; Sodium 210mg; Carbohydrate 15g (Dietary Fiber 0g); Protein 2g **Exchanges:** 1 Starch, 1 1/2 Fat **Carbohydrate Choices:** 1

EASY CREAM DROP BISCUITS

Provolone and Olive Biscuits

Prep Time: 20 min; Start to Finish: 35 min

10 biscuits

2 cups Gold Medal all-purpose flour*

2 teaspoons baking powder

1/2 teaspoon salt

2/3 cup butter or margarine

1/2 cup shredded provolone cheese (2 oz)

1/4 cup Kalamata or ripe olives, well drained and chopped

3/4 cup buttermilk

If using Gold Medal self-rising flour, omit baking powder and salt.

1 Heat oven to 425°F. In large bowl, mix flour, baking powder and salt. Cut in butter and cheese, using pastry blender (or pulling 2 table knives through ingredients in opposite directions), until mixture looks like coarse crumbs. Stir in olives and buttermilk just until moistened and soft dough forms.

2 On lightly floured surface, knead dough 5 or 6 times. Roll or pat dough 1/2 inch thick. Cut with 2 1/2-inch biscuit cutter. On ungreased cookie sheet, place biscuits 1 inch apart.

3 Bake 13 to 15 minutes or until light golden brown. Serve warm.

BAKING FOR TODAY

If you don't have buttermilk, add 2 teaspoons white vinegar or lemon juice plus enough milk to equal 3/4 cup. A round glass that's 2 1/2 inches in diameter makes a good stand-in for a biscuit cutter. Crazy about Cheddar? Try it instead of the provolone in these irresistible biscuits.

High Altitude (3500 to 6500 feet): Use 1/3 cup butter or margarine.

1 Biscuit: Calories 235 (Calories from Fat 135); Fat 15g (Saturated 9g); Cholesterol 40mg; Sodium 390mg; Carbohydrate 20g (Dietary Fiber 1g); Protein 5g **Exchanges:** 1 Starch, 3 Fat **Carbohydrate Choices:** 1

Currant Scones

Prep Time: 15 min; Start to Finish: 35 min

8 scones

1 3/4 cups Gold Medal all-purpose flour

3 tablespoons granulated sugar

2 1/2 teaspoons baking powder

1/2 teaspoon salt

1/3 cup firm butter or margarine

1 egg, beaten

1/2 teaspoon vanilla

4 to 6 tablespoons whipping (heavy) cream

1/2 cup currants or raisins

Additional whipping (heavy) cream

White coarse sugar crystals (decorating sugar) or granulated sugar

1 Heat oven to 400°F. In large bowl, mix flour, 3 tablespoons sugar, the baking powder and salt. Cut in butter, using pastry blender (or pulling 2 table knives through ingredients in opposite directions), until mixture looks like fine crumbs. Stir in egg, vanilla and just enough of the 4 to 6 tablespoons whipping cream so dough leaves side of bowl. Stir in currants.

2 On lightly floured surface, gently roll dough to coat with flour. Knead lightly 10 times. On ungreased cookie sheet, roll or pat dough into 8-inch circle. Cut into 8 wedges with sharp knife that has been dipped in flour, but do not separate wedges. Brush with additional whipping cream; sprinkle with sugar crystals.

3 Bake 14 to 16 minutes or until light golden brown. Immediately remove from cookie sheet; carefully separate wedges. Serve warm.

Chocolate Chip Scones: Omit currants. Stir in 1/2 cup miniature semisweet chocolate chips with the egg, vanilla and whipping cream.

Raspberry–White Chocolate Scones: Omit currants. Substitute almond extract for the vanilla; increase whipping cream to 1/2 cup. Stir in 3/4 cup frozen unsweetened raspberries (do not thaw) and 2/3 cup white baking chips with the egg, almond extract and whipping cream. Omit kneading step; pat dough into 8-inch circle on ungreased cookie sheet. Continue as directed.

BAKING FOR TODAY

A pizza cutter works great for cutting the scones before and after baking. In a hurry? Just drop dough from a large spoon into 8 equal mounds on ungreased cookie sheet. Flatten to about 1/2-inch thickness with floured fingers, and bake as directed.

High Altitude (3500 to 6500 feet): Use 1 teaspoon baking powder. Bake 20 to 22 minutes.

1 Scone: Calories 270 (Calories from Fat 110); Fat 12g (Saturated 7g); Cholesterol 60mg; Sodium 360mg; Carbohydrate 37g (Dietary Fiber 1g); Protein 4g **Exchanges:** 1 Starch; 1 1/2 Other Carbohydrates; 2 Fat **Carbohydrate Choices:** 2 1/2

Pear-Nut Scones

Prep Time: 15 min; Start to Finish: 35 min

8 scones

1 3/4 cups Gold Medal all-purpose flour

1/3 cup packed brown sugar

2 teaspoons baking powder

1/4 teaspoon salt

1/3 cup firm butter or margarine

1 egg

1/2 cup half-and-half

1 cup chopped peeled pear (1 medium)

1/3 cup chopped pecans

1 Heat oven to 400°F. In large bowl, mix flour, brown sugar, baking powder and salt. Cut in butter, using pastry blender (or pulling 2 table knives through ingredients in opposite directions), until mixture looks like fine crumbs. Stir in egg and half-and-half until soft dough forms. Stir in pear and pecans.

2 On ungreased cookie sheet, drop dough by slightly rounded 1/3 cupfuls.

3 Bake 16 to 18 minutes or until golden brown. Immediately remove from cookie sheet. Serve warm.

BAKING FOR TODAY

Scones are similar to biscuits, except they're sweet, buttery and more tender. They have become very popular in bakeries, restaurants and recipes in recent years. This tasty pear and pecan combination will become a winner in your household. If you prefer apple scones, just use chopped peeled apple in place of the pear and use any type of nuts you wish.

High Altitude (3500 to 6500 feet): Use 1 1/4 teaspoons baking powder.

1 Scone: Calories 285 (Calories from Fat 125); Fat 14g (Saturated 6g); Cholesterol 55mg; Sodium 270mg; Carbohydrate 35g (Dietary Fiber 2g); Protein 5g
Exchanges: 2 Starch, 3 Fat
Carbohydrate Choices: 2

PEAR-NUT SCONES

Sweet Corn–Pecan Bread

Corn has been a popular recipe ingredient since it was first cultivated. Many long-ago corn breads were named for their shapes or the way they were cooked. Ashcakes, corn pone, scratch back, hasty pudding, johnnycakes and slappers are a few of the corn-based breads that were familiar to early settlers.

Prep Time: 20 min; Start to Finish: 3 hr 5 min | **1 loaf (12 slices)**

1/2 cup butter or margarine, softened

1 cup sugar

2 eggs

1 can (14.75 oz) cream-style corn, undrained

2 cups Gold Medal all-purpose flour

1/2 cup cornmeal

3 teaspoons baking powder

1 teaspoon salt

1/2 cup chopped pecans

1 Heat oven to 350°F. Generously grease bottom and sides of 9 x 5-inch loaf pan with shortening or spray with cooking spray. In large bowl, beat butter and sugar with electric mixer on medium speed until fluffy. Beat in eggs and corn until well mixed. Stir in flour, cornmeal, baking powder and salt, scraping bowl once, just until blended. Stir in pecans. Pour into pan.

2 Bake 1 hour to 1 hour 15 minutes or until toothpick inserted in center comes out clean. Cool in pan 30 minutes. Remove from pan to wire rack. Cool completely, about 45 minutes, before slicing.

BAKING FOR TODAY

Filled with flecks of nutty pecans, a slice of this lightly sweetened loaf of corn bread makes a bowl of chili special.

High Altitude (3500 to 6500 feet): Heat oven to 375°F. Use 1 1/2 teaspoons baking powder. Bake 1 hour 5 minutes to 1 hour 15 minutes.

1 Slice: Calories 315 (Calories from Fat 115); Fat 13g (Saturated 5g); Cholesterol 55mg; Sodium 460mg; Carbohydrate 45g (Dietary Fiber 2g); Protein 5g **Exchanges:** 2 Starch, 1 Other Carbohydrates, 2 Fat **Carbohydrate Choices:** 3

SWEET CORN-PECAN BREAD

LEMON SQUARES AND APPLESAUCE JUMBLES

Chapter 3

Crazy About Cookies

Deluxe Brownies

Classic

Brownies first became popular in the 1920s. Could it be that they were originally a fallen chocolate cake? Or brownies could be an American version of Scottish cocoa scones. Whatever their pedigree, the first brownies in the United States were called Bangor Brownies after the city in Maine where they were first "discovered" by dessert fans.

Prep Time: 15 min; Start to Finish: 1 hr   16 brownies

2/3 cup butter or margarine

5 oz unsweetened baking chocolate, cut into pieces

1 3/4 cups sugar

2 teaspoons vanilla

3 eggs

1 cup Gold Medal all-purpose flour

1 cup chopped nuts

1 Heat oven to 350°F. Grease bottom and sides of 9-inch square pan with shortening or spray with cooking spray.

2 In 1-quart saucepan, melt butter and chocolate over low heat, stirring frequently; cool slightly. In medium bowl, beat sugar, vanilla and eggs with electric mixer on high speed 5 minutes. Beat in chocolate mixture on low speed. Beat in flour just until blended. Stir in nuts. Spread in pan.

3 Bake 40 to 45 minutes or just until edges crack and brownies pull away from sides of pan; cool. For brownies, cut into 4 rows by 4 rows.

BAKING FOR TODAY

Melting the butter and chocolate together gives a rich, chocolate flavor and fudginess to these long-time treasured brownies. You may be tempted to melt this mixture in your microwave, but that is not recommended because of the high wattage of today's microwaves and the fact that chocolate and butter can melt at different times. Sometimes slower is better, especially when it comes to flavor development.

High Altitude (3500 to 6500 feet): Grease bottom and sides of 13 x 9-inch pan. Bake 30 to 35 minutes.

1 Brownie: Calories 210 (Calories from Fat 170); Fat 19g (Saturated 8g); Cholesterol 60mg; Sodium 65mg; Carbohydrate 31g (Dietary Fiber 2g); Protein 4g
Exchanges: 1 Starch, 1 Other Carbohydrates, 4 Fat
Carbohydrate Choices: 2

Oatmeal Brownies

Classic

These scrumptious brownies were first featured in the Gold Medal recipe collection of 1925. The little oak recipe box, filled with recipes, was sold to consumers for just $1 and from 1925 to 1935, more than 350,000 boxes were sold.

Prep Time: 30 min; Start to Finish: 1 hr 5 min   **4 dozen brownies**

2 1/2 cups old-fashioned or quick-cooking oats

3/4 cup Gold Medal all-purpose flour

3/4 cup packed brown sugar

1/2 teaspoon baking soda

3/4 cup butter or margarine, melted

Deluxe Brownies (page 78)

1 Heat oven to 350°F. Grease bottom and sides of 13 x 9-inch pan with shortening or spray with cooking spray. In medium bowl, mix oats, flour, brown sugar and baking soda. Stir in butter. Reserve 3/4 cup oat mixture. Press remaining oat mixture in pan. Bake 10 minutes; cool 5 minutes.

2 Make batter for Deluxe Brownies as directed in step 2 except omit nuts. Spread batter over baked oat layer. Sprinkle with reserved oat mixture.

3 Bake 30 to 35 minutes or until brownies begin to pull away from sides of pan (do not overbake); cool. For brownies, cut into 8 rows by 6 rows.

BAKING FOR TODAY

With old-fashioned crumbly oat goodness on the bottom and top, these very fudgy treats store well and keep well, which makes them a great choice for giving or sending. To store, just keep tightly covered at room temperature, or freeze tightly covered for longer storage.

High Altitude (3500 to 6500 feet): In step 1, bake 13 minutes; cool 5 minutes.

1 Brownie: Calories 145 (Calories from Fat 65); Fat 7g (Saturated 5g); Cholesterol 30mg; Sodium 55mg; Carbohydrate 18g (Dietary Fiber 1g); Protein 2g
Exchanges: 1 Starch, 1 1/2 Fat
Carbohydrate Choices: 1

Lemon Squares

Classic

1 cup Gold Medal
all-purpose flour

1/2 cup butter or margarine,
softened

1/4 cup powdered sugar, plus
additional for sprinkling

1 cup granulated sugar

2 teaspoons grated lemon peel,
if desired

2 tablespoons lemon juice

1/2 teaspoon baking powder

1/4 teaspoon salt

2 eggs

1 Heat oven to 350°F. In small bowl, mix flour, butter and powdered sugar. Press in ungreased 8-inch square pan, building up 1/2-inch edge. Bake 20 minutes.

2 In small bowl, beat remaining ingredients with electric mixer on high speed about 3 minutes or until light and fluffy. Pour over hot crust.

3 Bake 25 to 30 minutes or until almost no indentation remains when touched lightly in center. Cool completely, about 1 hour. Sprinkle with additional powdered sugar. For squares, cut into 5 rows by 5 rows.

BAKING FOR TODAY

Bar cookies are popular because they save time in the kitchen. Get great results when making these ever-popular bars by using the correct size pan to prevent under- or overbaking. The three most common pan sizes are 13 x 9 inch, 9-inch square and 8-inch square; we developed this recipe to use an 8-inch pan.

High Altitude (3500 to 6500 feet): Use 3/4 cup granulated sugar. In step 1, bake 20 to 25 minutes.

1 Square: Calories 90 (Calories from Fat 35); Fat 4g (Saturated 2g); Cholesterol 30mg; Sodium 65mg; Carbohydrate 13g (Dietary Fiber 0g); Protein 1g
Exchanges: 1 Other Carbohydrates, 1 Fat
Carbohydrate Choices: 1

Hermits

Hermits originated in Cape Cod during the days of the clipper ships. The cookies kept well when stored in canisters aboard ships on long sea voyages. A Washburn Crosby cookbook of the late 1800s noted in a recipe for Hermits that the raisins, a traditional ingredient, must be "stoned and chopped." Now it's smooth sailing in the kitchen!

Prep Time: 10 min; Start to Finish: 50 min   **About 4 dozen cookies**

1 cup packed brown sugar

1/4 cup shortening

1/4 cup butter or margarine, softened

1/4 cup cold coffee or water

1/2 teaspoon baking soda

1/2 teaspoon salt

1/2 teaspoon ground cinnamon

1/2 teaspoon ground nutmeg

1 egg

1 3/4 cups Gold Medal all-purpose flour

1 1/4 cups raisins

3/4 cup chopped nuts

1 Heat oven to 375°F. In large bowl, mix brown sugar, shortening, butter, coffee, baking soda, salt, cinnamon, nutmeg and egg with spoon. Stir in flour, raisins and nuts.

2 On ungreased cookie sheet, drop dough by rounded teaspoonfuls about 2 inches apart.

3 Bake 8 to 10 minutes or until almost no indentation remains when touched. Immediately remove from cookie sheet to wire rack; cool.

Bran Hermits: Omit nuts. Stir in 1 1/4 cups Wheaties® cereal with the raisins.

Molasses Hermits: Decrease brown sugar to 3/4 cup. Increase shortening to 1/3 cup. Add 1/4 cup molasses.

BAKING FOR TODAY

A trick used in the Betty Crocker Kitchens to make drop cookies the same size and shape is to use a spring-handled cookie or ice-cream scoop. Scoops come in various sizes and have a corresponding number. The one most often used for cookies—and for this recipe—is a #70 scoop.

High Altitude (3500 to 6500 feet): Bake 10 to 12 minutes.

1 Cookie: Calories 85 (Calories from Fat 35); Fat 4g (Saturated 1g); Cholesterol 5mg; Sodium 50mg; Carbohydrate 11g (Dietary Fiber 0g); Protein 1g **Exchanges:** 1 Other Carbohydrates, 1/2 Fat **Carbohydrate Choices:** 1

Snickerdoodles

Classic

It's kind of a funny name for such a popular cookie. Way back when, there were also Petticoat Tails, Brambles, Tangle Breeches and Wasps Nests—names that gave away the nature of the cookies and that were given for fun—both to say and to eat.

Prep Time: 15 min; Start to Finish: 1 hr 5 min   **About 5 dozen cookies**

1/4 cup sugar

1 tablespoon ground cinnamon

1 1/2 cups sugar

1/2 cup shortening

1/2 cup butter or margarine, softened

2 eggs

2 3/4 cups Gold Medal all-purpose flour

2 teaspoons cream of tartar

1 teaspoon baking soda

1/4 teaspoon salt

1 Heat oven to 400°F. In small bowl, mix 1/4 cup sugar and the cinnamon; set aside. In large bowl, beat 1 1/2 cups sugar, the shortening, butter and eggs with electric mixer on medium speed, or mix with spoon. Stir in flour, cream of tartar, baking soda and salt.

2 Shape dough into 1 1/4-inch balls. Roll in sugar-cinnamon mixture. On ungreased cookie sheet, place balls about 2 inches apart.

3 Bake 8 to 10 minutes or until centers are almost set. Cool 1 minute; remove from cookie sheet to wire rack. Cool completely, about 30 minutes.

BAKING FOR TODAY

This classic and classy cookie gets its cracked, sugary look from being rolled in sugar and cinnamon before baking. Many popular foods from the past are making a comeback, including these semi-addictive Snickerdoodles.

High Altitude (3500 to 6500 feet): Before baking, flatten dough balls to 1/2-inch thickness with glass dipped in remaining sugar-cinnamon mixture.

1 Cookie: Calories 70 (Calories from Fat 25); Fat 3g (Saturated 1g); Cholesterol 10mg; Sodium 45mg; Carbohydrate 10g (Dietary Fiber 0g); Protein 1g
Exchanges: 1 Other Carbohydrates
Carbohydrate Choices: 1

Oatmeal-Raisin Cookies

2/3 cup granulated sugar

2/3 cup packed brown sugar

1/2 cup butter or margarine, softened

1/2 cup shortening

1 teaspoon baking soda

1 teaspoon ground cinnamon

1 teaspoon vanilla

1/2 teaspoon baking powder

1/2 teaspoon salt

2 eggs

3 cups quick-cooking or old-fashioned oats

1 cup Gold Medal all-purpose flour

1 cup raisins, chopped nuts or semisweet chocolate chips, if desired

1 Heat oven to 375°F. In large bowl, beat all ingredients except oats, flour and raisins with electric mixer on medium speed, or mix with spoon. Stir in oats, flour and raisins.

2 On ungreased cookie sheet, drop dough by rounded tablespoonfuls about 2 inches apart.

3 Bake 9 to 11 minutes or until light brown. Immediately remove from cookie sheet to wire rack.

Oatmeal-Raisin Squares: Press dough in ungreased 8-inch square pan. Bake about 25 minutes or until light brown. Cool in pan on wire rack. For squares, cut into 4 rows by 4 rows. 16 squares.

BAKING FOR TODAY

You can make a lighter version of these moist cookies by substituting unsweetened applesauce for the shortening and 1/2 cup fat-free cholesterol-free egg product for the eggs. Increase cinnamon and vanilla to 1 1/2 teaspoons each.

High Altitude (3500 to 6500 feet): Use 1/2 teaspoon baking soda; add additional 2 tablespoons flour. Cool cookies 1 minute before removing from cookie sheet.

1 Cookie: Calories 135 (Calories from Fat 55); Fat 6g (Saturated 2g); Cholesterol 20mg; Sodium 95mg; Carbohydrate 18g (Dietary Fiber 1g); Protein 2g
Exchanges: 1 Starch, 1 Fat
Carbohydrate Choices: 1

Farm-Style Oatmeal Cookies

Classic

These cookies were developed when most people lived on farms and baked large batches of cookies to feed their families. Cookies were real multi-taskers; kids loved them, they kept a long time and they were welcome treats in lunch boxes for school or in the fields.

Prep Time: 20 min; Start to Finish: 1 hr **About 4 dozen cookies**

2 cups packed brown sugar

1 cup butter or margarine, softened

1/2 cup buttermilk

1 teaspoon vanilla

3 1/2 cups old-fashioned or quick-cooking oats

1 3/4 cups Gold Medal all-purpose flour

1 teaspoon baking soda

3/4 teaspoon salt

1 Heat oven to 375°F. In large bowl, mix brown sugar, butter, buttermilk and vanilla. Stir in remaining ingredients.

2 Shape dough into 1-inch balls. On ungreased cookie sheet, place balls about 3 inches apart. Flatten cookies slightly with bottom of glass dipped in water.

3 Bake 8 to 10 minutes or until golden brown. Immediately remove from cookie sheet to wire rack; cool.

BAKING FOR TODAY

There are many versions of oatmeal cookies, as you'll see in this chapter. Like flour, oatmeal is also an American classic. In this cookie, the butter and brown sugar combination gives these treats an almost caramel-like flavor, a flavor your family is sure to love!

High Altitude (3500 to 6500 feet): Use 2 cups flour. Bake 9 to 11 minutes. Cool cookies 1 minute before removing from cookie sheet.

1 Cookie: Calories 110 (Calories from Fat 35); Fat 4g (Saturated 2g); Cholesterol 10mg; Sodium 95mg; Carbohydrate 16g (Dietary Fiber 1g); Protein 2g
Exchanges: 1 Starch, 1 Fat
Carbohydrate Choices: 1

Cream Wafers

Classic

Recipes have certainly changed over the years—they are much easier now. An 1894 Washburn Crosby cookbook included a rolled sugar cookie, similar to this one, instructing the cook to "roll the dough as thin as pasteboard" and "bake in a quick oven."

Prep Time: 10 min; Start to Finish: 1 hr 30 min	About 5 dozen sandwich cookies

1 cup butter or margarine, softened

1/3 cup whipping (heavy) cream

2 cups Gold Medal all-purpose flour

Granulated sugar

Creamy Filling (below)

1 In medium bowl, mix butter, whipping cream and flour thoroughly with spoon. Cover and refrigerate at least 1 hour.

2 Heat oven to 375°F. On lightly floured surface, roll about 1/3 of the dough at a time until 1/8 inch thick (keep remaining dough refrigerated until ready to roll). Cut into 1 1/2-inch rounds.

3 Cover a piece of waxed paper with a thick layer of granulated sugar. Transfer rounds with spatula to sugar-covered waxed paper; turn each round so that both sides are coated with sugar. On ungreased cookie sheet, place rounds about 1 inch apart. Prick rounds with fork about 4 times.

4 Bake 7 to 9 minutes or just until set but not brown. Remove from cookie sheet to wire rack. Cool completely, about 30 minutes. Put cookies together in pairs (bottoms together) with Creamy Filling.

Creamy Filling

1/4 cup butter or margarine, softened

3/4 cup powdered sugar

1 teaspoon vanilla

Food color

In small bowl, beat butter, powdered sugar and vanilla with spoon until smooth and fluffy. Stir in a few drops of food color. (A few drops of water can be added if necessary to make filling spreadable.)

High Altitude (3500 to 6500 feet): No changes.

1 Cookie: Calories 60 (Calories from Fat 35); Fat 4g (Saturated 3g); Cholesterol 10mg; Sodium 25mg; Carbohydrate 6g (Dietary Fiber 0g); Protein 0g **Exchanges:** 1/2 Other Carbohydrates, 1/2 Fat **Carbohydrate Choices:** 1/2

BAKING FOR TODAY

With only three ingredients, these buttery, rich cookies are so easy to mix, roll and bake in no time. While the cookies are cooling, you can make the filling. For special occasions, divide the filling and tint each amount with a different food color.

Butterscotch Shortbread

Classic

1/4 cup butter or margarine, softened

1/4 cup shortening

1/4 cup packed brown sugar

2 tablespoons granulated sugar

1 cup plus 2 tablespoons Gold Medal all-purpose flour

1/4 teaspoon salt

1 Heat oven to 300°F. In large bowl, beat butter, shortening and sugars with electric mixer on medium speed until creamy, or mix with spoon. Stir in flour and salt. (Dough will be dry and crumbly; use hands to mix completely.)

2 On lightly floured surface, roll dough into 9 x 6-inch rectangle. Cut into 1 1/2-inch squares. On ungreased cookie sheet, place squares about 1 inch apart.

3 Bake about 25 minutes or until set. Remove from cookie sheet to wire rack; cool.

BAKING FOR TODAY

This easy-to-work-with dough makes great cutout cookies. It's important to set the timer or watch the clock when baking them, because it's hard to tell by eye when they are done; they brown very little and the shape does not change. After baking, you can enjoy them plain, make sandwich cookies or frost them.

High Altitude (3500 to 6500 feet): Bake about 30 minutes.

1 Cookie: Calories 70 (Calories from Fat 35); Fat 4g (Saturated 2g); Cholesterol 5mg; Sodium 40mg; Carbohydrate 8g (Dietary Fiber 0g); Protein 1g
Exchanges: 1/2 Other Carbohydrates, 1 Fat
Carbohydrate Choices: 1/2

BUTTERSCOTCH SHORTBREAD

Ethel's Sugar Cookies

Classic

Refrigerated-dough cookies grew popular during World War II, when many women took jobs outside the home. With limited cooking time, Gold Medal users could prepare the dough ahead, refrigerate it and bake fresh cookies later, a practice that's alive and well today!

Prep Time: 15 min; Start to Finish: 1 hr 45 min   About 4 dozen cookies

1 cup granulated sugar

1/2 cup butter or margarine, softened

1/4 cup shortening

1 teaspoon vanilla

2 eggs

2 1/2 cups Gold Medal all-purpose flour

1 teaspoon baking powder

1 teaspoon salt

1 In medium bowl, mix sugar, butter, shortening, vanilla and eggs with spoon. Stir in flour, baking powder and salt. Cover and refrigerate at least 1 hour.

2 Heat oven to 400°F. On lightly floured surface, roll dough 1/8 inch thick. Cut into desired shapes with 3-inch cookie cutters. On ungreased cookie sheet, place shapes about 2 inches apart.

3 Bake 6 to 8 minutes or until very light brown. Immediately remove from cookie sheet to wire rack; cool.

Butterscotch Drop Sugar Cookies: Substitute 1 cup packed brown sugar for the granulated sugar. If desired, stir 1 cup chopped black or regular walnuts into dough. Do not refrigerate. On ungreased cookie sheet, drop dough by rounded teaspoonfuls about 2 inches apart. Bake as directed.

Chocolate Pinwheel Cookies: Melt 2 ounces unsweetened baking chocolate; cool. Make dough as directed. Divide dough in half. Stir chocolate into half of dough. Cover and refrigerate both doughs at least 1 hour. On lightly floured surface, roll plain dough into 12 x 9-inch rectangle. Repeat with chocolate dough. Place chocolate dough on plain dough. Roll doughs together until 3/16 inch thick. Roll up tightly, beginning at a long side; wrap roll and refrigerate 30 minutes. Cut roll into 1/8-inch slices. On ungreased cookie sheet, place slices 2 inches apart. Bake as directed.

Hand Cookies: Roll dough 3/16 inch thick. Place hand lightly on dough; trace around hand with pizza cutter. Bake 6 to 8 minutes or until no indentation remains when touched. Cool; decorate as desired.

High Altitude (3500 to 6500 feet): Bake 7 to 9 minutes.

1 Cookie: Calories 65 (Calories from Fat 25); Fat 3g (Saturated 2g); Cholesterol 15mg; Sodium 75mg; Carbohydrate 9g (Dietary Fiber 0g); Protein 1 g **Exchanges:** 1/2 Other Carbohydrates, 1/2 Fat **Carbohydrate Choices:** 1/2

Raisin Filled Sugar Cookies: Make dough as directed. Cover and refrigerate at least 1 hour. Heat oven to 400°F. Lightly grease cookie sheet with shortening or spray with cooking spray. Cut dough into 48 rounds with 2 1/2-inch doughnut cutter that has center removed. Cut out centers of 24 of the rounds with center of doughnut cutter. Place uncut rounds on cookie sheet. Top with Raisin Filling (below) or Date-Apricot Filling (page 109), spreading almost to edges. Top with remaining rounds. Press edges together with fingers or floured fork. Sprinkle tops with sugar. Bake 6 to 8 minutes or until very light brown.

Raisin Filling

1 3/4 cups raisins

3/4 cup water

1/2 cup sugar

2 tablespoons Gold Medal all-purpose flour

1 tablespoon lemon juice

In 1-quart saucepan, heat raisins and water to boiling; reduce heat. Cover and simmer 5 minutes. In small bowl, mix sugar and flour; stir into raisin mixture. Heat to boiling over medium heat, stirring constantly. Boil and stir 1 minute. Stir in lemon juice; cool.

BAKING FOR TODAY

You can add a mint frosting to these cookies in minutes. While cookies are warm, place 1 chocolate mint patty on each cookie; when softened, spread almost to edge of cookie. Remove cookies to wire rack to cool.

Old-Fashioned Molasses Cookies

Classic

With a delightful molasses, ginger and spice taste, these moist, cakelike cookies will remind you of the "good old days." The frosting is made just for this flavor-packed cookie—so make it when you can!

Prep Time: 25 min; Start to Finish: 4 hr 20 min — About 6 dozen cookies

1 1/2 cups sugar

1 cup butter or margarine, softened

1/2 cup molasses

2 eggs

3 teaspoons baking soda

1/2 cup water

5 1/2 cups Gold Medal all-purpose flour

1 1/2 teaspoons ground cinnamon

1 teaspoon ground ginger

1 teaspoon ground cloves

1 teaspoon salt

Vanilla Cooked Frosting (below)

1 In large bowl, mix sugar, butter, molasses and eggs with spoon. In small bowl, dissolve baking soda in water; stir into molasses mixture. Stir in remaining ingredients except Vanilla Cooked Frosting. Cover and refrigerate at least 2 hours.

2 Heat oven to 375°F. Lightly grease cookie sheet with shortening or spray with cooking spray. On lightly floured surface, roll dough 1/4 inch thick. Cut with floured 2 3/4-inch round cutter or other favorite cutter. On cookie sheet, place cutouts about 2 inches apart.

3 Bake 8 to 10 minutes or until light brown. Remove from cookie sheet to wire rack. Cool completely, about 30 minutes. Frost bottoms of cookies with Vanilla Cooked Frosting. Let stand 2 to 3 hours before storing to allow frosting to dry.

Vanilla Cooked Frosting

1 envelope plus 2 teaspoons unflavored gelatin

1 cup cold water

1 cup granulated sugar

2 1/4 cups powdered sugar

1 1/2 teaspoons vanilla

1 teaspoon baking powder

1/8 teaspoon salt

In 2-quart saucepan, sprinkle gelatin on cold water to soften; stir in granulated sugar. Heat to a rolling boil; reduce heat. Simmer uncovered 10 minutes. Place powdered sugar in large bowl. Pour hot mixture over powdered sugar; beat with electric mixer on medium speed about 2 minutes or until foamy. Beat in vanilla, baking powder and salt on high speed 12 to 15 minutes or until soft peaks form.

High Altitude (3500 to 6500 feet): Use 2 teaspoons baking soda.

1 Cookie: Calories 110 (Calories from Fat 25); Fat 3g (Saturated 2g); Cholesterol 15mg; Sodium 115mg; Carbohydrate 20g (Dietary Fiber 0g); Protein 1g **Exchanges:** 1 Other Carbohydrates, 1 Fat **Carbohydrate Choices:** 1

BAKING FOR TODAY

Make it easy on yourself! Make the dough one day, refrigerate it overnight, then cut out and bake the cookies the next day. All that's left is to make the frosting and frost the cookies. Or, skip the frosting—the cookies are just as delicious.

Chocolate Drop Cookies

Classic

Some recipes are just classics—like these rich chocolate cookies. Gold Medal flour has been publishing the recipe for these gems since 1903—more than a century of cookie satisfaction!

Prep Time: 15 min; Start to Finish: 1 hr 50 min   **About 4 1/2 dozen cookies**

1 cup sugar

1/2 cup butter or margarine, softened

1 egg

2 oz unsweetened baking chocolate, melted and cooled

1/3 cup buttermilk or water

1 teaspoon vanilla

1 3/4 cups Gold Medal all-purpose flour

1/2 teaspoon baking soda

1/2 teaspoon salt

1 cup chopped nuts, if desired

Chocolate Frosting (below)

1 Heat oven to 400°F. In medium bowl, mix sugar, butter, egg, chocolate, buttermilk and vanilla. Stir in flour, baking soda, salt and nuts.

2 On ungreased cookie sheet, drop dough by rounded teaspoonfuls about 2 inches apart.

3 Bake 8 to 10 minutes or until almost no indentation remains when touched. Immediately remove from cookie sheet to wire rack. Cool completely, about 30 minutes. Frost with Chocolate Frosting.

Chocolate Frosting

2 oz unsweetened baking chocolate   3 tablespoons water

2 tablespoons butter or margarine   About 2 cups powdered sugar

In 1 1/2-quart saucepan, melt chocolate and butter over low heat, stirring frequently; remove from heat. Stir in water and powdered sugar until smooth and spreadable.

BAKING FOR TODAY

These soft chocolate cookies will be a hit with your family, and you may remember them from your childhood. The kids can help by mixing the dough, dropping it onto the cookie sheets and then frosting the cookies. Before the frosting sets, kids can also decorate the cookies with candy sprinkles or colored sugar.

High Altitude (3500 to 6500 feet): No changes.

1 Cookie: Calories 80 (Calories from Fat 25); Fat 3g (Saturated 2g); Cholesterol 5mg; Sodium 50mg; Carbohydrate 12g (Dietary Fiber 0g); Protein 1g
Exchanges: 1 Other Carbohydrates, 1/2 Fat
Carbohydrate Choices: 1

Mary's Chocolate Chip Cookies

Classic

Chocolate chip cookies date back to 1940 when Ruth Wakefield of The Toll House Inn of Massachusetts chopped a bar of leftover semisweet chocolate and added it to a basic cookie recipe. Later that day, Toll House Cookies made the news when a visiting writer got a taste of the new cookie. That same year, chocolate chip cookies were introduced to homemakers on the Betty Crocker coast-to-coast radio series, "Famous Foods from Famous Places."

Prep Time: 15 min; Start to Finish: 1 hr   About 3 1/2 dozen cookies

1 1/2 cups butter or margarine, softened

1 1/4 cups granulated sugar

1 1/4 cups packed brown sugar

1 tablespoon vanilla

2 eggs

4 cups Gold Medal all-purpose flour

2 teaspoons baking soda

1/2 teaspoon salt

1 bag (24 oz) semisweet chocolate chips (4 cups)

1 Heat oven to 375°F. In large bowl, mix butter, sugars, vanilla and eggs with spoon. Stir in flour, baking soda and salt (dough will be stiff). Stir in chocolate chips.

2 On ungreased cookie sheet, drop dough by level 1/4 cupfuls about 2 inches apart. Flatten slightly with fork.

3 Bake 12 to 15 minutes or until light brown (centers will be soft). Cool slightly. Remove from cookie sheet to wire rack; cool.

BAKING FOR TODAY

These marvelous cookies are famous in the Betty Crocker Kitchens. Mary Bartz, former director of the kitchens and cookie expert, gives them as gifts for birthdays, anniversaries and other special occasions. Mary's special secret for making sure she has the proper amount of all ingredients? She always bakes a test cookie. You can also bake a test cookie; see page 19.

High Altitude (3500 to 6500 feet): Bake 10 to 13 minutes.

1 Cookie: Calories 245 (Calories from Fat 110); Fat 12g (Saturated 7g); Cholesterol 30mg; Sodium 140mg; Carbohydrate 32g (Dietary Fiber 1g); Protein 2g **Exchanges:** 1 Starch, 1 Other Carbohydrates, 2 1/2 Fat **Carbohydrate Choices:** 2

MARY'S CHOCOLATE CHIP COOKIES

Quick Chocolate Chip Sticks

1 1/3 cups sugar

1 cup plus 2 tablespoons butter or margarine, softened

1 teaspoon vanilla

2 eggs

3 cups Gold Medal all-purpose flour

1 teaspoon baking powder

1 bag (6 oz) semisweet chocolate chips (1 cup)

3 tablespoons sugar

3/4 teaspoon ground cinnamon

1 Heat oven to 350°F. In large bowl, beat 1 1/3 cups sugar, the butter, vanilla and eggs with electric mixer on medium speed, or mix with spoon. Stir in flour and baking powder. Stir in chocolate chips.

2 Divide dough into fourths. On lightly floured surface, shape each fourth into 15-inch roll, 1 inch in diameter. On ungreased cookie sheet, place rolls about 2 inches apart. Flatten slightly with fork to about 5/8-inch thickness. In small bowl, mix 3 tablespoons sugar and the cinnamon; sprinkle over dough.

3 Bake 13 to 15 minutes or until edges are light brown. Cut diagonally into about 1-inch strips while warm.

BAKING FOR TODAY

These delicious cookies are the ultimate in convenient cookie baking. You slice them into sticks after they are baked, saving yourself time in the kitchen.

High Altitude (3500 to 6500 feet): Use 1 cup butter. In step 2, use 2 cookie sheets with 2 rolls on each. Bake 18 to 20 minutes.

1 Cookie: Calories 80 (Calories from Fat 35); Fat 4g (Saturated 2g); Cholesterol 15mg; Sodium 30mg; Carbohydrate 10g (Dietary Fiber 0g); Protein 1g **Exchanges:** 1/2 Other Carbohydrates, 1 Fat **Carbohydrate Choices:** 1/2

Chocolate-Raspberry Triangles

Candylike cookies came into vogue around 1955. The headline on a Gold Medal flour advertisement that year said, "Bake as cookies. Eat as candy." Who can resist two desserts in one?

Prep Time: 20 min; **Start to Finish:** 2 hr 10 min   Makes 4 dozen triangles

1 1/2 cups Gold Medal all-purpose flour

3/4 cup sugar

3/4 cup butter or margarine, softened

1 box (10 oz) frozen raspberries in syrup, thawed and undrained

1/4 cup orange juice

1 tablespoon cornstarch

3/4 cup miniature semisweet chocolate chips

1 Heat oven to 350°F. In medium bowl, mix flour, sugar and butter with spoon. In bottom of ungreased 13 x 9-inch pan, press dough evenly. Bake 15 minutes.

2 In 1-quart saucepan, mix raspberries, orange juice and cornstarch. Heat to boiling, stirring constantly. Boil and stir 1 minute. Cool 10 minutes. Sprinkle chocolate chips over crust. Carefully spread raspberry mixture over chocolate chips.

3 Bake about 20 minutes or until raspberry mixture is set. Refrigerate about 1 hour or until chocolate is firm. For triangles, cut into 4 rows by 3 rows, then cut each square into 4 triangles.

BAKING FOR TODAY

These sensational bar cookies were developed to replicate popular restaurant and candy flavor combinations: chocolate with raspberry and orange. A great-looking and great-tasting treat, they look particularly fun when cut into triangles.

High Altitude (3500 to 6500 feet): In step 2, boil and stir about 3 minutes. In step 3, bake about 25 minutes.

1 Triangle: Calories 80 (Calories from Fat 35); Fat 4g (Saturated 2g); Cholesterol 10mg; Sodium 20mg; Carbohydrate 10g (Dietary Fiber 1g); Protein 1g **Exchanges:** 1/2 Other Carbohydrates, 1 Fat **Carbohydrate Choices:** 1/2

Chocolate Crinkles

Prep Time: 15 min; Start to Finish: 3 hr 45 min About 3 dozen cookies

1 cup granulated sugar

2 tablespoons butter or margarine, softened

1 teaspoon vanilla

2 oz unsweetened baking chocolate, melted and cooled

2 eggs

1 cup Gold Medal all-purpose flour

1 teaspoon baking powder

1/4 teaspoon salt

1/2 cup powdered sugar

1 In large bowl, mix granulated sugar, butter, vanilla and chocolate with spoon. Stir in eggs, one at a time. Stir in flour, baking powder and salt. Cover and refrigerate at least 3 hours.

2 Heat oven to 350°F. Grease cookie sheet with shortening or spray with cooking spray. Drop dough by teaspoonfuls into powdered sugar; roll around to coat. Shape into balls. On cookie sheet, place balls about 2 inches apart.

3 Bake 10 to 12 minutes or until almost no indentation remains when touched. Immediately remove from cookie sheet to wire rack; cool.

BAKING FOR TODAY

Always a classic, these family favorites seem to have been around forever. These delicious cookies look great, taste great and sell like hotcakes at bake sales. For added convenience to your cookie baking, try the new silicone baking mats and oven mitts.

High Altitude (3500 to 6500 feet): Bake 9 to 11 minutes.

1 Cookie: Calories 60 (Calories from Fat 20); Fat 2g (Saturated 1g); Cholesterol 15mg; Sodium 40mg; Carbohydrate 10g (Dietary Fiber 0g); Protein 1g
Exchanges: 1/2 Other Carbohydrates, 1/2 Fat
Carbohydrate Choices: 1/2

CHOCOLATE CRINKLES

Root Beer Float Cookies

Prep Time: 15 min; Start to Finish: 1 hr 15 min   **About 4 1/2 dozen cookies**

1 cup packed brown sugar

1/2 cup butter or margarine, softened

2 cups Gold Medal all-purpose flour

1/3 cup finely crushed root beer–flavored hard candies (about 10 candies)

1 teaspoon baking powder

1/2 teaspoon baking soda

1/4 teaspoon salt

1/8 teaspoon ground cinnamon

1/8 teaspoon ground allspice

2 eggs

Root Beer Glaze (below)

Additional finely crushed root beer–flavored hard candies, if desired

1 Heat oven to 350°F. Grease cookie sheet with shortening or spray with cooking spray. In large bowl, beat brown sugar and butter with electric mixer on medium speed until light and fluffy, or mix with spoon. Stir in remaining ingredients except Root Beer Glaze and additional candies.

2 On cookie sheet, drop dough by rounded teaspoonfuls about 2 inches apart.

3 Bake 8 to 10 minutes or until almost no indentation remains when touched in center and edges are golden brown. Cool 1 minute; remove from cookie sheet to wire rack. Cool completely, about 20 minutes.

4 Drizzle Root Beer Glaze over cookies. Sprinkle with additional candies.

Root Beer Glaze

1 cup powdered sugar   4 to 5 teaspoons root beer or milk

In small bowl, mix ingredients with spoon until smooth and thin enough to drizzle.

BAKING FOR TODAY

With flavors reminiscent of a soda fountain at an old-time drugstore, these cookies will be a hit with kids and adults alike. Favorite beverages of choice with these unique cookies? Milk or root beer to boost the cookie flavor, or hot chocolate or coffee for a new taste sensation.

High Altitude (3500 to 6500 feet): No changes.

1 Cookie: Calories 65 (Calories from Fat 20); Fat 2g (Saturated 1g); Cholesterol 15mg; Sodium 45mg; Carbohydrate 11g (Dietary Fiber 0g); Protein 1g
Exchanges: 1 Other Carbohydrates
Carbohydrate Choices: 1

ROOT BEER FLOAT COOKIES

Key Lime Coolers

1 cup butter or margarine, softened

1/2 cup powdered sugar

1 3/4 cups Gold Medal all-purpose flour

1/4 cup cornstarch

1 tablespoon grated lime peel

1/2 teaspoon vanilla

Granulated sugar

Key Lime Glaze (below)

1 Heat oven to 350°F. In large bowl, beat butter and powdered sugar with electric mixer on medium speed until light and fluffy, or mix with spoon. Stir in flour, cornstarch, lime peel and vanilla until well blended.

2 Shape dough into 1-inch balls. On ungreased cookie sheet, place balls about 2 inches apart. Press bottom of glass into dough to grease, then dip into granulated sugar; press on shaped dough until 1/4 inch thick.

3 Bake 9 to 11 minutes or until edges are light golden brown. Remove from cookie sheet to wire rack. Cool completely, about 30 minutes. Brush with Key Lime Glaze.

Key Lime Glaze

1/2 cup powdered sugar

2 teaspoons grated lime peel

4 teaspoons Key lime or regular lime juice

In small bowl, mix all ingredients with spoon until smooth.

BAKING FOR TODAY

These cookies, made with Key lime juice and peel, pack fresh, modern flavor. If you like using a cookie press, try making Key Lime Ribbons. Prepare dough as directed, but do not shape into balls. Place dough in cookie press fitted with a ribbon tip. Form long ribbons of dough on ungreased cookie sheet. Cut into 3-inch lengths. Continue as directed.

High Altitude (3500 to 6500 feet): Bake 10 to 12 minutes.

1 Cookie: Calories 70 (Calories from Fat 35); Fat 4g (Saturated 2g); Cholesterol 10mg; Sodium 25mg; Carbohydrate 8g (Dietary Fiber 0g); Protein 1g
Exchanges: 1/2 Other Carbohydrates, 1 Fat
Carbohydrate Choices: 1/2

KEY LIME COOLERS

Ginger Creams

Classic

Ginger Creams feature the flavor combination so popular during the early 1900s—molasses plus ginger, nutmeg, cinnamon and cloves—a rich, mellow taste that was more spicy than sweet. The cookies were then frosted with vanilla or lemon frosting.

Prep Time: 20 min; Start to Finish: 2 hr 30 min	About 4 dozen cookies

1/2 cup sugar

1/3 cup butter or margarine, softened

1 egg

1/2 cup molasses

1/2 cup water

2 cups Gold Medal all-purpose flour or whole wheat flour

1 teaspoon ground ginger

1/2 teaspoon salt

1/2 teaspoon baking soda

1/2 teaspoon ground nutmeg

1/2 teaspoon ground cloves

1/2 teaspoon ground cinnamon

Vanilla Butter Frosting (below)

1 In large bowl, mix sugar, butter, egg, molasses and water with spoon. Stir in remaining ingredients except frosting. Cover and refrigerate at least 1 hour.

2 Heat oven to 400°F. On ungreased cookie sheet, drop dough by rounded teaspoonfuls about 2 inches apart.

3 Bake about 8 minutes or until almost no indentation remains when touched. Immediately remove from cookie sheet to wire rack. Cool completely, about 30 minutes. Frost with Vanilla Butter Frosting.

Vanilla Butter Frosting

1/4 cup butter or margarine, softened

2 cups powdered sugar

1 teaspoon vanilla

About 1 tablespoon milk

In medium bowl, mix butter and powdered sugar with spoon. Beat in vanilla and milk until smooth and spreadable.

BAKING FOR TODAY

To add a frosty white finish to these cookies, omit the frosting, and dip half of each cookie in melted white chocolate. Let stand on waxed paper until the chocolate is set.

High Altitude (3500 to 6500 feet): No changes.

1 Cookie: Calories 75 (Calories from Fat 20); Fat 2g (Saturated 1g); Cholesterol 10mg; Sodium 55mg; Carbohydrate 13g (Dietary Fiber 0g); Protein 1g
Exchanges: 1 Other Carbohydrates
Carbohydrate Choices: 1

Applesauce Jumbles

Classic

Jumbles appeared on the cookie scene as early as Colonial days. When ingredients were scarce during the Great Depression and rationed in World War II, much of the sugar was replaced with molasses and the amount of shortening (now butter in this recipe) was reduced.

Prep Time: 20 min; **Start to Finish:** 1 hr 30 min | **4 1/2 to 5 dozen cookies**

2 3/4 cups Gold Medal all-purpose flour

1 1/2 cups packed brown sugar

1 cup chopped nuts, if desired

1 cup raisins

3/4 cup applesauce

1/2 cup butter or margarine, softened

1 teaspoon salt

1 teaspoon ground cinnamon

1 teaspoon vanilla

1/2 teaspoon baking soda

1/4 teaspoon ground cloves

2 eggs

Browned Butter Glaze (below)

1 In large bowl, mix all ingredients except Browned Butter Glaze with spoon. (If dough is soft, cover and refrigerate.)

2 Heat oven to 375°F. On ungreased cookie sheet, drop dough by rounded teaspoonfuls about 2 inches apart.

3 Bake about 10 minutes or until almost no indentation remains when touched. Immediately remove from cookie sheet to wire rack. Cool completely, about 30 minutes. Spread with Browned Butter Glaze.

Browned Butter Glaze

1/3 cup butter (do not use margarine)

2 cups powdered sugar

1 1/2 teaspoons vanilla

2 to 4 tablespoons hot water

In 1-quart saucepan, melt butter over low heat until golden brown. Remove from heat. Stir in powdered sugar and vanilla. Stir in hot water until smooth and spreadable.

BAKING FOR TODAY

If you've never tasted Browned Butter Glaze, you're in for a treat; it's the ultimate in buttery flavor and teams well with this classic cookie.

High Altitude (3500 to 6500 feet): Heat oven to 400°F.

1 Cookie: Calories 105 (Calories from Fat 25); Fat 3g (Saturated 2g); Cholesterol 15mg; Sodium 80mg; Carbohydrate 18g (Dietary Fiber 0g); Protein 1g
Exchanges: 1/2 Fruit, 1/2 Other Carbohydrates, 1 Fat
Carbohydrate Choices: 1

Classic Ranger Cookies

2 cups packed brown sugar

1 cup butter or margarine, softened

1 teaspoon vanilla

2 eggs

2 cups Gold Medal all-purpose flour

2 cups old-fashioned or quick-cooking oats

1 teaspoon baking powder

1 teaspoon baking soda

2 cups Wheaties cereal

1 cup salted peanuts

1 Heat oven to 350°F. In large bowl, mix brown sugar, butter, vanilla and eggs with spoon. Stir in flour, oats, baking powder and baking soda. Stir in cereal and peanuts.

2 Shape dough by rounded teaspoonfuls into balls. On ungreased cookie sheet, place balls about 2 inches apart. Flatten slightly with greased bottom of glass dipped into sugar.

3 Bake 10 to 12 minutes or until set. Cool 1 minute. Remove from cookie sheet to wire rack; cool.

BAKING FOR TODAY

If you bake cookies often, having several cookie sheets is convenient. As one sheet of cookies is baking, you can get another one ready to go. Also, it's important to let the cookie sheets cool a few minutes between bakings or the cookie dough will start to spread before it's placed in the oven.

High Altitude (3500 to 6500 feet): No changes.

1 Cookie: Calories 105 (Calories from Fat 45); Fat 5g (Saturated 2g); Cholesterol 15mg; Sodium 70mg; Carbohydrate 13g (Dietary Fiber 1g); Protein 2g
Exchanges: 1 Other Carbohydrates, 1 Fat
Carbohydrate Choices: 1

Banana Bars

Prep Time: 15 min; Start to Finish: 1 hr 50 min | **2 dozen bars**

1 cup sugar

1 cup mashed very ripe
bananas (2 medium)

1/3 cup vegetable oil

2 eggs

1 cup Gold Medal
all-purpose flour

1 teaspoon baking powder

1/2 teaspoon baking soda

1/2 teaspoon ground cinnamon

1/4 teaspoon salt

Cream Cheese Frosting (below)

1 Heat oven to 350°F. Grease bottom and sides of 13 x 9-inch pan with shortening or spray with cooking spray. In large bowl, mix sugar, bananas, oil and eggs with spoon. Stir in flour, baking powder, baking soda, cinnamon and salt. Spread in pan.

2 Bake 25 to 30 minutes or until toothpick inserted in center comes out clean. Cool completely, about 1 hour.

3 Frost with Cream Cheese Frosting. For bars, cut into 6 rows by 4 rows. Store covered in refrigerator.

Cream Cheese Frosting

1 package (3 oz) cream cheese, softened   1 teaspoon vanilla

1/3 cup butter or margarine, softened   2 cups powdered sugar

In medium bowl, mix cream cheese, butter and vanilla with electric mixer on medium speed until blended. Gradually beat in powdered sugar with spoon, scraping bowl occasionally, until smooth and spreadable.

Pumpkin-Spice Bars: Substitute 1 cup canned pumpkin (not pumpkin pie mix) for the bananas. Stir in 1/4 teaspoon ground ginger and 1/4 teaspoon ground cloves with the cinnamon. Sprinkle 1/4 cup chopped nuts over frosted bars if desired.

BAKING FOR TODAY

The special secret to making these old-fashioned bars moist and flavorful is to use very ripe bananas. And, if you love gadgets, there is a handy little tool called an "off-set spatula" or spreader. The spreader part has a bend in it, making it very easy to frost bars in pans. This offset spatula can be found in specialty cookware stores.

High Altitude (3500 to 6500 feet): Bake 27 to 32 minutes.

1 Bar: Calories 165 (Calories from Fat 65); Fat 7g (Saturated 3g); Cholesterol 30mg; Sodium 105mg; Carbohydrate 25g (Dietary Fiber 0g); Protein 1g **Exchanges:** 1/2 Fruit, 1 Other Carbohydrates, 1 1/2 Fat **Carbohydrate Choices:** 1 1/2

Salted Nut Bars

Prep Time: 20 min; Start to Finish: 40 min

32 bars

1 1/2 cups Gold Medal all-purpose flour

3/4 cup packed brown sugar

1/4 teaspoon salt

1/2 cup butter or margarine, softened

2 cups salted mixed nuts or peanuts

1 cup butterscotch-flavored chips

1/2 cup light corn syrup

2 tablespoons butter or margarine

1 Heat oven to 350°F. In medium bowl, mix flour, brown sugar and salt. Cut in 1/2 cup butter, using pastry blender (or pulling 2 table knives through ingredients in opposite directions), until evenly mixed.

2 In bottom of ungreased 13 x 9-inch pan, press dough evenly. Bake 15 minutes; cool slightly.

3 Cut up any large nuts. Sprinkle nuts evenly over crust. In 1-quart saucepan, heat remaining ingredients over low heat, stirring occasionally, just until chips are melted. Drizzle butterscotch mixture evenly over nuts. Bake 5 minutes. For bars, cut into 8 rows by 4 rows while warm for easiest cutting.

BAKING FOR TODAY

Love sweet and salty together? Then this yummy and easy-to-put-together bar cookie is made just for you. Delicious anytime, these bars are very popular—during the holidays we get a great many requests for this scrumptious recipe.

High Altitude (3500 to 6500 feet): In step 2, bake 15 to 20 minutes or until light brown; cool slightly.

1 Bar: Calories 150 (Calories from Fat 80); Fat 9g (Saturated 3g); Cholesterol 10mg; Sodium 110mg; Carbohydrate 15g (Dietary Fiber 1g); Protein 2g
Exchanges: 1 Other Carbohydrates, 2 Fat
Carbohydrate Choices: 1

SALTED NUT BARS

Sour Cream–Raisin Bars
Classic

Sour cream adds a special flavor to many foods, including these homespun bars. Through the ages, sour cream and raisin has been a popular flavor combination in pies, bars and cookies. Cooking the raisins a few minutes before adding them to the bars "plumps" them and adds moistness, a common practice in "old-fashioned" cooking that still works well today.

Prep Time: 30 min; Start to Finish: 1 hr 30 min   **Makes 24 bars**

2 cups raisins

1 cup butter or margarine, softened

1 cup packed brown sugar

2 cups old-fashioned or quick-cooking oats

1 1/2 cups Gold Medal all-purpose flour

1 teaspoon baking soda

1 cup sour cream

3/4 cup granulated sugar

2 tablespoons Gold Medal all-purpose flour

1 tablespoon grated lemon peel

1 teaspoon vanilla

1 egg

1 Heat oven to 350°F. In 2-quart saucepan, place raisins; add enough water to cover raisins. Cook over medium heat about 5 minutes or until softened; drain.

2 In large bowl, mix butter and brown sugar with spoon. Stir in oats, 1 1/2 cups flour and the baking soda. Reserve half of oat mixture. In bottom of ungreased 13 x 9-inch pan, pat remaining oat mixture. Bake 10 to 12 minutes or until golden brown.

3 In large bowl, mix raisins and remaining ingredients; pour over baked layer. Crumble reserved oat mixture over raisin mixture.

4 Bake 25 to 30 minutes or until top is golden brown and raisin mixture is set. Cool completely, about 30 minutes. For bars, cut into 8 rows by 3 rows.

BAKING FOR TODAY

For a different twist to this layered bar, omit the raisins and the cooking step for them. Instead, mix 2 cups sweetened dried cranberries or cherries with the sour cream and remaining ingredients in step 3.

High Altitude (3500 to 6500 feet): In step 2, bake 12 to 14 minutes. In step 4, bake 30 to 35 minutes.

1 Bar: Calories 250 (Calories from Fat 90); Fat 10g (Saturated 6g); Cholesterol 35mg; Sodium 115mg; Carbohydrate 37g (Dietary Fiber 1g); Protein 3g
Exchanges: 1 Starch, 1 1/2 Other Carbohydrates, 2 Fat
Carbohydrate Choices: 2 1/2

Date-Apricot Bars

Classic

These bar cookies have been loved throughout our culinary history. They have seen many different fillings, depending on the type of fruit people had on hand. Dried fruits like dates, apricots and raisins were popular and easy to use because they could be stored for a long time without refrigeration.

Prep Time: 25 min; Start to Finish: 55 min   About 40 bars

Date-Apricot Filling (below)

1/2 cup butter or margarine, softened

1 cup packed brown sugar

1 1/2 cups Gold Medal all-purpose flour

1 teaspoon salt

1/2 teaspoon baking soda

1 cup old-fashioned or quick-cooking oats

1/2 cup chopped walnuts or almonds

1 Make Date-Apricot Filling; set aside to cool.

2 Heat oven to 400°F. Grease bottom and sides of 13 x 9-inch pan with shortening or spray with cooking spray. In large bowl, mix butter and brown sugar with spoon. Stir in flour, salt, baking soda and oats. Press half of the crumbly mixture in pan. Spread filling over top. Sprinkle with walnuts. Sprinkle with remaining crumbly mixture; press lightly.

3 Bake 25 to 30 minutes or until light brown. While warm, make 1 diagonal cut from corner to corner. Continue cutting parallel to first cut, each about 1 1/2 inches apart. Repeat, cutting diagonally in opposite direction.

Date-Apricot Filling

1 1/2 cups cut-up dates   1/4 cup sugar

1 1/2 cups cut-up dried apricots   1 1/2 cups water

In 1 1/2-quart saucepan, heat all ingredients to boiling, stirring constantly; reduce heat. Simmer uncovered about 10 minutes, stirring occasionally, until thickened.

High Altitude (3500 to 6500 feet): No changes.

1 Bar: Calories 120 (Calories from Fat 35); Fat 4g (Saturated 2g); Cholesterol 5mg; Sodium 95mg; Carbohydrate 20g (Dietary Fiber 1g); Protein 1g
Exchanges: 1 Other Carbohydrates, 1 Fat
Carbohydrate Choices: 1

BAKING FOR TODAY

Such versatile bars! You can omit the apricots in the filling and just use 3 cups dates, or use half dates and half raisins. If you're feeling adventurous, you can try other dried fruit combinations, like mango-apricot, date-pineapple or any combination you like.

Chocolate Chip Dream Bars

Prep Time: 15 min; Start to Finish: 2 hr 45 min

Makes 32 bars

1/2 cup packed brown sugar

1/3 cup butter or margarine, softened

1 cup Gold Medal all-purpose flour

2 eggs

1 cup packed brown sugar

1 teaspoon vanilla

2 tablespoons Gold Medal all-purpose flour

1 teaspoon baking powder

1/2 teaspoon salt

1 bag (6 oz) semisweet chocolate chips (1 cup)

1 cup milk chocolate chips

Chocolate Glaze (below)

1 Heat oven to 350°F. In medium bowl, mix 1/2 cup brown sugar and the butter with spoon. Stir in 1 cup flour. In bottom of ungreased 13 x 9-inch pan, press mixture evenly. Bake 10 minutes.

2 In medium bowl, mix eggs, 1 cup brown sugar and the vanilla with spoon. Stir in 2 tablespoons flour, the baking powder and salt. Stir in semisweet and milk chocolate chips. Spread over crust.

3 Bake 15 to 20 minutes or until golden brown. Cool completely in pan on wire rack, about 1 hour. Drizzle with Chocolate Glaze. Refrigerate at least 1 hour until firm. For bars, cut into 8 rows by 4 rows. Store at room temperature.

Chocolate Glaze

3/4 cup milk chocolate chips

2 teaspoons vegetable oil

In 1-quart saucepan, heat ingredients over low heat, stirring constantly, until chocolate is melted.

BAKING FOR TODAY

An all-time favorite with a chocolate drizzle, Dream Bars have been popular decade after decade. If you like semisweet chocolate, you can use that instead of the milk chocolate in the glaze. For an easy way to drizzle, pour glaze into a small resealable plastic food-storage bag, seal the bag, snip off a tiny corner, then drizzle away!

High Altitude (3500 to 6500 feet): In step 1, bake 12 minutes.

1 Bar: Calories 160 (Calories from Fat 65); Fat 7g (Saturated 4g); Cholesterol 20mg; Sodium 80mg; Carbohydrate 22g (Dietary Fiber 1g); Protein 2g
Exchanges: 1/2 Starch, 1 Other Carbohydrates, 1 1/2 Fat
Carbohydrate Choices: 1 1/2

110 *BettyCrocker* Baking for Today

CHOCOLATE CHIP DREAM BARS

Russian Tea Cakes

Prep Time: 20 min; Start to Finish: 1 hr, 20 min   About 4 dozen cookies

1 cup butter or margarine, softened

1/2 cup powdered sugar

1 teaspoon vanilla

2 1/4 cups Gold Medal all-purpose flour

3/4 cup finely chopped nuts

1/4 teaspoon salt

Additional powdered sugar

1 Heat oven to 400°F. In large bowl, stir butter, 1/2 cup powdered sugar and the vanilla until well mixed. Stir in flour, nuts and salt until dough holds together.

2 Shape dough into 1-inch balls. On ungreased cookie sheet, place balls about 1 inch apart.

3 Bake 10 to 12 minutes or until set but not brown. Immediately remove from cookie sheet to wire rack; cool 5 minutes.

4 Place additional powdered sugar in small bowl. Roll warm cookies in powdered sugar; cool on wire rack 5 minutes. Roll in powdered sugar again.

Lemon Tea Cakes: Add 1/4 cup crushed lemon drop candies with the butter, powdered sugar and vanilla.

Peppermint Tea Cakes: Add 1/4 cup crushed hard peppermint candies with the butter, powdered sugar and vanilla.

BAKING FOR TODAY

Also known as Mexican Wedding Cookies, these delicate cookies are always a hit! To save time, you can use a food processor to chop the nuts and mix the dough. For best results, do not overmix the dough or the cookies will be tough.

High Altitude (3500 to 6500 feet): Heat oven to 350°F. Bake 15 to 17 minutes.

1 Cookie: Calories 75 (Calories from Fat 45); Fat 5g (Saturated 2g); Cholesterol 10mg; Sodium 40mg, Carbohydrate 7g (Dietary Fiber 0g); Protein 1g **Exchanges:** 1/2 Other Carbohydrates, 1 Fat **Carbohydrate Choices:** 1/2

Almond Biscotti

Prep Time: 25 min; **Start to Finish:** 1 hr, 45 min   **40 cookies**

1 cup slivered almonds

1 cup sugar

1/2 cup butter or margarine, softened

1 teaspoon almond extract

1 teaspoon vanilla

2 eggs

3 1/2 cups Gold Medal all-purpose flour

1 teaspoon baking powder

1/2 teaspoon baking soda

1 Heat oven to 350°F. Spread almonds in ungreased shallow pan. Bake uncovered 6 to 10 minutes, stirring occasionally, until golden brown; cool.

2 In large bowl, beat sugar, butter, almond extract, vanilla and eggs with electric mixer on medium speed, or mix with spoon. Stir in flour, baking powder and baking soda. Stir in almonds. On lightly floured surface, gently knead dough 2 to 3 minutes or until dough holds together and almonds are evenly distributed.

3 Divide dough in half. On one side of ungreased cookie sheet, shape half of dough into 10 x 3-inch rectangle, rounding edges slightly. Repeat with remaining dough on same cookie sheet.

4 Bake about 25 minutes or until center is firm to the touch. Cool on cookie sheet 15 minutes; move to cutting board. Cut each rectangle crosswise into 1/2-inch slices, using sharp knife.

5 Place 20 slices, cut sides down, on ungreased cookie sheet. Bake about 15 minutes or until crisp and light brown. Immediately remove from cookie sheet to wire rack; cool. Cool cookie sheet 5 minutes; repeat with remaining slices.

Hazelnut Biscotti: Substitute 1 cup hazelnuts (filberts), coarsely chopped, for the almonds.

BAKING FOR TODAY

Coming from Italy, *biscotti* literally means "twice baked." Using a serrated knife is a huge help when cutting the logs into slices before the second baking. Glaze cooled biscotti with Chocolate Glaze (page 110), if desired. Dunk in dessert wine, hot chocolate or coffee, and enjoy.

High Altitude (3500 to 6500 feet): In step 4, bake about 27 minutes. In step 5, bake about 20 minutes.

1 Cookie: Calories 100 (Calories from Fat 35); Fat 4g (Saturated 2g); Cholesterol 15mg; Sodium 45mg; Carbohydrate 14g (Dietary Fiber 1g); Protein 2g **Exchanges:** 1 Other Carbohydrates, 1 Fat **Carbohydrate Choices:** 1

TURKEY CHILI IN PARMESAN BREAD BOWLS

Chapter 4

Family-Pleasing Main Dishes

Quick Chicken Pot Pie

Classic

Love extra value? Then check out that bag of Gold Medal flour in your cupboard. Packing recipes free in flour bags began in 1928, to celebrate the newly formed company of General Mills, and has become a tasty Gold Medal tradition.

Prep Time: 10 min; Start to Finish: 40 min 6 servings

2 cups frozen mixed vegetables (from 1-lb bag), thawed and drained

2 cups cut-up cooked chicken

1 can (10.75 oz) condensed cream of mushroom soup

1/3 cup milk

1 cup Gold Medal all-purpose flour

1 1/2 teaspoons baking powder

2 tablespoons butter or margarine, melted

2/3 cup milk

1 egg

1 Heat oven to 425°F. In ungreased 8-inch square pan, stir vegetables, chicken, soup and 1/3 cup milk until mixed.

2 In medium bowl, stir remaining ingredients with fork until mixed. Pour over chicken mixture; spread evenly.

3 Bake uncovered 25 to 30 minutes or until golden brown.

BAKING FOR TODAY

This chicken pot pie comes together in a snap because the crust is poured, saving you the time of making a traditional roll-and-shape pastry. It's also a great take-and-bake option for your next potluck—use any frozen vegetable combination you like.

High Altitude (3500 to 6500 feet): Use 3/4 teaspoon baking powder. Bake 40 to 45 minutes.

1 Serving: Calories 270 (Calories from Fat 110); Fat 12g (Saturated 5g); Cholesterol 90mg; Sodium 570mg; Carbohydrate 22g (Dietary Fiber 2g); Protein 18g **Exchanges:** 1 Starch, 1 Vegetable, 2 Medium-Fat Meat, 1/2 Fat **Carbohydrate Choices:** 1 1/2

QUICK CHICKEN POT PIE

Pocket Pizza

Prep Time: 30 min; Start to Finish: 55 min

2 pocket pizzas (4 servings)

Pizza Dough (below)

Vegetable oil

1/2 cup pizza sauce

1/2 cup shredded mozzarella cheese (2 oz)

1 cup cooked mild Italian sausage

2 tablespoons finely chopped onion or 1/4 teaspoon onion powder

1/4 teaspoon garlic powder

About 1/2 package (3-oz size) sliced pepperoni

1/4 cup pizza sauce

1/2 cup shredded mozzarella cheese (2 oz)

1 Heat oven to 425°F. Lightly grease 2 cookie sheets with shortening or spray with cooking spray. Make Pizza Dough. On lightly floured surface, divide dough in half. Roll each half into 12-inch circle. Fold each circle loosely in half; place on cookie sheet and unfold. Brush each circle lightly with oil.

2 On one side of each dough circle, layer half each of remaining ingredients in order listed; fold dough over filling. Turn edge of lower dough over edge of top dough; pinch edge to seal. Prick top with fork. Bake 20 to 25 minutes or until golden brown.

Pizza Dough

2 cups Gold Medal all-purpose flour

2/3 cup milk

1/4 cup vegetable oil

2 teaspoons baking powder

1/2 teaspoon salt

In medium bowl, stir all ingredients vigorously until dough leaves side of bowl. (If dough seems dry, add 2 to 3 tablespoons milk.) On lightly floured surface, gather dough into a ball. Knead 10 times. Cover with bowl; let stand 15 minutes.

Pocket Ham and Cheese Sandwich: Substitute barbecue sauce for the pizza sauce, Monterey Jack cheese for the mozzarella cheese and 1 1/2 cups diced fully cooked smoked ham for the Italian sausage. Omit pepperoni.

BAKING FOR TODAY

You can make the dough when you have a few minutes, then refrigerate it for up to 24 hours. Place dough in a bowl lightly greased with shortening or sprayed with cooking spray, and turn to grease all sides. Cover tightly with plastic wrap; refrigerate. For easier shaping, let dough stand at room temperature at least 20 minutes.

High Altitude (3500 to 6500 feet): No changes.

1 Serving: Calories 640 (Calories from Fat 315); Fat 35g (Saturated 11g); Cholesterol 55mg; Sodium 1440mg; Carbohydrate 56g (Dietary Fiber 2g); Protein 25g **Exchanges:** 3 1/2 Starch, 2 High-Fat Meat, 3 1/2 Fat **Carbohydrate Choices:** 4

POCKET PIZZA

Turkey Chili in Parmesan Bread Bowls

Prep Time: 50 min; Start to Finish: 1 hr 20 min   6 servings (1 cup chili and 1 bread bowl each)

1 lb 4 oz ground turkey breast or lean (at least 80%) ground beef

1 large onion, chopped (1 cup)

2 cloves garlic, finely chopped

1 can (14.5 oz) stewed tomatoes, undrained

1 can (15 to 16 oz) kidney beans, undrained

1 can (15 oz) tomato sauce

1 can (4.5 oz) chopped green chiles, undrained

2 teaspoons chili powder

1 teaspoon sugar

1/4 teaspoon pepper

Parmesan Bread Bowls (below)

1 In 4-quart Dutch oven, cook turkey, onion and garlic over medium heat about 15 minutes, stirring occasionally, until turkey is no longer pink (or beef is brown) and onion is tender; drain if necessary.

2 Stir in remaining ingredients except Parmesan Bread Bowls. Heat to boiling, stirring frequently, reduce heat. Cover and simmer 30 minutes, stirring occasionally.

3 Meanwhile, make Parmesan Bread Bowls. Serve chili in bread bowls.

Parmesan Bread Bowls

1 package quick active dry yeast (2 1/4 teaspoons)

1/4 cup warm water (105°F to 115°F)

2 tablespoons sugar

3 cups Gold Medal all-purpose flour

3 teaspoons baking powder

1/2 teaspoon salt

1/3 cup grated Parmesan cheese

1/4 cup butter or margarine

About 1 cup buttermilk

1 In small bowl, dissolve yeast in warm water. Stir in sugar; set aside. In large bowl, mix flour, baking powder, salt and cheese. Cut in butter, using pastry blender (or pulling 2 table knives through ingredients in opposite directions), until mixture looks like fine crumbs. Stir in yeast mixture and just enough buttermilk so dough leaves side of bowl and forms a ball. On lightly floured surface, knead dough about 1 minute or until smooth. Cover and let rise in warm place 10 minutes.

2 Heat oven to 375°F. Grease outsides of six 10-ounce custard cups with shortening or spray with cooking spray. Place 3 cups upside down in ungreased 15 x 10 x 1-inch pan. Divide dough into 6 equal parts. Pat or roll 3 of the parts into 7-inch circles. Shape dough circles over outsides of custard cups; do not allow dough to curl under edges of cups. Bake 3 bread bowls at a time; pat or roll dough for remaining bread bowls while first 3 bowls are baking. Bake 18 to 22 minutes or until golden brown. Carefully lift bread bowls from custard cups—custard cups and bread will be hot. Cool bread bowls upright on wire rack 10 minutes.

High Altitude (3500 to 6500 feet): No changes.

1 Serving: Calories 615 (Calories from Fat 155); Fat 17g (Saturated 8g); Cholesterol 90mg; Sodium 1870mg; Carbohydrate 85g (Dietary Fiber 9g); Protein 39g **Exchanges:** 5 Starch, 2 Vegetable, 3 Lean Meat **Carbohydrate Choices:** 5 1/2

BAKING FOR TODAY

These savory bread bowls brimming with chili are just so cute—kids will love making (and eating) them again and again. Let them help by mixing the dough, rolling it into circles and shaping it onto the custard cups.

Easy Cheeseburger Pie

Classic

Beginning in 1942, flour was enriched to meet government regulations. Gold Medal ads explained the vitamin and mineral additions and offered consumers a booklet, *Thru Highway to Good Nutrition*, which earned national recognition from the American Red Cross. Many of these ads emphasized the importance of "nutritious, no-waste eating" during wartime. It's still a good idea today—and the principle is at work in this family-pleasing pie.

Prep Time: 25 min; Start to Finish: 1 hr | **6 servings**

Easy Pastry (below)

1 lb lean (at least 80%) ground beef

1/2 to 3/4 cup finely chopped onion

1 clove garlic, finely chopped

1/4 cup Gold Medal all-purpose flour

1/2 teaspoon salt

1/3 cup dill pickle liquid (from jar of pickles)

1/3 cup milk

1/2 cup chopped dill pickles

2 cups shredded American or Swiss cheese (8 oz)

1. Heat oven to 425°F. Make Easy Pastry. Pat pastry dough on bottom and up sides of ungreased 8-inch quiche dish or springform pan, 8-inch round pan or 8-inch ovenproof skillet. Bake 15 minutes.

2. In 10-inch skillet, cook beef, onion and garlic over medium heat 8 to 10 minutes, stirring occasionally, until beef is brown; drain. Sprinkle with flour and salt. Stir in pickle liquid and milk; stir in pickles and 1 cup of the cheese. Spoon into pastry-lined dish.

3. Bake uncovered 15 minutes. Sprinkle with remaining 1 cup cheese. Bake about 5 minutes longer or until crust is golden brown.

Easy Pastry

1 1/3 cups Gold Medal all-purpose flour | 1/2 cup shortening

1/2 teaspoon salt | 3 to 4 tablespoons cold water

In medium bowl, mix flour and salt. Cut in shortening, using pastry blender (or pulling 2 table knives through ingredients in opposite directions), until mixture looks like small peas. Sprinkle in water, 1 tablespoon at a time, stirring with fork after each addition. Mix lightly until all flour is moistened and dough almost cleans side of bowl (add 1 to 2 teaspoons more water if necessary).

High Altitude (3500 to 6500 feet): No changes.

1 Serving: Calories 580 (Calories from Fat 350); Fat 39g (Saturated 15g); Cholesterol 80mg; Sodium 790mg; Carbohydrate 29g (Dietary Fiber 1g); Protein 29g **Exchanges:** 2 Starch, 3 Medium-Fat Meat, 4 1/2 Fat **Carbohydrate Choices:** 2

BAKING FOR TODAY

Let the family help you make four Easy Individual Cheeseburger Pies: Make pastry and divide into 4 equal parts. Pat each part on bottom and up sides of four 10-ounce custard cups. Bake 10 minutes. Spoon about 3/4 cup beef mixture into each pastry-lined cup. Continue as directed.

Cheese-Crusted Meatball Pie

Prep Time: 20 min; Start to Finish: 1 hr 15 min

6 servings

1 lb lean (at least 80%) ground beef

1/4 cup dry bread crumbs

1/2 cup chopped onion

1/4 teaspoon salt

1/2 cup milk

1 jar (1 lb 10 oz) tomato pasta sauce (any variety)

1/2 cup sliced pimiento-stuffed olives

Cheese Pastry (below)

1 Heat oven to 425°F. In medium bowl, mix beef, bread crumbs, onion, salt and milk. Shape mixture into 18 meatballs. Place meatballs in 15 x 10 x 1-inch pan. Bake 15 to 18 minutes or until meat thermometer inserted in center of meatballs reads at least 160°F and meatballs are no longer pink in center.

2 Meanwhile, in 1-quart saucepan, heat pasta sauce and olives to boiling, stirring occasionally. Reduce heat to medium-low; keep warm.

3 Make Cheese Pastry. Place meatballs in 8-inch square glass baking dish. Top with hot pasta sauce. Cut slits in pastry; place over meatball mixture and tuck under edges. Bake 25 to 30 minutes or until pastry is golden brown.

Cheese Pastry

1 cup Gold Medal all-purpose flour

1/2 teaspoon salt

1/2 cup shredded Cheddar cheese (2 oz)

1/3 cup plus 1 tablespoon butter or shortening

2 to 3 tablespoons cold water

In medium bowl, mix flour, salt and cheese. Cut in butter, using pastry blender (or pulling 2 table knives through ingredients in opposite directions), until crumbly. Sprinkle with cold water, 1 tablespoon at a time, mixing with fork until all flour is moistened and dough almost leaves side of bowl (1 to 2 teaspoons more water can be added if necessary). On lightly floured surface, gather dough into a ball; shape into flattened round. Roll into 10-inch square.

BAKING FOR TODAY

The crust over this meaty main-dish pie is very tender. What's the secret? Heating the sauce is an important step in keeping the crust flaky.

High Altitude (3500 to 6500 feet): In step 3, bake 28 to 33 minutes.

1 Serving: Calories 555 (Calories from Fat 290); Fat 32g (Saturated 15g); Cholesterol 85mg; Sodium 1390mg; Carbohydrate 44g (Dietary Fiber 3g); Protein 22g **Exchanges:** 3 Starch, 2 Medium-Fat Meat, 3 1/2 Fat **Carbohydrate Choices:** 3

CHEESE-CRUSTED MEATBALL PIE

Company Beef Stew

Classic

Prep Time: 30 min; Start to Finish: 3 hr 20 min   6 to 8 servings

2 tablespoons vegetable oil

2 lb beef boneless chuck, tip or round, cut into 1 1/2-inch pieces

1 large onion, sliced

4 cups hot water

1 tablespoon salt

1 tablespoon lemon juice

1 teaspoon sugar

1 teaspoon Worcestershire sauce

1/2 teaspoon paprika

1 dried bay leaf

1 clove garlic

Dash of ground cloves

6 carrots, cut into 1-inch pieces

6 potatoes, cut into 1-inch pieces

1 lb fresh small whole pearl onions, if desired

Dumplings (below)

Chopped fresh parsley, if desired

1 In 4-quart Dutch oven, heat oil over high heat. Cook beef in oil, stirring occasionally, until brown. Stir in sliced onion, 4 cups water, the salt, lemon juice, sugar, Worcestershire sauce, paprika, bay leaf, garlic and cloves. Heat to boiling; reduce heat. Cover and simmer 2 hours (add up to 1/2 cup more water if mixture becomes too dry).

2 Stir in carrots, potatoes and whole onions. Cover and cook 30 minutes longer.

3 Make Dumplings. Drop dumpling dough by 6 to 8 spoonfuls onto hot stew (do not drop directly into liquid). Cook uncovered 10 minutes. Cover and cook 10 minutes longer. Sprinkle with parsley.

Dumplings

1 3/4 cups Gold Medal all-purpose flour

2 teaspoons baking powder

1/2 teaspoon salt

3 tablespoons firm butter or margarine

3/4 cup milk

In medium bowl, mix flour, baking powder and salt. Cut in butter, using pastry blender (or pulling 2 table knives through ingredients in opposite directions), until mixture looks like fine crumbs. Stir in milk until dough forms.

BAKING FOR TODAY

This stew is even more flavorful when made ahead. Just cook the stew, cover and refrigerate. The next day, heat the stew to simmering, prepare the Dumplings and continue as directed.

High Altitude (3500 to 6500 feet): In step 3, cook dumplings uncovered 12 minutes. Cover and cook 12 minutes longer.

1 Serving: Calories 520 (Calories from Fat 260); Fat 29g (Saturated 11g); Cholesterol 110mg; Sodium 1700mg; Carbohydrate 64g (Dietary Fiber 7g); Protein 39g **Exchanges:** 4 Starch, 1 Vegetable, 3 1/2 Lean Meat **Carbohydrate Choices:** 4

Three-Bean and Corn Bread Casserole

Classic

How does a classic begin? When the Washburn Crosby Company decided in 1921 to create the signature of Betty Crocker, a contest was held that included all the women employees of the company. The most distinctive and appropriate handwriting was chosen and that signature has remained pretty much the same over the years.

Prep Time: 15 min; Start to Finish: 45 min   **8 servings**

2 cans (21 oz each) baked beans

2 cans (15 to 16 oz each) kidney beans, drained

1 can (8.5 oz) lima beans, drained (1 cup)

1 can (8 oz) tomato sauce

1/4 cup ketchup

2 tablespoons packed brown sugar

2 tablespoons instant minced onion

1/2 teaspoon ground mustard

1/2 teaspoon salt

1/4 teaspoon pepper

Corn Bread Topping (below)

1 Heat oven to 425°F. In large bowl, mix all ingredients except Corn Bread Topping. Pour into ungreased 13 x 9-inch glass baking dish.

2 Make Corn Bread Topping; spoon evenly over bean mixture to within 1 inch of edges.

3 Bake uncovered 25 to 30 minutes or until topping is golden brown.

Corn Bread Topping

2/3 cup Gold Medal all purpose flour

1/3 cup yellow cornmeal

1/2 cup milk

1 tablespoon sugar

2 tablespoons butter or margarine, softened

1 teaspoon baking powder

1/2 teaspoon salt

1 egg

In small bowl, beat all ingredients with hand beater until smooth.

High Altitude (3500 to 6500 feet): In large pot, cook all ingredients except Corn Bread Topping over medium-high heat until very hot. Pour into ungreased 13 x 9-inch glass baking dish and continue as directed in step 2.

1 Serving: Calories 410 (Calories from Fat 55); Fat 6g (Saturated 3g); Cholesterol 45mg; Sodium 1640mg; Carbohydrate 83g (Dietary Fiber 17g); Protein 23g **Exchanges:** 5 Starch, 1 Very Lean Meat **Carbohydrate Choices:** 5 1/2

BAKING FOR TODAY

The ketchup and brown sugar bake together to create a barbecue taste that everyone loves, especially kids. It's a great choice for a meatless meal. The baked beans are a must because of their flavor and sauce, but you can use chili beans or black beans in place of the kidney and lima beans, if you like.

Pork and Spaetzle Soup

1 lb ground pork

1 egg

1/2 cup dry bread crumbs

1/2 teaspoon ground sage

1/4 teaspoon salt

1/4 teaspoon pepper

1 tablespoon vegetable oil

2 cans (14 oz each) beef broth

2 cups water

3/4 cup apple cider or
apple juice

1 large unpeeled all-purpose
apple, chopped

1/2 teaspoon salt

Spaetzle (below)

1/4 cup chopped fresh parsley

1 In medium bowl, mix pork, egg, bread crumbs, sage, salt and pepper. Shape mixture into 1-inch meatballs. In 4-quart Dutch oven, heat oil over medium heat. Cook meatballs in oil 6 to 8 minutes, turning frequently, until brown; drain.

2 Stir broth, water, apple cider, apple and salt into meatballs. Heat to boiling; reduce heat. Cover and simmer 10 minutes.

3 Heat meatball mixture to boiling. Make Spaetzle batter. Press batter, a few tablespoons at a time, through spaetzle press or colander (preferably one with large holes) into soup. Stir once or twice to prevent sticking. Cook 3 to 5 minutes or until spaetzle rise to surface and are tender. Stir in parsley.

Spaetzle

2 eggs

1 cup Gold Medal all-purpose flour

1/4 cup milk or water

1/4 teaspoon salt

Dash of pepper

In small bowl, beat eggs with fork or wire whisk. Mix in remaining ingredients (batter will be thick).

BAKING FOR TODAY

Spaetzle, tiny dumplings made with flour, came from Germans who settled in the Midwest region of America. Because spaetzle are so small, the cook time is conveniently short; however, try not to overcook them or they'll fall apart.

High Altitude (3500 to 6500 feet): No changes.

1 Serving: Calories 370 (Calories from Fat 155); Fat 17g (Saturated 5g); Cholesterol 155mg; Sodium 1140mg; Carbohydrate 32g (Dietary Fiber 2g); Protein 22g **Exchanges:** 2 Starch, 2 Medium-Fat Meat, 1 1/2 Fat **Carbohydrate Choices:** 2

PORK AND SPAETZLE SOUP

Vegetable Stew with Cheddar Cheese Dumplings

Prep Time: 20 min; Start to Finish: 1 hr 5 min   6 servings

2 tablespoons vegetable oil

2 large onions, coarsely chopped (3 1/2 cups)

2 medium stalks celery, coarsely chopped (3/4 cup)

2 cups frozen Italian green beans

1 can (28 oz) diced tomatoes, undrained

1 can (14 oz) chicken broth

1 teaspoon dried basil leaves

1/4 teaspoon pepper

Cheddar Cheese Dumplings (below)

1 In 4 1/2- to 5-quart Dutch oven, heat oil over medium-high heat. Cook onions and celery in oil, stirring frequently, until tender.

2 Stir in remaining ingredients except Cheddar Cheese Dumplings. Heat to boiling; reduce heat to low. Simmer uncovered 15 to 20 minutes or until beans are tender.

3 Meanwhile, make Cheddar Cheese Dumplings. Drop dough by rounded table-spoonfuls onto simmering stew. Cover and cook over medium-low heat 20 to 25 minutes or until dumplings are firm when pressed.

Cheddar Cheese Dumplings

1 1/2 cups Gold Medal all-purpose flour

2 teaspoons baking powder

1/2 teaspoon salt

1/2 teaspoon ground mustard

1/4 cup firm butter or margarine

1/2 cup shredded sharp Cheddar cheese (2 oz)

2/3 cup milk

In medium bowl, mix flour, baking powder, salt and mustard. Cut in butter, using pastry blender or fork, until mixture looks like coarse crumbs. Stir in cheese. Add milk; stir just until dry ingredients are moistened.

BAKING FOR TODAY

For the lightest, fluffiest dumplings, mix the dough just until the dry ingredients are moistened and resist the urge to stir too much. For a great salad with this family-style meal, add sunflower nuts and matchstick-cut carrots to your favorite salad greens and toss with ranch dressing.

High Altitude (3500 to 6500 feet): Use 2 cans chicken broth. In step 2, simmer 20 to 25 minutes. In step 3, cook 25 to 30 minutes.

1 Serving: Calories 350 (Calories from Fat 155); Fat 17g (Saturated 8g); Cholesterol 35mg; Sodium 990mg; Carbohydrate 39g (Dietary Fiber 4g); Protein 10g **Exchanges:** 2 Starch, 1 Vegetable, 3 1/2 Fat **Carbohydrate Choices:** 2 1/2

VEGETABLE STEW WITH CHEDDAR CHEESE DUMPLINGS

TRES LECHES CAKE

The Melting Pot

Blue Cornmeal Muffins

Classic

Corn was an important year-round staple for Native Americans and it also played a major role in the early days of our country's history. Today in Arizona and New Mexico, the Hopi Indians cultivate six varieties of corn—white, yellow, red, blue, black and speckled. Breads made from corn are among many favorite regional specialties.

Prep Time: 15 min; Start to Finish: 40 min   **14 muffins**

1 1/4 cups blue or yellow cornmeal

1 cup Gold Medal all-purpose flour

1/4 cup vegetable oil

2 teaspoons baking powder

1 teaspoon sugar

1 teaspoon salt

1/2 teaspoon baking soda

1 1/2 cups buttermilk

2 eggs

1 Heat oven to 450°F. Grease bottoms only of 14 medium muffin cups with shortening, or line with paper baking cups. In large bowl, mix all ingredients with spoon; beat vigorously 30 seconds. Fill muffin cups about 7/8 full.

2 Bake 20 to 25 minutes or until light golden brown. Immediately remove from pan. Serve warm.

BAKING FOR TODAY

There are many different versions of corn bread and corn muffins, and some are sweeter than others. This authentic one, from the Southwest, is not very sweet. If you want a sweeter corn muffin, just add more sugar, up to 1/3 cup, to get it just the way you like it.

High Altitude (3500 to 6500 feet): Heat oven to 425°F. Grease muffin cups with shortening or spray paper baking cups with cooking spray. Use 1 1/2 teaspoons baking powder. Bake 16 to 21 minutes.

1 Muffin: Calories 135 (Calories from Fat 45); Fat 5g (Saturated 1g); Cholesterol 30mg; Sodium 320mg; Carbohydrate 18g (Dietary Fiber 1g); Protein 4g **Exchanges:** 1 Starch, 1 Fat **Carbohydrate Choices:** 1

BLUE CORNMEAL MUFFINS

Spicy Sausage 'n Greens Pizza Pie

Prep Time: 35 min; Start to Finish: 1 hr 5 min

4 servings

4 large collard green leaves

1 cup water

1 package (12 oz) bulk
hot pork sausage

1 can (8 oz) pizza sauce

1/2 teaspoon dried
oregano leaves

1 3/4 cups Gold Medal
all-purpose flour

1/4 to 1/2 teaspoon crushed
red pepper

1/2 cup cheese dip
(room temperature)

1/4 cup water

8 thin rings red and/or green
bell pepper

1 cup shredded mozzarella
cheese (4 oz)

1 Wash collard green leaves. Cut off long stem at the base of each leaf; carefully shave the remaining thick stem. Chop leaves. In 2-quart saucepan, heat 1 cup water to boiling. Add chopped collard greens. Boil 15 to 18 minutes or until softened; drain. Pat dry with paper towels.

2 Meanwhile, heat oven to 375°F. Grease large cookie sheet with shortening or spray with cooking spray. In 10-inch skillet, cook sausage over medium heat 8 to 10 minutes, stirring occasionally, until no longer pink; drain. Stir in pizza sauce, collard greens and oregano; set aside.

3 In medium bowl, stir flour, red pepper, cheese dip and 1/4 cup water until soft dough forms. (If dough is dry, stir in additional 1 to 2 tablespoons water.) Gather dough into a ball. On lightly floured surface, roll dough into 14-inch circle. Place dough on cookie sheet. Spread sausage mixture over dough to within 2 inches of edge. Fold dough over edge of sausage mixture. Top with bell pepper rings; sprinkle with cheese.

4 Bake 25 to 30 minutes or until crust is light golden brown and cheese is melted.

BAKING FOR TODAY

Here's an Italian idea fused with favorite African-American ingredients—hot pork sausage, flavorful greens, crushed red pepper—and wrapped in a cheesy pastry crust. If you'd like this dish to be less spicy, you can use mild pork sausage and leave out the crushed red pepper.

High Altitude (3500 to 6500 feet): Bake 30 to 35 minutes.

1 Serving: Calories 520 (Calories from Fat 215); Fat 24g (Saturated 10g); Cholesterol 60mg; Sodium 1120mg; Carbohydrate 52g (Dietary Fiber 4g); Protein 25g **Exchanges:** 3 Starch, 1 Vegetable, 2 High-Fat Meat, 1 Fat **Carbohydrate Choices:** 3 1/2

SPICY SAUSAGE 'N GREENS PIZZA PIE

Salmon and Corn Cakes

Prep Time: 30 min; Start to Finish: 45 min | 8 servings

1 can (14.75 oz) pink
salmon, drained

1 can (6 to 7.5 oz) pink
salmon, drained

1 cup frozen (thawed) whole
kernel corn (from 1-lb bag)

1/3 cup chopped bell pepper

1/3 cup chopped onion

3 cloves garlic, finely chopped

2 eggs, beaten

1/4 cup teriyaki marinade

3 tablespoons lemon juice

1 tablespoon dry bread crumbs

1 teaspoon dried seafood
seasoning (from 6-oz container)

1 teaspoon pepper

1/2 teaspoon celery seed

Pinch of sugar

1/2 cup Gold Medal
all-purpose flour

1/4 cup vegetable oil

1 In large bowl, stir together salmon, corn, bell pepper, onion and garlic; stir in eggs. Stir in remaining ingredients except flour and oil; gradually stir in flour. Shape mixture into eight 3-inch patties, using about 1/3 cup mixture for each.

2 In 10- or 12-inch skillet, heat oil over medium heat. Cook patties in oil about 8 minutes, turning once, until deep golden brown. Drain on paper towels.

BAKING FOR TODAY

These delightful salmon cakes literally burst with flavor and color. You can use frozen or canned corn and red salmon in place of the pink, if you like.

High Altitude (3500 to 6500
feet): Use 3/4 cup flour. Cook
patties 8 to 10 minutes.

1 Serving: Calories 225 (Calories
from Fat 100); Fat 11g (Saturated
2g); Cholesterol 95mg; Sodium
780mg; Carbohydrate 14g
(Dietary Fiber 1g); Protein 18g
Exchanges: 1 Starch, 2 Medium-
Fat Meat
Carbohydrate Choices: 1

SALMON AND CORN CAKES

Smothered Chicken and Gravy

2 tablespoons vegetable oil

3- to 3 1/2-lb cut-up broiler-fryer chicken

1/2 teaspoon salt

1/2 teaspoon pepper

1/2 medium yellow onion, thinly sliced

3 green onions, cut into 1-inch pieces

3/4 cup Gold Medal all-purpose flour

1/3 cup soy sauce

3 1/2 cups hot water

1 teaspoon onion powder

1. In deep 12-inch skillet, heat oil over low heat 5 minutes. Sprinkle chicken with salt and pepper; place in hot skillet. Cover chicken with yellow and green onions.

2. Cook chicken over medium heat 10 minutes. Turn chicken; cook about 10 minutes longer or until golden. Reduce heat to low; cook 5 minutes longer. Turn; cook 5 minutes. Remove chicken from skillet. Place in large pot or Dutch oven; set aside.

3. Continue heating skillet over low heat. In medium bowl, stir together flour, soy sauce, 2 cups of the hot water and the onion powder with wire whisk or fork until smooth.

4. Cook flour mixture in hot skillet over medium heat, stirring constantly with wire whisk or fork, until mixture boils and thickens. Gradually stir in remaining 1 1/2 cups hot water until smooth.

5. Pour gravy over chicken in large pot. Heat to boiling; reduce heat to low. Cover and simmer 1 hour, stirring occasionally. (Gravy may stick to pot.)

BAKING FOR TODAY

Smothered chicken and gravy is a *real* southern specialty. Just add some warm-from-the-oven biscuits (try Easy Cream Drop Biscuits, page 68) with honey butter, and pass around the platter for a second helping.

High Altitude (3500 to 6500 feet): No changes.

1 Serving: Calories 245 (Calories from Fat 115); Fat 13g (Saturated 3g); Cholesterol 65mg; Sodium 820mg; Carbohydrate 11g (Dietary Fiber 1g); Protein 22g
Exchanges: 1 Starch, 3 Lean Meat
Carbohydrate Choices: 1

SMOTHERED CHICKEN AND GRAVY

Baked Lemon Chicken

Classic

1 egg white

1 teaspoon water

4 boneless skinless chicken breast halves (about 1 1/4 lb)

1/2 cup Gold Medal all-purpose flour

1 teaspoon baking soda

1/4 to 1/2 teaspoon ground red pepper (cayenne), if desired

Cooking spray

Chinese Lemon Sauce (below)

1/2 lemon, cut into thin slices

1 medium green onion, chopped (1 tablespoon), if desired

1 In medium glass or plastic bowl, mix egg white and water. Add chicken; turn chicken to coat both sides.

2 Heat oven to 425°F. Spray 15 x 10 x 1-inch pan with cooking spray. In resealable plastic food-storage bag, mix flour, baking soda and red pepper. Remove chicken from egg mixture; discard egg mixture. Add 1 chicken breast at a time to flour mixture. Seal bag; shake to coat chicken. Place chicken in pan; spray with cooking spray about 5 seconds or until surface of chicken appears moist.

3 Bake uncovered 20 to 25 minutes or until juice of chicken is no longer pink when centers of thickest pieces are cut.

4 Meanwhile, make Chinese Lemon Sauce. Let chicken stand 5 minutes; cut each breast diagonally into about 5 slices. Pour warm sauce over chicken. Garnish with lemon slices and green onion.

Chinese Lemon Sauce

1/4 cup sugar

1/3 cup chicken broth

1 teaspoon grated lemon peel

3 tablespoons lemon juice

2 tablespoons light corn syrup

2 tablespoons rice vinegar

1/4 teaspoon salt

1 clove garlic, finely chopped

2 teaspoons cornstarch

2 teaspoons cold water

In 1-quart saucepan, heat all ingredients except cornstarch and cold water to boiling, stirring occasionally. In small bowl, mix cornstarch and cold water; stir into sauce. Cook and stir about 30 seconds or until thickened. Serve warm.

High Altitude (3500 to 6500 feet): No changes.

1 Serving: Calories 295 (Calories from Fat 35); Fat 4g (Saturated 1g); Cholesterol 75mg; Sodium 640mg; Carbohydrate 35g (Dietary Fiber 1g); Protein 30g **Exchanges:** 1 Starch, 1 Other Carbohydrates, 4 Very Lean Meat **Carbohydrate Choices:** 2

BAKING FOR TODAY

This recipe is much easier than the traditional twice-fried Lemon Chicken. This baked version retains the tangy lemon and garlic flavors of the original while eliminating half the fat. Serve with jasmine rice or fried rice.

Navajo Fry Breads

Prep Time: 40 min; Start to Finish: 1 hr   **12 breads**

2 cups Gold Medal
all-purpose flour

2 teaspoons baking powder

1 teaspoon salt

2 tablespoons firm butter, firm
margarine or shortening

2/3 cup warm water

Vegetable oil

1 In medium bowl, mix flour, baking powder and salt. Cut in butter, using pastry blender (or pulling 2 table knives through ingredients in opposite directions), until mixture looks like fine crumbs. Sprinkle with water, 1 tablespoon at a time, tossing with fork until all flour is moistened and dough almost cleans side of bowl. Gather into a ball; cover and refrigerate 30 minutes.

2 In 4-quart Dutch oven, heat 1 inch oil to 400°F. Divide dough into 12 equal parts. On lightly floured surface, roll each part into 6-inch circle. Let rest a few minutes.

3 Make a hole about 1/2 inch in diameter in center of each circle. Fry circles in oil about 1 minute on each side, turning once, until puffed and golden; drain on paper towels. Serve warm.

BAKING FOR TODAY

Every cuisine has its own version of fry bread—this is a Native American fry bread. Go international—try Green Onion–Sesame Flatbreads (page 142) for an Asian fry bread, and Cake Doughnuts (page 53) for a sweet one. Another thing these breads have in common? They all use Gold Medal flour, a staple in Americans' diets.

High Altitude (3500 to 6500
feet): No changes.

1 Bread: Calories 100 (Calories
from Fat 25); Fat 3g (Saturated 1g);
Cholesterol 5mg; Sodium 290mg;
Carbohydrate 16g (Dietary
Fiber 1g); Protein 2g
Exchanges: 1 Starch, 1/2 Fat
Carbohydrate Choices: 1

Green Onion–Sesame Flatbreads

Prep Time: 20 min; Start to Finish: 40 min

6 flatbreads (24 servings)

3 cups Gold Medal
all-purpose flour

2 tablespoons sesame seed

1 1/2 teaspoons baking powder

1 teaspoon salt

1 tablespoon sesame oil

1 cup plus 1 to 2 tablespoons
cold water

1/3 cup chopped green onions
(about 4 medium)

1/2 cup vegetable oil

1 In medium bowl, mix flour, sesame seed, baking powder and salt. Stir in sesame oil and enough cold water to make a smooth, soft dough. On floured surface, knead dough 3 minutes. Divide dough into 6 equal parts; keep covered. Roll each part into 7-inch circle.

2 Sprinkle each circle with about 1 tablespoon of the onions. Roll each circle up tightly, pinching side and ends to seal. Roll into 12-inch rope. Shape each rope to form a coil, tucking end under coil; roll into 7-inch circle.

3 In 8-inch skillet, heat vegetable oil over medium heat to 375°F. Cook 1 circle in oil 1 to 3 minutes, turning once, until golden brown. Drain on paper towels. Repeat with remaining circles. Cut each into 4 wedges. Serve warm.

BAKING FOR TODAY

This Asian bread is easy to make in advance; just roll it out in the morning and refrigerate, covered, until ready to cook. It is traditionally used to sop up the juices of stews, soups, gravies or other liquids. Serve it with pot roast, curried dishes or barbecued meats.

High Altitude (3500 to 6500 feet): No changes.

1 Serving: Calories 75 (Calories from Fat 20); Fat 2g (Saturated 0g); Cholesterol 0mg; Sodium 130mg; Carbohydrate 12g (Dietary Fiber 1g); Protein 2g **Exchanges:** 1 Starch **Carbohydrate Choices:** 1

GREEN ONION-SESAME FLATBREADS

Pumpkin-Honey Sopaipillas

2 cups Gold Medal
all-purpose flour

2 tablespoons shortening

1 tablespoon granulated sugar

2 teaspoons baking powder

1/2 teaspoon salt

2/3 to 3/4 cup water

Pumpkin Honey (below) or
regular honey, if desired

Vegetable oil

Powdered sugar

1 In medium bowl, mix flour, shortening, granulated sugar, baking powder and salt with spoon. Stir in enough of the water to make stiff dough; let rest 15 minutes. Make Pumpkin Honey; set aside.

2 In 3-quart saucepan, heat 2 inches oil to 375°F. On lightly floured surface, roll dough into 15 x 12-inch rectangle. Cut into 3-inch squares.

3 Fry a few squares at a time in oil, turning occasionally, until golden brown. Remove with slotted spoon and drain on paper towels; sprinkle with powdered sugar. Serve warm with Pumpkin Honey.

Pumpkin Honey

1/2 cup canned pumpkin (not pumpkin pie mix)

1/4 cup honey

1/4 teaspoon ground cinnamon

1/8 teaspoon ground nutmeg

In small bowl, stir together all ingredients.

BAKING FOR TODAY

Sopaipillas are deep-fried pastries and the Pumpkin Honey adds a wonderful sweet-spice flavor, or just dip the sopaipillas in regular honey—that tastes great, too.

High Altitude (3500 to 6500 feet): No changes.

1 Sopaipilla: Calories 100 (Calories from Fat 35); Fat 4g (Saturated 1g); Cholesterol 0mg; Sodium 110mg; Carbohydrate 15g (Dietary Fiber 1g); Protein 1g
Exchanges: 1 Other Carbohydrates, 1 Fat
Carbohydrate Choices: 1

PUMPKIN-HONEY SOPAIPILLAS AND MANGO-LIME COOKIES (PAGE 149)

Sweet Potato–Banana Empanadas

2 1/2 cups Gold Medal all-purpose flour

1/2 teaspoon salt

2/3 cup firm butter or margarine, cut into pieces

1/3 cup cold water

3/4 cup mashed cooked sweet potato

1/4 cup chopped pecans

2 tablespoons sugar

1 teaspoon ground cinnamon

1/4 teaspoon ground nutmeg

1/8 teaspoon ground cloves

1 medium banana, cut into 1/4-inch pieces (3/4 cup)

2 tablespoons sugar

3/4 teaspoon ground cinnamon

1 In medium bowl, mix flour and salt. Cut in butter, using pastry blender (or pulling 2 table knives through ingredients in opposite directions), until particles are size of small peas. Sprinkle with cold water, 1 tablespoon at a time, tossing with fork until all flour is moistened and dough almost leaves side of bowl.

2 Divide dough in half; shape each half into flattened round. Wrap rounds in plastic wrap. Cover and refrigerate about 1 hour or until easy to handle.

3 Meanwhile, in small bowl, mix sweet potato, pecans, 2 tablespoons sugar, 1 teaspoon cinnamon, the nutmeg, cloves and banana; set aside. In another small bowl, mix 2 tablespoons sugar and 3/4 teaspoon cinnamon; set aside.

4 Heat oven to 400°F. On lightly floured surface, roll each half of dough into 16 x 8-inch rectangle. Cut each rectangle into 8 squares. Place about 1 tablespoon sweet potato–banana filling on center of each square. Brush edges of squares with water. Fold squares in half diagonally to form triangles, pressing edges firmly to seal or crimping with fork dipped in flour. Lightly brush tops with water. Sprinkle with cinnamon-sugar.

5 On ungreased cookie sheet, place empanadas about 1 inch apart. Bake 15 to 20 minutes or until golden brown. Serve warm.

BAKING FOR TODAY

If you don't happen to have leftover sweet potatoes, you can microwave 1 large sweet potato (8 to 10 ounces) in its skin. Pierce the potato with a fork several times, then microwave on High 8 to 12 minutes or until tender. Let it cool about 5 minutes until you can handle it easily, then peel and mash.

High Altitude (3500 to 6500 feet): No changes.

1 Empanada: Calories 185 (Calories from Fat 80); Fat 9g (Saturated 5g); Cholesterol 20mg; Sodium 125mg; Carbohydrate 23g (Dietary Fiber 1g); Protein 3g **Exchanges:** 1 Starch, 1/2 Fruit, 1 1/2 Fat **Carbohydrate Choices:** 1 1/2

SWEET POTATO-BANANA EMPANADAS

Crepes with Easy Caramel Filling

Prep Time: 60 min; **Start to Finish:** 1 hr 30 min

12 servings

Easy Caramel Custard (below)

1 cup Gold Medal
all-purpose flour

1 tablespoon powdered sugar

1 teaspoon baking powder

1/2 teaspoon salt

1 cup milk

1/2 teaspoon vanilla

2 eggs, slightly beaten

1/4 cup brandy, if desired

2 tablespoons powdered sugar

1/2 teaspoon ground cinnamon

Sliced strawberries, if desired

1 Make Easy Caramel Custard.

2 In medium bowl, mix flour, 1 tablespoon powdered sugar, the baking powder and salt. Stir in milk, vanilla and eggs. Beat with hand beater until smooth.

3 Lightly butter 6- to 8-inch skillet; heat over medium heat until bubbly. For each crepe, pour scant 1/4 cup of the batter into skillet; immediately rotate skillet until thin film covers bottom.

4 Cook until light brown. Run wide spatula around edge to loosen; turn and cook other side until light brown. Stack crepes, placing waxed paper between each. Keep covered.

5 Spread about 2 measuring tablespoons custard on each warm crepe; roll up. Drizzle each crepe with 1 teaspoon brandy; sprinkle with powdered sugar and cinnamon. Serve with sliced strawberries, if desired.

Easy Caramel Custard

Heat oven to 425°F. In 8-inch square coated pan, pour 1 can (14 oz) sweetened condensed milk. Cover tightly with foil. Place square pan in 13 x 9-inch pan; place on oven rack. Pour very hot water into 13 x 9-inch pan to within 1/2 inch of top of square pan. Bake about 1 hour or until thick and golden brown. Carefully remove square pan from hot water. Remove foil; cool slightly or completely.

High Altitude (3500 to 6500 feet): No changes.

1 Serving: Calories 210 (Calories from Fat 45); Fat 5g (Saturated 3g); Cholesterol 50mg; Sodium 220mg; Carbohydrate 35g (Dietary Fiber 0g); Protein 6g **Exchanges:** 2 Starch, 1 Fat **Carbohydrate Choices:** 2

BAKING FOR TODAY

The caramel filling for these crepes is so rich and flavorful that no one will guess it was so simple to make. Turning canned milk into caramel is a trick that's been around about as long as canned milk has; good ideas are worth sticking with. Sliced fresh strawberries or other fruit and a little ice cream on the side make great accompaniments to this delicious dessert.

Mango-Lime Cookies

Mango Filling (below)

1 cup granulated sugar

1/2 cup butter or
margarine, softened

1 teaspoon vanilla

1 egg

1 2/3 cups Gold Medal
all-purpose flour

1 teaspoon grated lime peel

1 teaspoon baking powder

1/4 teaspoon salt

1 cup powdered sugar

1 tablespoon lime juice

1 Make Mango Filling.

2 In large bowl, beat granulated sugar, butter, vanilla and egg with spoon. Stir in flour, lime peel, baking powder and salt. Divide dough in half; shape each half into flattened round. Wrap rounds in plastic wrap; refrigerate about 30 minutes or until easy to roll.

3 Heat oven to 350°F. On lightly floured surface, roll each round of dough 1/8 inch thick. Cut with 3-inch round cookie cutter. On ungreased cookie sheet, place rounds about 1 inch apart. Place about 1 teaspoon filling in center of each cookie. Fold each cookie in half, pressing around edge to seal.

4 Bake 12 to 15 minutes or until light golden. Remove from cookie sheet to wire rack. Cool completely, about 30 minutes. In small bowl, mix powdered sugar, lime juice and enough water to make a glaze that's easy to spread. Spread over cookies.

Mango Filling

3/4 cup dried mangoes, finely chopped

1/2 cup water

3 tablespoons granulated sugar

1 teaspoon lime juice

In 2-quart saucepan, mix mangoes, water and sugar. Heat to boiling over high heat, stirring occasionally. Reduce heat to medium. Cover and simmer about 10 minutes or until mangoes are softened and mixture is slightly thickened. Stir in lime juice. Cool 30 minutes.

Apricot-Lime Cookies: Omit Mango Filling. In small bowl, mix 2/3 cup apricot preserves and 1 teaspoon lime juice. Use to fill cookies.

High Altitude (3500 to 6500
feet): Use 2 cups flour.

1 Cookie: Calories 130 (Calories
from Fat 26); Fat 4g (Saturated
2g); Cholesterol 20mg; Sodium
75mg; Carbohydrate 23g
(Dietary Fiber 0g); Protein 1g
Exchanges: 1/2 Starch, 1 Fruit,
1/2 Fat
Carbohydrate Choices: 1 1/2

BAKING FOR TODAY

Want an easy way to chop dried mangoes? Sprinkle some of the sugar on the cutting board first; the sugar helps ease the cutting. Put the fruit and sugar along with the water into the saucepan, and continue as directed.

Coconut-Pecan Bars

Classic

A version of this popular bar was published in the 1978 *Century of Success Cookbook* that celebrated 100 years of Gold Medal flour. That version won raves from Gold Medal users, and a packaged mix was developed using the bar cookies as the model.

Prep Time: 20 min; Start to Finish: 2 hr 15 min   16 bars

6 tablespoons butter or margarine, softened

1/4 cup granulated sugar

1/4 teaspoon salt

1 cup Gold Medal all-purpose flour

2 eggs

1 teaspoon vanilla

1 cup packed brown sugar

2 tablespoons Gold Medal all-purpose flour

1/2 teaspoon salt

1 cup flaked coconut

1/2 cup chopped pecans

1 Heat oven to 350°F. In small bowl, beat butter, granulated sugar and 1/4 teaspoon salt with electric mixer on medium speed until light and fluffy. Stir in 1 cup flour. On bottom of ungreased 9-inch square pan, pat mixture evenly. Bake 12 to 17 minutes or until very light brown.

2 Meanwhile, in medium bowl, beat eggs slightly with wire whisk. Stir in vanilla. Gradually beat in brown sugar just until blended. Beat in 2 tablespoons flour and 1/2 teaspoon salt. Stir in coconut and pecans. Carefully spoon coconut mixture evenly over baked layer.

3 Bake 20 to 25 minutes or until golden brown and filling is set. Cool 10 minutes. Run knife around edges of pan to loosen. Cool completely, about 1 hour. For bars, cut into 4 rows by 4 rows.

BAKING FOR TODAY

Add a new shape to your cookie tray. Cut bars diagonally in half to make 32 triangles. To store these sensational bars, keep tightly covered at room temperature for up to two days or freeze for longer storage.

High Altitude (3500 to 6500 feet): In step 1, bake 15 to 19 minutes. In step 3, bake 23 to 27 minutes.

1 Bar: Calories 205 (Calories from Fat 90); Fat 10g (Saturated 5g); Cholesterol 50mg; Sodium 170mg; Carbohydrate 26g (Dietary Fiber 1g); Protein 3g
Exchanges: 1 Starch, 1 Other Carbohydrates, 1 1/2 Fat
Carbohydrate Choices: 2

Tres Leches Cake

4 eggs

3/4 cup sugar

1/4 cup cold water

1 teaspoon vanilla

1 cup Gold Medal
all-purpose flour

1 teaspoon baking powder

1/4 teaspoon salt

Tres Leches Sauce (below)

Sweetened Whipped Cream
(page 232)

1 cup flaked coconut, toasted*

1 pound sliced strawberries

5 kiwifruit, peeled
and chopped

*To toast coconut, bake
uncovered in ungreased shallow
pan in 350°F oven 5 to 7
minutes, stirring occasionally,
until golden brown.*

1 Heat oven to 350°F. Grease bottom and sides of 11 x 7-inch glass baking dish with shortening or spray with cooking spray. In large bowl, beat eggs with electric mixer on high speed until frothy. Gradually beat in sugar; beat on high speed about 5 minutes or until very thick and lemon colored. Beat in water and vanilla on low speed. Gradually add flour, baking powder and salt, beating just until batter is smooth. Pour into pan.

2 Bake 20 to 25 minutes or until toothpick inserted in center comes out clean. Cool 1 hour on wire rack.

3 Make Tres Leches Sauce. Poke top of cake all over with toothpick or fork; slowly pour sauce over cake, allowing it to soak in. Cover and refrigerate at least 2 hours until most of the sauce is absorbed. Serve cake topped with Sweetened Whipped Cream, coconut, strawberries and kiwifruit.

Tres Leches Sauce

1 can (14 ounces) sweetened condensed milk

1 cup whipping (heavy) cream

1/2 cup canned cream of coconut
(not coconut milk)

3 tablespoons light rum or 1 tablespoon vanilla

In medium bowl, stir together all ingredients. Refrigerate until ready to use.

BAKING FOR TODAY

Tres Leches Cake is a classic Nicaraguan cake soaked with three forms of *leches*, or "milks." It is a very moist cake and becomes more flavorful as it is stored. Refrigerate it, tightly covered, for up to three days.

High Altitude (3500 to 6500 feet): Use 13 x 9-inch glass baking dish.

1 Serving: Calories 330 (Calories from Fat 155); Fat 17g (Saturated 11g); Cholesterol 90mg; Sodium 135mg; Carbohydrate 38g (Dietary Fiber 2g); Protein 6g **Exchanges:** 2 Starch, 1/2 Fruit, 3 Fat **Carbohydrate Choices:** 2 1/2

TURTLE BREAD

Baking with the Kids

Turtle Bread

Classic

A little light verse adds even more fun to baking bread. In the aptly named "A Good Bread Recipe" from the 1910 *Gold Medal Flour Cookbook*, this poem adds charm:

"Now let the mixture stand a minute or two,
You've got other things of great importance to do.
First sift the flour, the finest in the land.
Three quarts is the measure,
Gold Medal the brand."

Prep Time: 20 min; Start to Finish: 1 hr 10 min	1 turtle bread (16 servings)

2 1/2 to 3 cups Gold Medal all-purpose flour

1 package quick active dry yeast*

1 tablespoon sugar

1 teaspoon salt

1/2 cup water

1/3 cup milk

1 tablespoon butter or margarine

1 egg

2 raisins

Regular active dry yeast can be substituted for quick active dry yeast. In large bowl, dissolve yeast in 1/2 cup warm water (105°F to 115°F). Stir in sugar, salt, warmed milk, melted butter and 1 1/2 cups of the flour. Stir in egg. Stir in enough remaining flour to make dough easy to handle. Continue as directed.

High Altitude (3500 to 6500 feet): No changes. Refrigerating dough is not recommended.

1 Serving: Calories 85 (Calories from Fat 10); Fat 1g (Saturated 0g); Cholesterol 15mg; Sodium 160mg; Carbohydrate 16g (Dietary Fiber 1g); Protein 3g
Exchanges: 1 Starch
Carbohydrate Choices: 1

1 In large bowl, mix 1 1/2 cups of the flour, the yeast, sugar and salt; set aside.

2 In 1-quart saucepan, heat water, milk and butter over medium heat, stirring occasionally, to 125°F to 130°F; stir into yeast mixture. Stir in egg. Stir in enough remaining flour to make dough easy to handle. On lightly floured surface, knead dough about 5 minutes or until smooth and springy. Cover and let rest 10 minutes.

3 Lightly grease cookie sheet with shortening or spray with cooking spray. Shape a 2-inch piece of dough into a ball for turtle's head. Shape 4 walnut-size pieces of dough into balls for feet. Shape 1 walnut-size piece of dough into tail. Shape remaining dough into ball for turtle body; place on cookie sheet and flatten slightly. Attach head, feet and tail by placing 1 end of each under edge of body to secure. Press raisins into head for eyes. Cover and let rise in warm place 20 minutes.

4 Heat oven to 400°F. Make 1/4-inch-deep circular cut around top edge of body, then make crisscross cuts in center to look like a turtle's shell. Bake 20 to 25 minutes or until golden brown.

Animal Breads: Shape dough into alligator, bear, cow, dog, ladybug or other animals. Cover and let rise in warm place 20 minutes. Cut an X in dough for eyes, buttons, nose, etc., using kitchen scissors. Bake as directed. For a shiny surface, brush baked bread with softened butter or margarine. Cool bread; decorate with raisins, currants, chocolate chips, etc., by attaching with a drop of honey.

BAKING FOR TODAY

You can refrigerate this dough for up to 24 hours. Here's how: Grease a large bowl with shortening or spray with cooking spray. Place dough in bowl, turning dough to grease all sides. Cover tightly with plastic wrap; refrigerate. For easier shaping, let dough stand at room temperature at least 20 minutes.

You Can Dough It!
(Baked Dough Creations)

Prep Time: 20 min; Start to Finish: 1 hr 20 min   About 4 cups dough

4 cups Gold Medal
all-purpose flour

1 cup salt

1 1/2 cups warm water

Paste food color or tempera
powder, if desired

Clear sealing spray for
crafts, if desired

1 Heat oven to 300°F. In large bowl, stir flour and salt until well mixed. Stir in water. Stir in food color. On lightly floured surface, shape dough into a ball, using floured hands. Knead 5 to 10 minutes or until dough is smooth and springy. Wrap dough tightly in plastic wrap. Take out only as much dough as you will use at one time because dough dries out quickly.

2 Use dough to make fun shapes. See below for how to make a hand creation and a necklace. On ungreased cookie sheet, place shapes. Bake about 1 hour or until dough is dry and just begins to brown (bake time will depend on size of shapes). If more bake time is needed, turn shapes over and continue baking until dough is dry. Remove shapes from cookie sheet to wire rack. Cool completely.

BAKING FOR TODAY

Let them play with their food by making a dough for just that reason! Kids can trace their hands, make a necklace or create any shape. There is a lot of salt in the dough, so it's recommended to play with only, not to eat.

3 Paint shapes with tempera paint or watercolors, if desired. Spray sealing spray on shapes to keep them longer. Store unbaked dough tightly wrapped in refrigerator up to 30 days.

Remember, this dough is to play with, not to eat!

Make a Hand Creation

1 Shape 1/3 of the dough into a ball.

2 On a lightly floured surface, roll or pat the ball to make a circle that is 3/4 inch thick.

3 Press your hand into dough, then write your name and the date around edge with a toothpick. Bake your hand creation.

Make a Necklace

High Altitude (3500 to 6500 feet): No changes.

1 For beads, shape some of the dough into about 1-inch balls.

2 Push a toothpick through each bead to make a hole. Bake and cool beads.

3 Paint beads, then string them on cord.

Bread Machine
Frosty Snowman

Prep Time: 15 min; Start to Finish: 3 hr 10 min 24 servings

1 cup water

2 tablespoons butter or margarine, softened

3 cups Gold Medal Better for Bread flour

3 tablespoons granulated sugar

1 teaspoon ground cinnamon

1 1/2 teaspoons salt

2 1/4 teaspoons bread machine yeast

2 cups powdered sugar

About 3 tablespoons milk

Pretzel rods, if desired

2 round cookies, if desired

Assorted candies, if desired

Chewy fruit snack roll, if desired

White candy sprinkles or edible glitter, if desired

1 Measure carefully, placing water, butter, flour, granulated sugar, cinnamon, salt and yeast in bread machine pan in the order recommended by the manufacturer.

2 Select Dough/Manual cycle. Do not use Delay cycle. Remove dough from pan, using lightly floured hands.

3 Heat oven to 375°F. Grease cookie sheet with shortening or spray with cooking spray. Divide dough into 2 parts, 1 part slightly smaller than the other. Shape smaller part of dough into 4-inch ball; place on cookie sheet. Shape remaining dough into 6-inch ball; place next to 4-inch ball with sides touching. Cover and let rise in warm place 15 minutes.

4 Bake 25 to 28 minutes or until bread is golden and sounds hollow when tapped. Cool 10 minutes. Carefully remove from cookie sheet to wire rack. Cool completely, about 2 hours.

5 Place bread on serving platter. In small bowl, mix powdered sugar and milk until smooth and thin enough to drizzle; spoon over bread, allowing glaze to drizzle down sides. Attach pretzel rods for arms and cookies for earmuffs. Decorate with candies. Cut fruit snack, and add for scarf. Sprinkle with candy sprinkles.

BAKING FOR TODAY

Gift a family with fun! Package the unfrosted baked bread, a tub of vanilla frosting and containers of decorations, and let the fun begin.

High Altitude (3500 to 6500 feet): In step 3, cover and let rise about 20 minutes.

1 Serving: Calories 115 (Calories from Fat 10); Fat 1g (Saturated 1g); Cholesterol 5mg; Sodium 155mg; Carbohydrate 25g (Dietary Fiber 1g); Protein 2g
Exchanges: 1 Starch, 1/2 Other Carbohydrates
Carbohydrate Choices: 1 1/2

BREAD MACHINE FROSTY SNOWMAN

Pepperoni Spinners

Prep Time: 50 min; Start to Finish: 1 hr 20 min

9 servings

1 3/4 cups Gold Medal all-purpose flour

1/4 teaspoon salt

1 package quick active dry yeast

1 tablespoon vegetable oil

2/3 cup very warm water (120°F to 130°F)

1/2 package (3 1/4-oz size) sliced pepperoni

1/2 cup shredded mozzarella cheese (2 oz)

1/4 teaspoon dried oregano leaves

Pizza sauce, heated, if desired

1 In medium bowl, stir flour, salt and yeast until mixed. Stir in oil and warm water until a soft dough forms. On lightly floured surface, shape dough into a ball, using floured hands. Knead 5 times. Place bowl over dough; let rest 5 minutes.

2 Grease bottom and side of 9-inch round pan with shortening or spray with cooking spray. On floured surface, press dough with hands or rolling pin into 9-inch square. Place pepperoni on dough. Sprinkle with cheese and oregano. Tightly roll up dough, and pinch edge to seal. Cut roll into nine 1-inch slices. Put slightly apart in pan. Cover and let rise in warm place about 30 minutes or until dough has doubled in size.

3 Heat oven to 375°F. Bake 25 to 30 minutes or until golden brown. Serve warm with pizza sauce.

BAKING FOR TODAY

When measuring flour and other dry ingredients, have the kids spoon it lightly into a dry-ingredient measuring cup until full, then level off the top with a flat spatula or table knife. Measuring ingredients properly is very important to baking and can mean the difference between success and disappointment.

High Altitude (3500 to 6500 feet): Bake 30 to 35 minutes.

1 Serving: Calories 145 (Calories from Fat 45); Fat 5g (Saturated 2g); Cholesterol 5mg; Sodium 200mg; Carbohydrate 19g (Dietary Fiber 1g); Protein 6g **Exchanges:** 1 Starch, 1/2 High-Fat Meat **Carbohydrate Choices:** 1

Monkey See, Monkey Dough

2 cups Gold Medal all-purpose flour

1 tablespoon sugar

1 tablespoon baking powder

1 teaspoon salt

1/2 cup butter or margarine, softened

3/4 cup milk

1/3 cup grated Parmesan cheese

1 teaspoon Italian seasoning

2 tablespoons butter or margarine, melted

Tomato pasta sauce, cheese sauce or pizza sauce, heated, if desired

1 Heat oven to 425°F. In medium bowl, stir flour, sugar, baking powder and salt until mixed. Cut in 1/2 cup butter, using pastry blender (or pulling 2 table knives through ingredients in opposite directions), until crumbly. Stir in milk until soft dough forms.

2 On lightly floured surface, shape dough into a ball, using floured hands. Knead 10 times. Divide dough into 32 pieces.

3 In small bowl, mix cheese and Italian seasoning. Roll dough pieces in cheese mixture. In ungreased 9-inch round pan, place coated dough pieces. Sprinkle with rest of cheese mixture. Drizzle 2 tablespoons melted butter over top.

4 Bake 15 to 20 minutes or until light golden brown. Remove bread from pan. Serve warm with heated tomato pasta sauce, cheese sauce or pizza sauce for dipping.

BAKING FOR TODAY

Kids love dipping! This interactive snack bread is great anytime, and it makes a perfect after-school snack. Keep leftovers in an airtight bag and refresh in the microwave for a few seconds before serving.

High Altitude (3500 to 6500 feet): No changes.

1 Serving: Calories 275 (Calories from Fat 145); Fat 16g (Saturated 10g); Cholesterol 45mg; Sodium 660mg; Carbohydrate 27g (Dietary Fiber 1g); Protein 5g
Exchanges: 2 Starch, 2 1/2 Fat
Carbohydrate Choices: 2

Cheesy Pretzels

Classic

Kneading instructions have changed a bit over the years. The 1910 *Gold Medal Flour Cookbook* gives these instructions: "TO KNEAD: Push the dough with palm, curving the fingers to keep the ball from flattening too much. With every push turn the dough one-quarter way round and fold over. Do not make it too stiff. Knead until the dough has a silky smoothness, is full of blisters and does not stick to the hands or dough (about 20 minutes)." No "knead" to worry, our modern instructions work just as well!

Prep Time: 20 min; Start to Finish: 45 min | **16 pretzels**

1 1/2 cups Gold Medal all-purpose flour

2/3 cup milk

1/2 cup shredded Cheddar cheese (2 oz)

2 tablespoons butter or margarine, softened

2 teaspoons baking powder

1 teaspoon sugar

1/2 teaspoon salt

1 egg

Coarse salt, if desired

1. Heat oven to 400°F. Grease cookie sheet with shortening or spray with cooking spray.

2. In a bowl, mix all ingredients except egg and coarse salt with fork. On lightly floured surface, gently smooth dough into a ball. Knead 10 times. Divide dough in half.

3. Roll 1/2 of the dough into 12 x 8-inch rectangle. Cut rectangle lengthwise into eight 1-inch strips. Make each strip narrower by folding it in half lengthwise. Pinch edges to seal. Twist each strip into a pretzel shape and place, seam side down, on cookie sheet.

4. In small bowl, beat egg with fork. Brush egg over pretzels; sprinkle lightly with coarse salt.

5. Bake 20 to 25 minutes or until golden brown. Remove from cookie sheet to wire rack. Repeat with remaining half of dough.

Peanutty Pretzels: Substitute 2 tablespoons crunchy peanut butter for the butter. Omit shredded cheese. Substitute 2 tablespoons chopped salted peanuts for the coarse salt.

High Altitude (3500 to 6500 feet): No changes.

1 Serving: Calories 80 (Calories from Fat 25); Fat 3g (Saturated 2g); Cholesterol 20mg; Sodium 180mg; Carbohydrate 10g (Dietary Fiber 0g); Protein 3g **Exchanges:** 1/2 Starch, 1 Fat **Carbohydrate Choices:** 1/2

BAKING FOR TODAY

You and the kids will have as much fun making these cheesy pretzels as eating them. Let the kids do the kneading by folding and pushing the dough with the palms of their hands, then make a quarter turn and repeat folding and pushing to knead 10 times. This is a great opportunity for kids to learn how important kneading dough is to baking great bread and for you to share your love of baking with them.

Twisters Biscuit Sticks

Classic

In 1895, the Sperry Flour Company—one of the flour firms that joined General Mills—produced the recipe booklet, *Easy Cooking for Little Cooks.* No matter what the century, kids love to bake!

Prep Time: 16 min; Start to Finish: 30 min   **6 twisters**

1 1/4 cups Gold Medal all-purpose flour*

1 teaspoon baking powder

1/2 teaspoon salt

2 tablespoons vegetable oil

1/2 cup milk

1 egg, beaten

Topping (such as cinnamon-sugar, oats, sesame seed or shredded cheese), if desired

If using Gold Medal self-rising flour, omit baking powder and salt.

1 In medium bowl, stir all ingredients except egg and topping until a soft dough forms. On lightly floured surface, shape dough into a ball, using floured hands. Knead 10 times. Place bowl over dough; let rest 15 minutes.

2 Heat oven to 425°F. Divide dough into 6 parts. Roll each part into 15-inch rope. On ungreased cookie sheet, place ropes. Fold each rope crosswise in half, and twist halves together. Brush egg over dough. Sprinkle with topping.

3 Bake 9 to 11 minutes or until light golden brown. Remove from cookie sheet to wire rack.

BAKING FOR TODAY

You can add drops of food color when you stir in the milk for a fanciful, colorful bread. Make twisters a special treat by dipping them into applesauce or warm cheese sauce.

High Altitude (3500 to 6500 feet): Use 1/2 teaspoon baking powder.

1 Serving: Calories 155 (Calories from Fat 55); Fat 6g (Saturated 1g); Cholesterol 35mg; Sodium 300mg; Carbohydrate 21g (Dietary Fiber 1g); Protein 4g **Exchanges:** 1 Starch, 1/2 Other Carbohydrates, 1 Fat **Carbohydrate Choices:** 1 1/2

Berry-Streusel Muffins

Classic

During the early 1930s, Gold Medal ads featured winning recipes from state fair competitions across the country. This blueberry muffin recipe (minus the streusel) took top prize at the Illinois State Fair. It will be prized at your house as well.

Prep Time: 20 min; Start to Finish: 50 min   **12 muffins**

Streusel Topping (below)
3/4 cup milk
1/4 cup vegetable oil
1 egg
2 cups Gold Medal
all-purpose flour
1/2 cup sugar
2 teaspoons baking powder
1/2 teaspoon salt
1 cup fresh, canned (drained)
or frozen blueberries

1 Heat oven to 400°F. Grease bottoms only of 12 medium muffin cups with shortening, or line with paper baking cups.

2 Make Streusel Topping; set aside.

3 In large bowl, beat milk, oil and egg with fork or wire whisk. Stir in flour, sugar, baking powder and salt all at once just until flour is moistened (batter will be lumpy). Fold in blueberries. Divide batter evenly among muffin cups. Sprinkle each with about 1 tablespoon topping.

4 Bake 20 to 25 minutes or until golden brown. If baked in greased pan, let stand about 5 minutes in pan, then remove from pan to wire rack; if baked in paper baking cups, immediately remove from pan to wire rack. Serve warm if desired.

BAKING FOR TODAY

If you have mini-muffin pans, bring them out and make mini-muffins. The wee muffins will only need to bake for 10 to 15 minutes.

High Altitude (3500 to 6500 feet): Use 1 teaspoon baking powder.

1 Muffin: Calories 210 (Calories from Fat 65); Fat 7g (Saturated 2g); Cholesterol 25mg; Sodium 210mg; Carbohydrate 33g (Dietary Fiber 1g); Protein 4g **Exchanges:** 1 Starch, 1 Fruit, 1 1/2 **Fat Carbohydrate Choices:** 2

Streusel Topping

1/4 cup Gold Medal all-purpose flour   1/4 teaspoon ground cinnamon
1/4 cup packed brown sugar   2 tablespoons firm butter or margarine

In medium bowl, mix flour, brown sugar and cinnamon. Cut in butter, using pastry blender (or pulling 2 table knives through ingredients in opposite directions), until crumbly.

Apple-Cinnamon Muffins: Omit blueberries. Beat in 1 cup chopped peeled apple (about 1 medium) with the milk. Stir in 1/2 teaspoon ground cinnamon with the flour. Bake 25 to 30 minutes.

Banana Muffins: Omit blueberries. Decrease milk to 1/3 cup. Beat in 1 cup mashed very ripe bananas (about 2 medium) with the milk. Use packed brown sugar for the sugar.

Cranberry-Orange Muffins: Omit blueberries. Beat in 1 tablespoon grated orange peel with the milk. Fold 1 cup cranberry halves into batter.

BERRY-STREUSEL MUFFINS

Oatmeal Pancakes

12 to 14 pancakes

1 egg

3/4 cup buttermilk

1/2 cup old-fashioned or
quick-cooking oats

1/2 cup Gold Medal
all-purpose flour

1/4 cup milk

1 tablespoon sugar

2 tablespoons vegetable oil

1 teaspoon baking powder

1/2 teaspoon baking soda

1/2 teaspoon salt

1 In medium bowl, beat egg with hand beater until fluffy. Beat in remaining ingredients. (For thinner pancakes, stir in additional 2 to 4 tablespoons milk.)

2 Heat griddle or skillet over medium heat or to 375°F. (To test griddle, sprinkle with a few drops of water. If bubbles jump around, heat is just right.) Grease griddle with vegetable oil if necessary (or spray with cooking spray before heating).

3 For each pancake, pour about 3 tablespoons batter from cup or pitcher onto hot griddle. Cook pancakes until puffed and dry around edges. Turn and cook other sides until golden brown.

BAKING FOR TODAY

Cooking gives kids a chance to learn about how foods are prepared and served in other cultures. In Scandinavia, for instance, oatmeal pancakes are traditionally served with lingonberry preserves and sour cream. Look for the preserves when you shop—when you find them, why not pick them up and create a Scandinavian food experience?

High Altitude (3500 to 6500 feet): No changes.

1 Pancake: Calories 65 (Calories from Fat 25); Fat 3g (Saturated 1g); Cholesterol 20mg; Sodium 210mg; Carbohydrate 8g (Dietary Fiber 1g); Protein 2g
Exchanges: 1/2 Starch, 1/2 Fat
Carbohydrate Choices: 1/2

Flying Apple Flapjack

Prep Time: 10 min; Start to Finish: 45 min   2 to 4 servings

2 tablespoons butter
or margarine

2 tablespoons packed
brown sugar

1/4 teaspoon ground
cinnamon

1 medium cooking apple,
thinly sliced (1 cup)

2 eggs

1/2 cup Gold Medal
all-purpose flour

1/2 cup milk

1/4 teaspoon salt

1 Heat oven to 400°F. In 9-inch glass pie plate, melt butter in oven. Sprinkle brown sugar and cinnamon over butter. Place apple slices on cinnamon-sugar mixture.

2 In medium bowl, beat eggs slightly with wire whisk or hand beater. Beat in flour, milk and salt just until mixed (do not overbeat). Pour batter over apple slices.

3 Bake 30 to 35 minutes or until puffy and deep golden brown. Immediately loosen edge of pancake. Place heatproof serving plate upside down on pie plate; turn serving plate and pie plate over to remove pancake.

BAKING FOR TODAY

Learning to clean up is almost as important as learning to cook, so make picking up after cooking a family affair. Even small kids can help by putting food and dishes away, wiping off counters and wiping dishes. When everyone helps, you'll be done in no time.

High Altitude (3500 to 6500 feet): No changes.

1 Serving: Calories 210 (Calories from Fat 80); Fat 9g (Saturated 5g); Cholesterol 125mg; Sodium 240mg; Carbohydrate 26g (Dietary Fiber 1g); Protein 6g
Exchanges: 2 Starch, 1 Fat
Carbohydrate Choices: 2

Wonderful Waffles

Classic

A picture puzzle contest appeared in a Gold Medal advertisement in the *Saturday Evening Post* in 1921. Nearly 30,000 people sent in the correct solution, along with an avalanche of consumer mail requesting recipes and asking about baking.

Prep Time: 15 min; Start to Finish: 30 min   **3 waffles (7 to 8 inch)**

1 cup Gold Medal all-purpose flour

2 teaspoons baking powder

1 teaspoon sugar

1/4 teaspoon salt

1 cup milk

1/4 cup butter or margarine, melted

1 egg, separated

1 Heat waffle iron. (Waffle irons without a nonstick coating may need to be brushed with vegetable oil or sprayed with cooking spray before batter for each waffle is added.)

2 In small bowl, mix flour, baking powder, sugar and salt. Stir in milk, butter and egg yolk until blended. In medium bowl, beat egg white with electric mixer on high speed until stiff peaks form; fold flour mixture into egg white.

3 Pour about 2/3 cup batter from cup or pitcher onto center of hot waffle iron. (Check manufacturer's directions for recommended amount of batter.) Close lid of waffle iron.

4 Bake about 5 minutes or until steaming stops. Carefully remove waffle. Repeat with remaining batter.

BAKING FOR TODAY

Serve these waffles with maple-flavored syrup and fresh fruit, or add easy toppings like equal parts peanut butter and maple-flavored syrup.

High Altitude (3500 to 6500 feet): No changes.

1 Waffle: Calories 185 (Calories from Fat 90); Fat 10g (Saturated 6g); Cholesterol 60mg; Sodium 340mg; Carbohydrate 19g (Dietary Fiber 1g); Protein 5g
Exchanges: 1 Starch, 2 Fat
Carbohydrate Choices: 1

Pizza Stampede

1 1/3 cups Gold Medal all-purpose flour

1/2 cup shredded Cheddar cheese (2 oz)

1 teaspoon baking powder

1/2 teaspoon salt

2 tablespoons vegetable oil

1/2 cup milk

1 can (8 oz) pizza sauce

Meat toppings (such as sliced pepperoni, cut-up cooked chicken, cooked ground beef or sausage)

Vegetable toppings (such as broccoli, carrots, corn or olives)

1 1/2 cups shredded mozzarella cheese (6 oz)

1 Heat oven to 425°F. Grease 2 cookie sheets with shortening or spray with cooking spray. In medium bowl, stir flour, Cheddar cheese, baking powder, salt, oil and milk until a soft dough forms. Divide dough into 6 parts. Press each part into 6-inch circle on cookie sheet. Pinch edge to form rim.

2 Spread pizza sauce over dough. Top with meat and vegetable toppings. Sprinkle with mozzarella cheese.

3 Bake 11 to 15 minutes or until crust is golden brown and cheese is melted.

BAKING FOR TODAY

This recipe combines many favorite flavors—cheese, meat and tomato—in kids' favorite form, pizza. Be sure to have lots of different veggie and meat toppings on hand for them to choose from.

High Altitude (3500 to 6500 feet): No changes.

1 Pizza: Calories 405 (Calories from Fat 200); Fat 22g (Saturated 9g); Cholesterol 50mg; Sodium 770mg; Carbohydrate 29g (Dietary Fiber 2g); Protein 23g **Exchanges:** 2 Starch, 2 Medium-Fat Meat, 2 Fat **Carbohydrate Choices:** 2

Veggie Bites

1/3 cup butter or
margarine, melted

1 egg

2 teaspoons water

1/2 cup Gold Medal
all-purpose flour

1/2 teaspoon salt or
seasoned salt

2 cups fresh vegetables
(such as broccoli flowerets,
cauliflowerets, 1/4-inch carrot
slices, 1/2-inch zucchini
slices, 1/2-inch strips green
or red bell pepper)

Grated Parmesan cheese,
if desired

1 Heat oven to 475°F. On bottom of 15 x 10 x 1-inch or 13 x 9-inch pan, brush about 2 tablespoons of the melted butter.

2 In shallow dish, beat egg and water with fork. In another shallow dish, mix flour and salt. Dip about 1/4 of the vegetables into egg mixture. Remove 1 piece at a time with slotted spoon, fork or hands; roll in flour mixture to coat. Place in pan. Repeat with remaining vegetables. Pour remaining butter carefully over each vegetable piece and into pan.

3 Bake 10 to 12 minutes, turning once, until vegetables are tender and coating is light golden brown; drain. Sprinkle lightly with cheese.

BAKING FOR TODAY

Learning to bake and cook is a wonderful opportunity for creativity. Preparing a food from beginning to end gives kids a sense of accomplishment and helps build confidence. They'll learn that home-baked food tastes better and is better for them; making recipes like Veggie Bites can be the beginning step for kids to learn to make healthy food choices.

High Altitude (3500 to 6500
feet): No changes.

1/4 Cup: Calories 110 (Calories
from Fat 70); Fat 8g (Saturated
5g); Cholesterol 45mg; Sodium
210mg; Carbohydrate 8g (Dietary
Fiber 1g); Protein 2g
Exchanges: 1/2 Starch, 1 1/2 Fat
Carbohydrate Choices: 1/2

VEGGIE BITES

Pup-Tent Pie

1/2 lb hot dogs, sliced

1 can (15 oz) pork and beans

1 can (8 oz) tomato sauce

3 tablespoons packed
brown sugar

1 1/2 cups Gold Medal
all-purpose flour

2 teaspoons baking powder

1/2 teaspoon salt

2/3 cup water

3 tablespoons butter or
margarine, melted

1 Heat oven to 450°F. In 9-inch square pan, stir hot dogs, pork and beans, tomato sauce and brown sugar until mixed. Bake about 15 minutes or until bubbly.

2 Meanwhile, in medium bowl, stir remaining ingredients until a soft dough forms. Drop dough by 8 spoonfuls onto hot dog mixture.

3 Bake 15 to 20 minutes or until dumplings are golden brown.

BAKING FOR TODAY

If you have school-age kids, this may be a recipe that the kids can make all on their own. Be sure to stay close by in case they have questions or need advice. When done, they can see, taste and share the results of their efforts. Let them sprinkle their favorite shredded cheese over this dish before serving.

High Altitude (3500 to 6500 feet): No changes.

1 Serving: Calories 300 (Calories from Fat 115); Fat 13g (Saturated 6g); Cholesterol 30mg; Sodium 1050mg; Carbohydrate 37g (Dietary Fiber 4g); Protein 9g **Exchanges:** 2 Starch, 1/2 Other Carbohydrates, 1/2 High-Fat Meat, 1 1/2 Fat **Carbohydrate Choices:** 2 1/2

Fruitzzas

1/2 cup sugar

1/2 cup butter or
margarine, softened

1/4 teaspoon vanilla

1 egg

1 1/2 cups Gold Medal
all-purpose flour

1 box (4-serving size)
vanilla instant pudding
and pie filling mix

1 3/4 cups milk

1 can (21 oz) blueberry, cherry
or strawberry pie filling

1 Heat oven to 375°F. In large bowl, stir sugar, butter, vanilla and egg until mixed. Stir in flour until a soft dough forms. Divide dough into 8 equal parts. On ungreased cookie sheet, press each part into 4-inch circle.

2 Bake 8 to 10 minutes or until edges are light golden brown. Cool 1 minute; remove from cookie sheet to wire rack. Cool completely.

3 Make vanilla pie filling mix as directed on box for pie directions, using milk. Spread about 2 tablespoons vanilla pie filling on each cookie crust. Top each with 1 tablespoon fruit pie filling.

BAKING FOR TODAY

Kids love foods in individual servings that are all their own, so they'll love creating their own little pies. They can customize this recipe with their favorite fruit pie filling or use fresh fruit. Instead of the vanilla pudding mix, vanilla custard-style yogurt can be used.

High Altitude (3500 to 6500
feet): No changes.

1 Pizza: Calories 395 (Calories
from Fat 125); Fat 14g (Saturated
8g); Cholesterol 60mg; Sodium
290mg; Carbohydrate 62g
(Dietary Fiber 2g); Protein 5g
Exchanges: 2 Starch, 2 Other
Carbohydrates, 2 Fat
Carbohydrate Choices: 4

On-the-Double Peanut Butter Cookies

1/2 cup granulated sugar

1/2 cup packed brown sugar

1/2 cup peanut butter

1/3 cup vegetable oil

1 egg

1 cup Gold Medal
all-purpose flour

1/2 teaspoon baking powder

1/2 teaspoon baking soda

1/4 teaspoon salt

1/2 cup peanut butter chips

1 Heat oven to 375°F. In large bowl, mix sugars, peanut butter, oil and egg with spoon until smooth. Stir in flour, baking powder, baking soda and salt.

2 Divide dough into fourths. On ungreased cookie sheet, shape each fourth into 14-inch roll; place 2 rolls on a cookie sheet. Pat each roll to about 1/2-inch thickness. Sprinkle 2 tablespoons of the peanut butter chips on each strip; press lightly.

3 Bake 6 to 8 minutes until golden brown. Cool on cookie sheet 2 minutes. Cut each strip crosswise at an angle into 2-inch slices; cut slices crosswise at an angle the other direction to make triangle shapes. Remove from cookie sheet to wire rack; cool.

BAKING FOR TODAY

Not only is this recipe doubly delicious with a double taste of peanut butter and peanut butter chips, it is doubly easy as well. The dough is divided into four logs, then baked and sliced, so each cookie isn't shaped individually. To shave off even more minutes, try baking both cookie sheets at one time.

High Altitude (3500 to 6500 feet): Use 1 cup plus 2 tablespoons flour. Bake 7 to 9 minutes.

1 Cookie: Calories 65 (Calories from Fat 25); Fat 3g (Saturated 1g); Cholesterol 5mg; Sodium 45mg; Carbohydrate 7g (Dietary Fiber 0g); Protein 1g
Exchanges: 1/2 Starch, 1/2 Fat
Carbohydrate Choices: 1/2

ON-THE-DOUBLE PEANUT BUTTER COOKIES

Paintbrush Cookies
Classic

This recipe was first published in the 1957 *Betty Crocker's Cookbook for Boys and Girls*. The first version of it had honey as the sweetener but now uses powdered sugar, giving the cookie a light, airy texture and yummy butter cookie flavor. The 1957 cookbook says, "If you have cooky cutters that you like, you'll use them, of course. Always dip them in flour so they won't stick to the dough."

Prep Time: 15 min; Start to Finish: 3 hr 30 min   **About 5 dozen 2- to 2 1/2-inch cookies or about 3 1/2 dozen 3-inch cookies**

1 1/2 cups powdered sugar

1 cup butter or margarine, softened

1 teaspoon vanilla

1/2 teaspoon almond extract

1 egg

2 1/2 cups Gold Medal all-purpose flour

1 teaspoon baking soda

1 teaspoon cream of tartar

Egg Yolk Paint (below)

1 In large bowl, mix powdered sugar, butter, vanilla, almond extract and egg. Stir in flour, baking soda and cream of tartar. Cover and refrigerate 2 to 3 hours.

2 Heat oven to 375°F. Lightly grease cookie sheet with shortening or spray with cooking spray. Divide dough in half. On lightly floured surface, roll each half 3/16 inch thick. Cut into desired shapes with cookie cutters. On cookie sheet, place cookies about 2 inches apart.

3 Make Egg Yolk Paint; paint designs on cookies with small paintbrushes. Bake 7 to 8 minutes or until edges are light brown. Remove from cookie sheet to wire rack; cool.

Egg Yolk Paint: In small bowl, mix 1 egg yolk and 1/4 teaspoon water. Divide mixture among several small custard cups. Tint each with different food colors to make bright colors. If paint thickens while standing, stir in a few drops of water.

BAKING FOR TODAY

Kids will have fun mixing the dough, cutting it into shapes and "painting" the cookies. Even if their painting doesn't look the greatest, you'll be pleasantly surprised to see how adorable the baked cookies turn out. After cooling, sugar cookies can be frozen up to 9 months. Thaw uncovered at room temperature 20 minutes.

High Altitude (3500 to 6500 feet): Bake 8 to 9 minutes.

1 Cookie: Calories 60 (Calories from Fat 25); Fat 3g (Saturated 2g); Cholesterol 15mg; Sodium 45mg; Carbohydrate 7g (Dietary Fiber 0g); Protein 1g
Exchanges: 1/2 Starch, 1/2 Fat
Carbohydrate Choices: 1/2

PAINTBRUSH COOKIES

Trail Mix Cookies

Prep Time: 20 min; Start to Finish: 1 hr 10 min   About 5 dozen cookies

1 cup granulated sugar

1 cup packed brown sugar

1 cup peanut butter

1/2 cup butter or
margarine, softened

1/2 cup shortening

2 teaspoons vanilla

2 eggs

2 cups Gold Medal
all-purpose flour

1 1/2 cups old-fashioned or
quick-cooking oats

1 teaspoon baking powder

1 teaspoon baking soda

2 cups candy-coated
chocolate candies

1 cup peanuts

3/4 cup raisins

1 Heat oven to 375°F. In large bowl, beat sugars, peanut butter, butter, shortening, vanilla and eggs with electric mixer on medium speed until creamy, or mix with spoon. Stir in flour, oats, baking powder and baking soda thoroughly. Stir in candies, peanuts and raisins.

2 On ungreased cookie sheet, drop dough by rounded tablespoonfuls about 2 inches apart; flatten slightly with fork.

3 Bake 9 to 10 minutes or until light brown. Cool 1 minute. Remove from cookie sheet to wire rack; cool.

BAKING FOR TODAY

Named because they contain the original "gorp" ingredients (good old raisins and peanuts) along with chocolate candies, these great-tasting cookies will be a hit on or off the trail. Pack them for your next outing, whether it's to the park, a sports event, a bike path or a picnic.

High Altitude (3500 to 6500 feet): No changes.

1 Cookie: Calories 160 (Calories from Fat 70); Fat 8g (Saturated 3g); Cholesterol 10mg; Sodium 80mg; Carbohydrate 19g (Dietary Fiber 1g); Protein 3g
Exchanges: 1 Starch, 2 Fat
Carbohydrate Choices: 1

TRAIL MIX COOKIES

Chocolate Teddy Bear Pops

1 cup sugar

1 cup butter or
margarine, softened

1/2 teaspoon vanilla

1 egg

2 cups Gold Medal
all-purpose flour

1/4 cup baking cocoa

20 wooden sticks with rounded
ends or lollipop sticks

1 package (16 oz) chocolate-
flavored candy coating
(almond bark)

Chocolate candy sprinkles,
if desired

40 small gumdrops, if desired

1 bag (9 oz) candy-coated
chocolate candies, if desired

60 red cinnamon candies or
ready-to-eat cereal pieces,
if desired

1 tube (4.25 oz) decorating
icing (any color), if desired

1 In large bowl, beat sugar, butter, vanilla and egg with spoon until smooth. Stir in flour and cocoa. Cover and refrigerate at least 1 hour.

2 Heat oven to 375°F. Shape dough into twenty 1-inch balls and twenty 3/4-inch balls. On ungreased cookie sheet, arrange 1 large ball and 1 small ball with sides touching. Insert about 1 1/2 inches of wooden stick through center of 1-inch ball and into smaller ball. Press floured bottom of glass on dough until about 1/4 thick. Repeat with remaining balls of dough, placing pairs of dough balls about 2 inches apart on cookie sheet.

3 Bake 10 to 12 minutes or until set. Cool 1 minute; remove from cookie sheet to wire rack. Cool completely, about 30 minutes.

4 Place waxed paper on tray. Melt candy coating as directed on package. Spoon coating over cookies; place on waxed paper. Sprinkle with chocolate sprinkles. Add gumdrops for ears. Add chocolate candies for hands and feet. Add cinnamon candies for eyes and nose. Personalize teddies by writing names with decorating icing.

BAKING FOR TODAY

Not only is baking with your kids fun and a good family bonding time, there are lots of things kids learn by baking. Reading and math skills and hand-eye coordination are enhanced by measuring the ingredients, and cooking is a skill that will serve them well throughout life.

High Altitude (3500 to 6500 feet): Use 3/4 cup butter or margarine.

1 Cookie: Calories 410 (Calories from Fat 180); Fat 20g (Saturated 13g); Cholesterol 40mg; Sodium 95mg; Carbohydrate 54g (Dietary Fiber 2g); Protein 4g
Exchanges: 1 1/2 Starch, 2 Other Carbohydrates, 3 1/2 Fat
Carbohydrate Choices: 3 1/2

CHOCOLATE TEDDY BEAR POPS

CHOCOLATE-RASPBERRY CAKE AND SLICE OF CHERRY PIE

Home-Baked Cakes and Pies

Pound Cake

Classic

Pound cakes date back to the late 1800s. In 1895, Sperry Flour Company (a firm that joined General Mills) produced a recipe booklet called *Easy Cooking for Little Cooks*. Included in this booklet was a recipe for Pound Cake, given its name because the primary ingredients originally were one pound each of butter, powdered sugar and sifted flour.

Prep Time: 15 min; Start to Finish: 3 hr 55 min   **16 servings**

3 cups Gold Medal all-purpose flour

1 teaspoon baking powder

1/4 teaspoon salt

2 3/4 cups sugar

1 1/4 cups butter or margarine, softened

1 teaspoon vanilla

5 eggs

1 cup evaporated milk

1 Heat oven to 350°F. Grease bottom and side of 12-cup fluted tube cake pan or 10 x 4-inch angel food cake pan (tube pan) with shortening or spray with cooking spray; lightly flour.

2 In medium bowl, mix flour, baking powder and salt; set aside. In large bowl, beat sugar, butter, vanilla and eggs with electric mixer on low speed 30 seconds, scraping bowl constantly. Beat on high speed 5 minutes, scraping bowl occasionally. Beat in flour mixture alternately with milk on low speed. Pour into pan.

3 Bake 1 hour 10 minutes to 1 hour 20 minutes or until toothpick inserted in center comes out clean. Cool 20 minutes; remove from pan to wire rack. Cool completely, about 2 hours.

Almond Pound Cake: Substitute almond extract for the vanilla.

Lemon Pound Cake: Substitute lemon extract for the vanilla; fold 2 to 3 teaspoons grated lemon peel into batter.

Orange-Coconut Pound Cake: Fold 1 1/3 cups flaked coconut and 2 to 3 tablespoons grated orange peel into batter.

High Altitude (3500 to 6500 feet): Use 2 1/4 cups sugar and 3/4 cup butter or margarine. Bake 1 hour 5 minutes to 1 hour 10 minutes.

1 Serving: Calories 395 (Calories from Fat 155); Fat 17g (Saturated 10g); Cholesterol 105mg; Sodium 200mg; Carbohydrate 54g (Dietary Fiber 1g); Protein 6g **Exchanges:** 2 Starch, 1 1/2 Other Carbohydrates, 3 Fat **Carbohydrate Choices:** 3 1/2

BAKING FOR TODAY

This moist, lovely cake is a classic and very versatile. You can dust it with cocoa or powdered sugar for a dramatic look, drizzle with a vanilla or Chocolate Glaze (page 53) for extra homemade flavor, or serve with any fresh fruit. Pound cakes keep very well and often taste even better a day or two after baking.

Cocoa Fudge Cake with Fudge Frosting

Classic

General Mills made history in 1943 with a streamlined method for making cakes that cut mixing time in half. It used only one mixing bowl and eliminated creaming butter and sugar and the separate beating of eggs. Dry ingredients were sifted together, then shortening and the liquid was added.

Prep Time: 15 min; Start to Finish: 1 hr 55 min   **12 servings**

1 2/3 cups Gold Medal all-purpose flour

1 1/2 cups sugar

2/3 cup baking cocoa

1/2 cup butter or margarine, softened

1 1/2 cups buttermilk

1 1/2 teaspoons baking soda

1 teaspoon salt

1 teaspoon vanilla

2 eggs

Fudge Frosting (below)

1. Heat oven to 350°F. Grease bottom and sides of one 13 x 9-inch pan, two 8-inch or 9-inch round pans or one 12-cup fluted tube cake pan with shortening or spray with cooking spray; lightly flour.

2. In large bowl, beat all ingredients except Fudge Frosting with electric mixer on low speed 30 seconds, scraping bowl constantly. Beat on high speed 3 minutes, scraping bowl occasionally. Pour into pan(s).

3. Bake 13 x 9-inch pan 35 to 40 minutes, round pans 30 to 35 minutes, fluted tube cake pan 40 to 45 minutes, or until toothpick inserted in center comes out clean. Cool 13 x 9-inch cake in pan on wire rack. Cool rounds 10 minutes; remove from pans to wire rack. Cool fluted cake 20 minutes; remove from pan to wire rack. Cool completely, about 1 hour.

4. Frost 13 x 9-inch or fluted cake or fill and frost round layers with Fudge Frosting.

High Altitude (3500 to 6500 feet): Heat oven to 375°F. Do not use 8-inch round pans or fluted tube cake pan. Decrease sugar to 1 1/3 cups and baking soda to 1 1/4 teaspoons. Increase buttermilk to 1 2/3 cups and eggs to 3. Bake 13 x 9-inch pan 33 to 37 minutes, 9-inch rounds 25 to 30 minutes and cupcakes 15 to 20 minutes.

1 Serving: Calories 535 (Calories from Fat 180); Fat 20g (Saturated 12g); Cholesterol 80mg; Sodium 560mg; Carbohydrate 82g (Dietary Fiber 3g); Protein 6g **Exchanges:** 2 Starch, 3 1/2 Other Carbohydrates, 3 1/2 Fat **Carbohydrate Choices:** 5 1/2

Fudge Frosting

2 cups sugar

1/4 cup light corn syrup

1/2 cup milk

1/2 cup butter or margarine

2 oz unsweetened baking chocolate

1/4 teaspoon salt

1 teaspoon vanilla

In 2-quart saucepan, mix sugar, corn syrup, milk, butter, chocolate and salt. Cook over medium heat, stirring constantly, until chocolate is melted and sugar is dissolved. Heat to rolling boil, stirring constantly. Boil rapidly 1 minute, stirring constantly, to 220°F on candy thermometer. Remove from heat; stir in vanilla. Place in pan of ice and water; let cool 5 minutes. Beat with electric mixer on medium speed about 10 minutes or until dull in color and spreadable.

BAKING FOR TODAY

If you have mini-muffin pans, make mini-cupcakes! The kids will love frosting them with this yummy frosting. Then get out the decorating gel and candy sprinkles, and let them decorate to their heart's content!

Lazy Daisy Cake

Classic

In the 1890s, this recipe was popular as One-Egg Cake. During the 1920s and '30s, it was promoted as Emergency Cake or Lazy Daisy Cake. A 1940 Gold Medal ad called it Busy Day Cake. Still popular in 1955, it was referred to as Kitchenette or Dinette Cake.

Prep Time: 15 min; Start to Finish: 1 hr　　　　　　　　　　　　　　　　　　　**9 servings**

1 1/4 cups Gold Medal all-purpose flour

1 cup granulated sugar

1/3 cup butter or margarine, softened

3/4 cup milk

1 1/2 teaspoons baking powder

1 teaspoon vanilla

1/2 teaspoon salt

1 egg

Broiled Coconut Frosting (below)

1 Heat oven to 350°F. Grease bottom and sides of 8-inch or 9-inch square pan with shortening or spray with cooking spray; lightly flour.

2 In medium bowl, beat all ingredients except Broiled Coconut Frosting with electric mixer on low speed 30 seconds, scraping bowl constantly. Beat on high speed 3 minutes, scraping bowl occasionally. Pour into pan.

3 Bake 35 to 40 minutes or until toothpick inserted in center comes out clean.

4 Meanwhile, make Broiled Coconut Frosting. Set oven control to broil. Carefully spread frosting over hot cake. Broil with top of cake about 4 inches from heat about 2 minutes or until frosting is light brown.

Broiled Coconut Frosting

1 cup flaked coconut

1/3 cup packed brown sugar

1/4 cup butter or margarine, softened

2 tablespoons half-and-half

In small bowl, stir all ingredients until mixed.

BAKING FOR TODAY

High Altitude (3500 to 6500 feet): Use 1 teaspoon baking powder.

1 Serving: Calories 355 (Calories from Fat 145); Fat 16g (Saturated 11g); Cholesterol 60mg; Sodium 340mg; Carbohydrate 49g (Dietary Fiber 1g); Protein 4g **Exchanges:** 1 1/2 Starch, 1 1/2 Other Carbohydrates, 3 Fat **Carbohydrate Choices:** 3

When choosing the right pan for your cake, measure the pan across the top from inside edge to inside edge. Cakes baked in dark pans with a nonstick finish often bake faster and have a darker crust. To compensate for that, lower your oven temperature 25°F.

LAZY DAISY CAKE WITH BROILED COCONUT FROSTING

Silver White Cake

Classic

In 1962, Gold Medal revolutionized cake baking again with the first "no-sift" flour. An ad that year described the flour as being milled through sifters "97 times finer than yours . . . the only flour that promises success without sifting or altering your recipes."

Prep Time: 15 min; **Start to Finish:** 2 hr   12 servings

2 1/4 cups Gold Medal all-purpose flour

1 2/3 cups sugar

2/3 cup shortening

1 1/4 cups milk

3 1/2 teaspoons baking powder

1 teaspoon salt

1 teaspoon vanilla

5 egg whites

Lemon Filling (below)

White Mountain Frosting (page 187)

1 Heat oven to 350°F. Grease bottom and side of two 9-inch round pans, three 8-inch round pans or one 13 x 9-inch pan with shortening or spray with cooking spray; lightly flour.

2 In large bowl, beat flour, sugar, shortening, milk, baking powder, salt and vanilla with electric mixer on low speed 30 seconds, scraping bowl constantly. Beat on high speed 2 minutes, scraping bowl occasionally. Beat in egg whites on high speed 2 minutes, scraping bowl occasionally. Pour into pan(s).

3 Bake 9-inch rounds 30 to 35 minutes, 8-inch rounds 23 to 28 minutes, 13 x 9-inch pan 40 to 45 minutes, or until toothpick inserted in center comes out clean or until cake springs back when touched lightly in center. Cool rounds 10 minutes; remove from pans to wire rack. Cool 13 x 9-inch cake in pan on wire rack. Cool completely, about 1 hour.

4 Fill layers with Lemon Filling or spread Lemon Filling over 13 x 9-inch cake. Frost cake with White Mountain Frosting.

Lemon Filling

3/4 cup sugar

3 tablespoons cornstarch

1/4 teaspoon salt

3/4 cup water

1 teaspoon grated lemon peel

1 tablespoon butter or margarine

1/3 cup lemon juice

4 drops yellow food color, if desired

In 1-quart saucepan, mix sugar, cornstarch and salt. Gradually stir in water. Cook over medium heat, stirring constantly, until mixture thickens and boils. Boil and stir 5 minutes. Remove from heat; stir in lemon peel and butter. Stir in lemon juice and food color; cool. If filling is too soft, refrigerate until set.

High Altitude (3500 to 6500 feet): Heat oven to 375°F. Decrease sugar to 1 1/2 cups and baking powder to 2 1/4 teaspoons. Increase milk to 1 1/3 cups. Bake 8-inch rounds 20 to 25 minutes, 9-inch rounds 25 to 30 minutes, rectangle 35 to 40 minutes.

1 Serving: Calories 405 (Calories from Fat 115); Fat 13g (Saturated 4g); Cholesterol 5mg; Sodium 450mg; Carbohydrate 67g (Dietary Fiber 1g); Protein 5g **Exchanges:** 2 Starch, 2 1/2 Other Carbohydrates, 2 Fat **Carbohydrate Choices:** 4 1/2

White Mountain Frosting

1/2 cup sugar

1/4 cup light corn syrup

2 tablespoons water

2 egg whites

1 teaspoon vanilla

In 1-quart saucepan, stir sugar, corn syrup and water until well mixed. Cover and heat to rolling boil over medium heat. Uncover and boil 4 to 8 minutes, without stirring, to 242°F on candy thermometer or until small amount of mixture dropped into cup of very cold water forms a firm ball that holds its shape until pressed. While mixture is boiling, in medium bowl, beat egg whites with electric mixer on high speed just until stiff peaks form. Pour hot syrup very slowly in thin stream into egg whites, beating constantly on medium speed. Add vanilla. Beat on high speed about 10 minutes or until stiff peaks form.

Silver White Cupcakes: Fill paper-lined muffin cups 1/2 full. Bake 20 to 25 minutes. 2 1/2 dozen cupcakes.

Silver White Sheet Cake: Pour batter into greased and floured 15 x 10 x 1-inch pan. Bake 25 minutes.

Small Silver White Cake: Decrease flour to 1 cup plus 2 tablespoons, sugar to 3/4 cup, shortening to 1/3 cup, milk to 2/3 cup, baking powder to 1 3/4 teaspoons, salt to 1/2 teaspoon, vanilla to 1/2 teaspoon and egg whites to 3. Pour batter into greased and floured 8-inch or 9-inch square pan. Bake 35 to 40 minutes.

BAKING FOR TODAY

This elegant classic cake has a few steps for making it, but the results are well worth the effort! Be sure to store any leftovers of this filled and frosted cake in the refrigerator.

Date–Chocolate Chip Cake

Prep Time: 20 min; **Start to Finish:** 3 hr 20 min · 12 servings

1 1/4 cups boiling water

1 cup chopped dates

1 teaspoon baking soda

Chocolate Chip Topping (below)

1 3/4 cups Gold Medal all-purpose flour

1/2 cup granulated sugar

1/2 cup packed brown sugar

2/3 cup vegetable oil

1 teaspoon baking soda

1 teaspoon vanilla

1/2 teaspoon salt

2 eggs

1 In large bowl, pour boiling water on dates. Stir in 1 teaspoon baking soda. Cool about 15 minutes or until lukewarm.

2 Make Chocolate Chip Topping; set aside.

3 Heat oven to 350°F. Stir remaining ingredients into date mixture. Pour into ungreased 9-inch square pan. Sprinkle with topping.

4 Bake 50 to 55 minutes or until toothpick inserted in center comes out clean. Cool completely, about 2 hours.

Chocolate Chip Topping

1/2 cup semisweet chocolate chips

1/4 cup packed brown sugar

1/4 cup Gold Medal all-purpose flour

1 tablespoon butter or margarine, softened

In small bowl, mix all ingredients.

BAKING FOR TODAY

The chocolate chip topping and dates make this cake look special, but it's really very easy and is great served with ice cream or whipped cream. Make chocolate shavings by pulling a vegetable peeler or thin sharp knife across a block of white or milk chocolate, using long, thin strokes. Sprinkle shavings over the top of the ice cream and cake.

High Altitude (3500 to 6500 feet): No changes.

1 Serving: Calories 385 (Calories from Fat 155); Fat 17g (Saturated 5g); Cholesterol 40mg; Sodium 340mg; Carbohydrate 53g (Dietary Fiber 2g); Protein 4g **Exchanges:** 1 1/2 Starch, 2 Other Carbohydrates, 3 Fat **Carbohydrate Choices:** 3 1/2

DATE-CHOCOLATE CHIP CAKE

Applesauce Bundt Cake

Classic

Applesauce Cake was one of the recipes contributed by world-famous chefs to the handsome cookbook, *Betty Crocker's $25,000 Recipe Set*. Printed in France, the book was brought home on the *Normandie*'s maiden voyage.

Prep Time: 20 min; Start to Finish: 3 hr 20 min   16 servings

1 tablespoon Gold Medal all-purpose flour

1 cup dried cranberries

2 1/2 cups Gold Medal all-purpose flour

1 1/2 teaspoons salt

1 tablespoon pumpkin pie spice

1 teaspoon baking powder

1/2 teaspoon baking soda

1 1/2 cups granulated sugar

1/2 cup butter or margarine, softened

2 eggs

1 1/2 cups applesauce

1/2 cup chopped walnuts or pecans

2 tablespoons powdered sugar

1 Heat oven to 350°F. Grease bottom and side of 12-cup fluted tube cake pan with shortening or spray with cooking spray; lightly flour. In small bowl, toss 1 tablespoon flour and the cranberries to coat; set aside. In medium bowl, mix 2 1/2 cups flour, the salt, pumpkin pie spice, baking powder and baking soda; set aside.

2 In large bowl, beat granulated sugar and butter with electric mixer on low speed 30 seconds, scraping bowl constantly. Beat on high speed, scraping bowl occasionally, until light and fluffy. Beat in eggs, one at a time, until smooth and blended. Reduce mixer speed to medium. Gradually beat in flour mixture alternately with applesauce until smooth. Stir in cranberry-flour mixture and walnuts. Pour into pan.

3 Bake 50 to 60 minutes or until toothpick inserted in center comes out clean. Cool 10 minutes; remove from pan to wire rack. Cool completely, about 2 hours. Sprinkle powdered sugar over cake.

BAKING FOR TODAY

Applesauce is the ingredient that adds moistness and depth to this updated favorite, and cranberries add a new, trendy look and taste. If you don't have pumpkin pie spice handy, you can use 1 1/2 teaspoons ground cinnamon, 1 teaspoon ground nutmeg and 1/4 teaspoon ground allspice instead.

High Altitude (3500 to 6500 feet): No changes.

1 Serving: Calories 280 (Calories from Fat 80); Fat 9g (Saturated 4g); Cholesterol 40mg; Sodium 340mg; Carbohydrate 46g (Dietary Fiber 2g); Protein 4g **Exchanges:** 1 Starch, 1 Fruit, 1 Other Carbohydrates, 2 Fat **Carbohydrate Choices:** 3

Chocolate-Raspberry Cake

3 cups Gold Medal
all-purpose flour

2 cups granulated sugar

1/2 cup baking cocoa

2 teaspoons baking soda

1 teaspoon salt

2/3 cup vegetable oil

2 teaspoons white vinegar

1 teaspoon vanilla

2 cups cold water

1/4 cup raspberry jam

About 1 tablespoon powdered
sugar, if desired

Fresh raspberries, if desired

1 Heat oven to 350°F. Grease bottoms and sides of two 9-inch round pans with shortening or spray with cooking spray; lightly flour.

2 In large bowl, mix flour, granulated sugar, cocoa, baking soda and salt. In small bowl, mix oil, vinegar and vanilla. Vigorously stir oil mixture and water into flour mixture with spoon about 1 minute or until well blended. Immediately pour into pans.

3 Bake 30 to 35 minutes or until toothpick inserted in center comes out clean. Cool 10 minutes; remove from pans to wire rack. Cool completely, about 1 hour.

4 Place 1 cake layer, top side down, on serving platter; spread with jam. Top with second layer, top side up; dust with powdered sugar. Garnish with raspberries.

BAKING FOR TODAY

Delight in made-from-scratch goodness with this easy cake mixed in just one bowl. If you love frosting, go ahead and fill and top this super-moist chocoholic's dream with your favorite chocolate frosting, and then "let them eat cake"!

High Altitude (3500 to 6500 feet): Use 1 teaspoon baking soda. Bake 35 to 40 minutes.

1 Serving: Calories 295 (Calories from Fat 90); Fat 10g (Saturated 2g); Cholesterol 0mg; Sodium 310mg; Carbohydrate 48g (Dietary Fiber 2g); Protein 3g **Exchanges:** 1 Starch, 2 Other Carbohydrates, 2 Fat **Carbohydrate Choices:** 3

Sugar and Spice Cake

Prep Time: 15 min; **Start to Finish:** 50 min   **9 servings**

1 1/4 cups Gold Medal all-purpose flour

1 cup sugar

3 teaspoons ground cinnamon

1/4 teaspoon salt

1/2 cup shortening

3/4 cup sour cream

1 teaspoon baking soda

1 teaspoon baking powder

2 eggs

1 Heat oven to 350°F. Grease bottom and side(s) of 9-inch round pan or 8-inch square pan with shortening or spray with cooking spray; lightly flour.

2 In large bowl, mix flour, sugar, cinnamon and salt. Cut in shortening, using pastry blender (or pulling 2 table knives through ingredients in opposite directions), until particles are size of small peas; reserve 1/3 cup.

3 Stir remaining ingredients into flour mixture with spoon until well blended. Pour into pan. Sprinkle reserved flour mixture over batter.

4 Bake 30 to 35 minutes or until toothpick inserted in center comes out clean. Serve warm or cool.

BAKING FOR TODAY

For an extra spice hit, serve this easy-yet-sensational cake warm from the oven with a spoonful of cinnamon ice cream.

High Altitude (3500 to 6500 feet): Use 3/4 cup sugar, 1/4 cup shortening, 1/2 teaspoon baking soda and 1/2 teaspoon baking powder.

1 Serving: Calories 310 (Calories from Fat 145); Fat 16g (Saturated 6g); Cholesterol 60mg; Sodium 280mg; Carbohydrate 37g (Dietary Fiber 1g); Protein 4g **Exchanges:** 1 1/2 Starch, 1 Other Carbohydrates, 3 Fat **Carbohydrate Choices:** 2 1/2

SUGAR AND SPICE CAKE

Molten Chocolate Cakes

Baking cocoa

6 oz semisweet baking chocolate, chopped

1/2 cup plus 2 tablespoons butter or margarine

3 whole eggs

3 egg yolks

1 1/2 cups powdered sugar

1/2 cup Gold Medal all-purpose flour

Additional powdered sugar, if desired

1 Heat oven to 450°F. Grease bottoms and sides of six 6-ounce custard cups with shortening; dust with cocoa.

2 In 2-quart saucepan, melt chocolate and butter over low heat, stirring frequently. Cool slightly.

3 In large bowl, beat whole eggs and egg yolks with wire whisk or hand beater until well blended. Beat in 1 1/2 cups powdered sugar. Beat in melted chocolate mixture and flour. Divide batter evenly among custard cups. Place cups on cookie sheet with sides.

4 Bake 12 to 14 minutes or until sides are set and centers are still soft (tops will be puffed and cracked). Let stand 3 minutes. Run small knife or metal spatula along sides of cakes to loosen. Immediately place heatproof serving plate upside down onto each cup; turn plate and cup over and remove cup. Sprinkle with additional powdered sugar. Serve warm.

Note: Be sure to grease the custard cups with shortening, dust the cups with cocoa and bake the cakes at the correct oven temperature for the right time. These steps are critical to the success of this recipe. If the centers are too cakelike in texture, bake a few minutes less the next time; if they're too soft, bake a minute or two longer.

BAKING FOR TODAY

Now you can make this sensational restaurant favorite at home. These cakes have a hot, flowing chocolate center that oozes out when you cut into them. You can make the batter up to 24 hours ahead. After pouring batter into custard cups, cover with plastic wrap and refrigerate up to 24 hours. You may need to bake the cakes 1 to 2 minutes longer.

High Altitude (3500 to 6500 feet): Bake 14 to 16 minutes.

1 Serving: Calories 475 (Calories from Fat 225); Fat 25g (Saturated 14g); Cholesterol 245mg; Sodium 115mg; Carbohydrate 56g (Dietary Fiber 2g); Protein 7g
Exchanges: 2 Starch, 2 Other Carbohydrates, 4 1/2 Fat
Carbohydrate Choices: 4

Carrot Cake
Classic

Prep Time: 25 min; **Start to Finish:** 2 hr   **9 servings**

1 1/4 cups Gold Medal all-purpose flour

3/4 cup granulated sugar

3/4 cup vegetable oil

2 teaspoons ground cinnamon

1 teaspoon baking soda

2 teaspoons vanilla

1/2 teaspoon salt

1/4 teaspoon ground nutmeg

2 eggs

1 1/2 cups grated or finely shredded carrots (about 3 medium)

Cream Cheese Frosting (below)

1 Heat oven to 350°F. Grease bottom and sides of 8-inch or 9-inch square pan with shortening or spray with cooking spray.

2 In large bowl, beat all ingredients except carrots and Cream Cheese Frosting with electric mixer on low speed 30 seconds. Beat on medium speed 3 minutes. Stir in carrots. Pour into pan.

3 Bake 30 to 35 minutes or until toothpick inserted in center comes out clean. Cool completely, about 1 hour. Frost with Cream Cheese Frosting. Store covered in refrigerator.

Cream Cheese Frosting

1 package (3 oz) cream cheese, softened

1/4 cup butter or margarine, softened

2 cups powdered sugar

1 teaspoon vanilla

In medium bowl, beat cream cheese and butter on medium speed until smooth. Gradually stir in powdered sugar and vanilla until smooth and spreadable.

BAKING FOR TODAY

If you like ginger, you can add crystallized ginger to this classic carrot cake to give it a unique flavor. Toss 1/4 cup finely chopped crystallized ginger and 1 tablespoon Gold Medal all-purpose flour to coat, and stir into the cake batter.

High Altitude (3500 to 6500 feet): Bake about 40 minutes.

1 Serving: Calories 505 (Calories from Fat 250); Fat 28g (Saturated 8g); Cholesterol 70mg; Sodium 350mg; Carbohydrate 59g (Dietary Fiber 1g); Protein 4g **Exchanges:** 1 Starch, 3 Other Carbohydrates, 5 1/2 Fat **Carbohydrate Choices:** 4

French Silk Pie

Classic

Pastry for 9-Inch One-Crust Pie (page 197) or Easy-Roll Buttermilk Pastry (page 204)

1 cup sugar

3/4 cup butter, softened (do not use margarine)

1 1/2 teaspoons vanilla

3 oz unsweetened baking chocolate, melted and cooled

3/4 cup fat-free cholesterol-free egg product

1 1/2 cups Sweetened Whipped Cream (page 232)

Chocolate curls, if desired

1 Heat oven to 475°F. Make pastry. On lightly floured surface, roll pastry into circle 2 inches larger than upside-down 9-inch glass pie plate with floured rolling pin. Fold pastry into fourths; place in pie plate. Unfold and ease into plate, pressing firmly against bottom and side. Trim overhanging edge of pastry 1 inch from rim of plate. Fold and roll pastry under, even with plate; press with tines of fork or flute if desired. Prick bottom and side of pastry thoroughly with fork. Bake 8 to 10 minutes or until light brown. Cool completely, about 30 minutes.

2 In medium bowl, beat sugar and butter with electric mixer on medium speed until light and fluffy. Beat in vanilla and chocolate. Gradually beat in egg product on high speed or until light and fluffy (about 3 minutes). Pour into pie crust. Refrigerate until set, at least 2 hours but no longer than 24 hours.

3 Spread with Sweetened Whipped Cream. Garnish with chocolate curls. Store covered in refrigerator.

Mocha French Silk Pie: Beat in 1 1/2 teaspoons instant coffee (dry) with the chocolate.

BAKING FOR TODAY

This French Silk Pie is a *classic* and is loved by adults and kids alike. You can use egg product substitute with confidence; since it is pasteurized, the risk of contracting salmonella (associated with using raw eggs) is eliminated.

High Altitude (3500 to 6500 feet): No changes.

1 Serving: Calories 460 (Calories from Fat 295); Fat 33g (Saturated 17g); Cholesterol 55mg; Sodium 260mg; Carbohydrate 37g (Dietary Fiber 1g); Protein 5g **Exchanges:** 2 Starch, 1/2 Other Carbohydrates, 6 Fat **Carbohydrate Choices:** 2 1/2

Classic Deep-Dish Apple Pie

This round, flat apple pie featured in a Washburn Crosby Cookbook of 1894 is truly an American classic. The pie shape was created by thrifty American colonists so that "a little would go a long way." The original apple "pye" of old England was made in a long, deep dish called a "coffin."

Prep Time: 45 min; Start to Finish: 3 hr 30 min — 12 servings

Pastry for 9-Inch One-Crust Pie (below) or Easy-Roll Buttermilk Pastry (page 204)

1 1/2 cups sugar

1/2 cup Gold Medal all-purpose flour

1 teaspoon ground nutmeg

1 teaspoon ground cinnamon

1/4 teaspoon salt

12 cups thinly sliced peeled tart apples (about 11 medium)

2 tablespoons butter or margarine

Ice cream, if desired

1 Heat oven to 375°F. Make pastry. On lightly floured surface, roll pastry into 10-inch square with floured rolling pin. Fold pastry in half; cut slits near center so steam can escape.

2 In extra-large bowl, mix sugar, flour, nutmeg, cinnamon and salt. Stir in apples. In ungreased 9-inch square pan, spread apple mixture. Cut butter into small pieces; sprinkle over top.

3 Cover with pastry; fold edges under just inside edges of pan. Line 15 x 10 x 1-inch pan with foil; place on oven rack below the rack pie will be baked on to catch any spillover. Bake 1 hour to 1 hour 10 minutes or until juice begins to bubble through slits in crust. Cool 1 hour before serving. Serve with ice cream.

Pastry for 9-Inch One-Crust Pie

1 cup Gold Medal all-purpose flour

1/2 teaspoon salt

1/3 cup plus 1 tablespoon shortening

2 to 3 tablespoons cold water

In medium bowl, mix flour and salt. Cut in shortening, using pastry blender (or pulling 2 table knives through ingredients in opposite directions), until particles are size of small peas. Sprinkle with cold water, 1 tablespoon at a time, tossing with fork until all flour is moistened and pastry almost leaves side of bowl (1 to 2 teaspoons more water can be added if necessary). Gather pastry into a ball. On lightly floured surface, shape into flattened round. Wrap flattened round of pastry in plastic wrap and refrigerate about 45 minutes or until dough is firm and cold, yet pliable. This allows the shortening to become slightly firm, which helps make the baked pastry more flaky. If refrigerated longer, let pastry soften slightly before rolling.

High Altitude (3500 to 6500 feet): No changes.

1 Serving: Calories 305 (Calories from Fat 80); Fat 9g (Saturated 3g); Cholesterol 5mg; Sodium 160mg; Carbohydrate 54g (Dietary Fiber 3g); Protein 2g **Exchanges:** 1 Starch, 1 1/2 Fruit, 1 Other Carbohydrates, 1 1/2 Fat **Carbohydrate Choices:** 3 1/2

BAKING FOR TODAY

With more fruit to pastry than regular pies, deep-dish pies are also easier to make because there is only one pastry that fits beautifully over the top of the fruit. If you like, you can serve the pie for breakfast with a slice of cheese, as people did in the 1920s.

Classic Raspberry Pie

Berry pies, featured in a 1943 Gold Medal ad, can be traced back more than 375 years. New England colonists made blueberry and raspberry pies. The Pennsylvania Dutch settlers used currants, blackberries, elderberries and gooseberries.

Prep Time: 25 min; Start to Finish: 1 hr 55 min — **8 servings**

Pastry for 9-Inch Two-Crust Pie (below)

1 cup sugar

1/3 cup Gold Medal all-purpose flour

4 cups fresh raspberries

2 tablespoons butter or margarine

1 Heat oven to 425°F. Make pastry. On lightly floured surface, roll 1 round of pastry into circle 2 inches larger than upside-down 9-inch glass pie plate with floured rolling pin. Fold pastry into fourths; place in pie plate. Unfold and ease into plate, pressing firmly against bottom and side. Trim overhanging edge of bottom pastry 1/2 inch from rim of plate (if making Lattice Top, trim bottom pastry 1 inch from rim of plate).

2 In large bowl, mix sugar and flour. Gently stir in berries. Spoon into pastry-lined pie plate. Cut butter into small pieces; sprinkle over berries.

3 Roll second round of pastry (if making Lattice Top, see page 199). Fold top pastry into fourths and cut slits so steam can escape. Place pastry over filling and unfold. Trim overhanging edge of top pastry 1 inch from rim of plate. Fold and roll top edge under lower edge, pressing on rim to seal; flute.

4 Cover edge with 2- to 3-inch strip of foil to prevent excessive browning; remove foil for last 15 minutes of baking. Bake 35 to 45 minutes or until crust is golden brown and juice begins to bubble through slits in crust. Serve slightly warm.

BAKING FOR TODAY

Make cutouts of holiday shapes in the top crust. Using mini-cutters, cut out 15 designs in the top pastry before folding the pastry into fourths (do not cut slits).

High Altitude (3500 to 6500 feet): Heat oven to 450°F.

1 Serving: Calories 470 (Calories from Fat 215); Fat 24g (Saturated 7g); Cholesterol 10mg; Sodium 320mg; Carbohydrate 60g (Dietary Fiber 5g); Protein 4g **Exchanges:** 1 1/2 Starch, 1 1/2 Fruit, 1 Other Carbohydrates, 4 1/2 Fat **Carbohydrate Choices:** 4

Pastry for 9-Inch Two-Crust Pie

2 cups Gold Medal all-purpose flour

1 teaspoon salt

2/3 cup plus 2 tablespoons shortening

4 to 5 tablespoons cold water

In medium bowl, mix flour and salt. Cut in shortening, using pastry blender (or pulling 2 table knives through ingredients in opposite directions), until particles are size of small peas. Sprinkle with cold water, 1 tablespoon at a time, tossing with fork until all flour is moistened and pastry almost leaves side of bowl (1 to 2 teaspoons more water can be added if necessary). Gather pastry into a ball; divide in half. On lightly floured surface, shape each half into flattened round. Wrap flattened rounds of pastry in plastic wrap and refrigerate about 45 minutes or until dough is firm and cold, yet pliable. This allows the shortening to become slightly firm, which helps make the baked pastry more flaky. If refrigerated longer, let pastry soften slightly before rolling.

Cherry Pie
Classic

Pastry for 9-Inch Two-Crust Pie
(page 198)

1 1/3 cups sugar

1/2 cup Gold Medal
all-purpose flour

6 cups fresh sour cherries,
pitted

2 tablespoons butter or
margarine, if desired

1 Heat oven to 425°F. Make pastry. On lightly floured surface, roll 1 round of pastry into circle 2 inches larger than upside-down 9-inch glass pie plate with floured rolling pin. Fold pastry into fourths; place in pie plate. Unfold and ease into plate, pressing firmly against bottom and side. Trim overhanging edge of bottom pastry 1/2 inch from rim of plate (if making Lattice Top, trim bottom pastry 1 inch from rim of plate).

2 In large bowl, mix sugar and flour. Stir in cherries. Spoon into pastry-lined pie plate. Cut butter into small pieces; sprinkle over cherries.

3 Roll second round of pastry (if making Lattice Top, see below). Fold top pastry into fourths and cut slits so steam can escape. Place pastry over filling and unfold. Trim overhanging edge of top pastry 1 inch from rim of plate. Fold and roll top edge under lower edge, pressing on rim to seal; flute.

4 Cover edge with 2- to 3-inch strip of foil to prevent excessive browning; remove foil for last 15 minutes of baking. Bake 35 to 45 minutes or until crust is golden brown and juice begins to bubble through slits in crust. Cool on wire rack at least 2 hours.

Quick Cherry Pie: Substitute 6 cups frozen unsweetened pitted red tart cherries, thawed and drained, or 3 cans (14.5 oz each) pitted red tart cherries, drained, for the fresh cherries.

Lattice Top: Roll second round of pastry. Cut into 10 strips, about 1/2 inch wide. Place 5 strips of pastry across filling. Weave a cross-strip through center by first folding back every other strip of the first 5 strips. Continue weaving, folding back alternate strips before adding each cross-strip, until lattice is complete; trim ends of strips. Fold trimmed edge of bottom crust over ends of strips, forming a high stand-up rim; seal and flute. Brush pastry with milk; sprinkle with sugar if desired.

High Altitude (3500 to 6500 feet): Place cookie sheet on oven rack below pie to catch any spillover. Cover edge of crust with foil for first 40 minutes of baking; uncover for last 10 minutes. Bake 40 to 50 minutes.

1 Serving: Calories 570 (Calories from Fat 225); Fat 25g (Saturated 7g); Cholesterol 10mg; Sodium 320mg; Carbohydrate 81g (Dietary Fiber 4g); Protein 5g **Exchanges:** 2 Starch, 2 Fruit, 1 1/2 Other Carbohydrates, 4 1/2 Fat **Carbohydrate Choices:** 5 1/2

BAKING FOR TODAY

There are two types of cherries—sweet and sour. Sour cherries are sometimes called pie cherries, tart cherries or tart red cherries. Sour cherries make wonderful pies, which become showpieces when topped with a lattice crust (above).

Pear-Cranberry Pie

Prep Time: 35 min; Start to Finish: 2 hr 10 min   8 servings

Pastry for 9-Inch Two-Crust Pie
(page 198)

4 cups sliced peeled pears
(5 medium)

1 1/2 cups fresh or frozen
(thawed) cranberries

1 cup sugar

1/4 cup cornstarch

1 teaspoon ground cinnamon

2 tablespoons butter or
margarine

1 egg, beaten

1 Heat oven to 425°F. Make pastry. On lightly floured surface, roll 1 round of pastry into circle 2 inches larger than upside-down 9-inch glass pie plate with floured rolling pin. Fold pastry into fourths; place in pie plate. Unfold and ease into plate, pressing firmly against bottom and side. Trim overhanging edge of bottom pastry 1/2 inch from rim of plate.

2 In large bowl, place pears, cranberries, sugar, cornstarch and cinnamon; toss to coat. Spoon into pastry-lined pie plate. Cut butter into small pieces; sprinkle over fruit mixture.

3 Roll second round of pastry. Cut out and remove leaf shapes from center of pastry, using 1 1/2-inch leaf-shaped cookie cutter and leaving 3-inch solid border around edge. Place pastry over filling. Trim overhanging edge of top pastry 1 inch from rim of plate. Fold and roll top edge under lower pastry edge, pressing on rim to seal. Arrange leaves on pie and around edge, using beaten egg to attach. Brush pastry and leaves with remaining beaten egg.

4 Cover edge of pastry with 2- to 3-inch strip of foil to prevent excessive browning; remove foil for last 15 minutes of baking. Bake 40 to 50 minutes or until crust is brown and juice begins to bubble through holes in crust. Serve warm.

BAKING FOR TODAY

Cranberries' tart flavor and beautiful color have made them natural additions to apple, pear and other fruit pies. If you prefer apple or pear pie without cranberries, use 6 cups peeled apple or pear slices.

High Altitude (3500 to 6500 feet): Use 1/2 cup cornstarch. Bake 45 to 55 minutes; remove foil for last 10 minutes of baking.

1 Serving: Calories 515 (Calories from Fat 225); Fat 25g (Saturated 7g); Cholesterol 35mg; Sodium 320mg; Carbohydrate 68g (Dietary Fiber 4g); Protein 4g **Exchanges:** 1 1/2 Starch, 2 Fruit, 1 Other Carbohydrates, 5 Fat **Carbohydrate Choices:** 4 1/2

PEAR-CRANBERRY PIE

Best-Ever Lemon Meringue Pie

Classic

Prep Time: 50 min; Start to Finish: 3 hr 5 min   8 servings

Easy-Roll Buttermilk Pastry (page 204) or Pastry for 9-Inch One-Crust Pie (page 197)

1/2 cup sugar

4 teaspoons cornstarch

1/2 cup cold water

3 egg yolks

1 1/2 cups sugar

1/3 cup plus 1 tablespoon cornstarch

1 1/2 cups water

3 tablespoons butter or margarine

2 teaspoons grated lemon peel

1/2 cup lemon juice

2 drops yellow food color, if desired

4 egg whites

1/8 teaspoon salt

1 Heat oven to 475°F. Make pastry. On lightly floured surface, roll pastry into circle 2 inches larger than upside-down 9-inch glass pie plate with floured rolling pin. Fold pastry into fourths; place in pie plate. Unfold and ease into plate, pressing firmly against bottom and side. Trim overhanging edge of pastry 1 inch from rim of plate. Fold and roll pastry under, even with plate; press with tines of fork or flute if desired. Prick bottom and side of pastry thoroughly with fork. Bake 8 to 10 minutes or until light brown. Cool completely, about 30 minutes.

2 Heat oven to 350°F. In 1-quart saucepan, mix 1/2 cup sugar and 4 teaspoons cornstarch. Stir in 1/2 cup cold water. Cook over medium heat, stirring constantly, until mixture thickens and boils. Boil and stir 1 minute; remove from heat. Cool completely. (To cool more quickly, place in freezer about 10 minutes.) Reserve for step 4.

3 While sugar mixture for meringue is cooling, in small bowl, beat egg yolks with fork; set aside. In 2-quart saucepan, mix 1 1/2 cups sugar and 1/3 cup plus 1 tablespoon cornstarch. Gradually stir in 1 1/2 cups water. Cook over medium heat, stirring constantly, until mixture thickens and boils. Boil and stir 1 minute. Immediately stir at least half of the hot mixture into egg yolks, then stir back into hot mixture in saucepan. Boil and stir 2 minutes or until very thick; remove from heat. Stir in butter, lemon peel, lemon juice and food color. Press plastic wrap on filling to prevent a tough layer from forming on top.

4 In large bowl, beat egg whites and salt with electric mixer on high speed until soft peaks just begin to form. Very gradually beat in sugar mixture from step 2 until stiff peaks form.

5 Pour hot lemon filling into pie crust. Spoon meringue onto hot lemon filling. Spread over filling, carefully sealing meringue to edge of crust to prevent shrinking or weeping.

6 Bake about 15 minutes or until meringue is light brown. Cool away from draft 2 hours. Refrigerate cooled pie until serving. Store covered in refrigerator. (This pie is best served the day it is made. If refrigerated more than 1 day, the filling may become soft.)

High Altitude (3500 to 6500 feet): In step 1, bake 10 to 12 minutes. In step 6, bake 20 minutes.

1 Serving: Calories 460 (Calories from Fat 160); Fat 18g (Saturated 7g); Cholesterol 95mg; Sodium 230mg; Carbohydrate 70g (Dietary Fiber 1g); Protein 5g **Exchanges:** 2 Starch, 1 Fruit, 1 1/2 Other Carbohydrates, 3 1/2 Fat **Carbohydrate Choices:** 4 1/2

BAKING FOR TODAY

When you separate the eggs for the lemon filling, use the egg whites left over from separating the eggs to make the meringue (you'll need an additional egg white). Room-temperature eggs whites beat up more quickly than cold whites. Egg whites can stand up to 30 minutes at room temperature to warm.

BEST-EVER LEMON MERINGUE PIE

Key Lime Pie

Prep Time: 25 min; Start to Finish: 3 hr

8 servings

Easy-Roll Buttermilk Pastry (below) or Pastry for 9-Inch One-Crust Pie (page 197)

4 egg yolks

1 can (14 oz) sweetened condensed milk

1/2 cup Key lime juice or regular lime juice

1 or 2 drops green food color, if desired

1 1/2 cups Sweetened Whipped Cream (page 232)

1 Heat oven to 475°F. Make pastry. On lightly floured surface, roll pastry into circle 2 inches larger than upside-down 9-inch glass pie plate with floured rolling pin. Fold pastry into fourths; place in pie plate. Unfold and ease into plate, pressing firmly against bottom and side. Trim overhanging edge of pastry 1 inch from rim of plate. Fold and roll pastry under, even with plate; press with tines of fork or flute if desired. Prick bottom and side of pastry thoroughly with fork. Bake 8 to 10 minutes or until light brown. Cool completely, about 30 minutes.

2 Heat oven to 375°F. In medium bowl, beat egg yolks, milk, lime juice and food color with electric mixer on medium speed about 1 minute or until well blended. Pour into pastry-lined pie plate.

3 Bake 14 to 16 minutes or until center is set.

4 Cool on wire rack 15 minutes. Cover and refrigerate until chilled, at least 2 hours but no longer than 3 days. Spread with Sweetened Whipped Cream. Store covered in refrigerator.

Easy-Roll Buttermilk Pastry

1 cup Gold Medal all-purpose flour

1/2 teaspoon salt

1/3 cup shortening

1 tablespoon plus 1 1/2 teaspoons butter or margarine

1 teaspoon vegetable oil

2 1/2 to 3 tablespoons buttermilk

In medium bowl, mix flour and salt. Cut in shortening and butter, using pastry blender (or pulling 2 table knives through ingredients in opposite directions), until particles are size of small peas. Mix in oil and buttermilk with fork until all flour is moistened and pastry leaves side of bowl.

High Altitude (3500 to 6500 feet): In step 1, bake 10 to 12 minutes. In step 3, bake 15 to 17 minutes.

1 Serving: Calories 470 (Calories from Fat 225); Fat 25g (Saturated 11g); Cholesterol 150mg; Sodium 250mg; Carbohydrate 52g (Dietary Fiber 0g); Protein 9g **Exchanges:** 3 Starch, 1/2 Fruit, 4 1/2 Fat **Carbohydrate Choices:** 3 1/2

BAKING FOR TODAY

Key limes, found in the Florida Keys, are smaller and rounder than the more familiar Persian limes and can sometimes be difficult to find. The good news is that bottled Key lime juice is available in most large supermarkets.

Kentucky Pecan Pie

Classic

Betty Crocker's Picture Cook Book of 1950 sold a million copies in its first year, establishing an all-time record in the book trade for a nonfiction best-seller. The book was so popular that consumer requests brought it back in facsimile form, so now you can buy it again at your local bookstore. This tempting recipe was a part of that success story—enjoy this "best-seller" pie soon!

Prep Time: 30 min; Start to Finish: 3 hr 30 min   **8 servings**

Easy-Roll Buttermilk Pastry (page 204) or Pastry for 9-Inch One-Crust Pie (page 197)

2/3 cup sugar

1/3 cup butter or margarine, melted

1 cup corn syrup

2 tablespoons bourbon, if desired

1/2 teaspoon salt

3 eggs

1 cup pecan halves or broken pecans

1 cup semisweet chocolate chips

1 Heat oven to 375°F. Make pastry. On lightly floured surface, roll pastry into circle 2 inches larger than upside-down 9-inch glass pie plate with floured rolling pin. Fold pastry into fourths; place in pie plate. Unfold and ease into plate, pressing firmly against bottom and side. Trim overhanging edge of pastry 1 inch from rim of plate. Fold and roll pastry under, even with plate; press with tines of fork or flute if desired.

2 In large bowl, beat sugar, butter, corn syrup, bourbon, salt and eggs with hand beater. Stir in pecans and chocolate chips. Pour into pastry-lined pie plate.

3 Cover edge of pastry with 2- to 3-inch strip of foil to prevent excessive browning; remove foil for last 15 minutes of baking. Bake 40 to 50 minutes or until set. Refrigerate at least 2 hours until chilled. Store covered in refrigerator.

Brandy Pecan Pie: Decrease corn syrup to 3/4 cup. Substitute 1/4 cup brandy for the bourbon. Omit chocolate chips.

Chocolate Pecan Pie: Melt 2 oz unsweetened baking chocolate with the butter. Omit bourbon and chocolate chips.

Pecan Pie: Omit bourbon and chocolate chips.

High Altitude (3500 to 6500 feet): Bake 50 to 55 minutes.

1 Serving: Calories 650 (Calories from Fat 325); Fat 36g (Saturated 13g); Cholesterol 100mg; Sodium 420mg; Carbohydrate 75g (Dietary Fiber 3g); Protein 6g **Exchanges:** 2 Starch, 3 Other Carbohydrates, 6 Fat **Carbohydrate Choices:** 5

BAKING FOR TODAY

Nothing compares to pecan pie! Kentuckians bake their specialty using chocolate chips and bourbon at Derby time. Native southern pecans paired with southern cane sugar make this pie a matchless creation.

Pumpkin Pie
Classic

Easy-Roll Buttermilk Pastry
(page 204) or Pastry for 9-Inch
One-Crust Pie (page 197)

2 eggs

1/2 cup sugar

1 teaspoon ground cinnamon

1/2 teaspoon salt

1/2 teaspoon ground ginger

1/8 teaspoon ground cloves

1 can (15 oz) pumpkin
(not pumpkin pie mix)

1 can (12 oz) evaporated milk

Spiced Cream Clouds (below)

1 Heat oven to 425°F. Make pastry. On lightly floured surface, roll pastry into circle 2 inches larger than upside-down 9-inch glass pie plate with floured rolling pin. Fold pastry into fourths; place in pie plate. Unfold and ease into plate, pressing firmly against bottom and side. Trim overhanging edge of pastry 1 inch from rim of plate. Fold and roll pastry under, even with plate; press with tines of fork or flute if desired.

2 In medium bowl, beat eggs slightly with wire whisk or hand beater. Beat in remaining ingredients except Spiced Cream Clouds.

3 Place pastry-lined pie plate on oven rack to prevent spilling the filling. Pour filling into pie plate. Cover edge of pastry with 2- to 3-inch strip of foil to prevent excessive browning; remove foil for last 15 minutes of baking. Bake 15 minutes.

4 Reduce oven temperature to 350°F. Bake about 45 minutes longer or until knife inserted in center comes out clean. Cool 30 minutes. Refrigerate about 4 hours or until chilled. Meanwhile, make Spiced Cream Clouds.

5 Top slices of pie with frozen Spiced Cream Clouds; let stand 5 minutes before serving. Store pie covered in refrigerator.

Spiced Cream Clouds

1/2 cup whipping (heavy) cream

1 tablespoon packed brown sugar

1/4 teaspoon pumpkin pie spice or ground cinnamon

In chilled small bowl, beat all ingredients with electric mixer on high speed until stiff. Place waxed paper on cookie sheet. Drop whipped cream by 8 spoonfuls onto waxed paper. Freeze uncovered at least 2 hours. Place in freezer container; cover tightly and freeze no longer than 2 months.

High Altitude (3500 to 6500 feet): No changes.

1 Serving: Calories 340 (Calories from Fat 160); Fat 18g (Saturated 7g); Cholesterol 75mg; Sodium 370mg; Carbohydrate 37g (Dietary Fiber 2g); Protein 8g **Exchanges:** 2 Starch, 1 Vegetable, 3 1/2 Fat **Carbohydrate Choices:** 2 1/2

BAKING FOR TODAY

You can decorate your pies with pretty pastry shapes cut from leftover unbaked pastry. Cut the pastry into shapes with a leaf-shaped or other cookie cutter, sprinkle with a little granulated sugar and cinnamon, and bake on an ungreased cookie sheet at 425°F for 8 to 10 minutes or until lightly browned.

Fresh Blueberry Tart

1 cup Gold Medal
all-purpose flour

2 tablespoons granulated sugar

1/8 teaspoon salt

1/2 cup butter or margarine

1 tablespoon white vinegar

1 cup granulated sugar

2 tablespoons Gold Medal
all-purpose flour

1/4 teaspoon ground cinnamon

3 cups fresh blueberries

2 tablespoons powdered sugar

1 In small bowl, mix 1 cup flour, 2 tablespoons granulated sugar and the salt. Cut in butter, using pastry blender (or pulling 2 table knives through ingredients in opposite directions), until particles are size of small peas. Stir in vinegar until dough forms. Press dough evenly on bottom and 1 inch up side of ungreased 9-inch springform pan or 8-inch square pan. (Be sure there are no thin areas at bottom seam of springform pan.) Refrigerate at least 15 minutes.

2 Heat oven to 400°F. In medium bowl, mix 1 cup granulated sugar, 2 tablespoons flour and the cinnamon. Reserve 1 cup of the largest blueberries. Gently stir remaining blueberries into sugar mixture. Spread evenly in tart shell.

3 Bake 50 to 60 minutes or until crust is golden brown. Sprinkle with reserved 1 cup blueberries and the powdered sugar; cool. Loosen tart from side of pan; remove side of pan.

BAKING FOR TODAY

Tart or pie? What's the difference? A tart is baked in a tart pan or springform pan, and the crust is often more sweet and more tender than a pie crust. Some tarts are baked in individual tart pans. If you don't have a tart or springform pan, you can still make this wonderful pie; just use your 8-inch square pan.

High Altitude (3500 to 6500 feet): No changes.

1 Serving: Calories 320 (Calories from Fat 110); Fat 12g (Saturated 7g); Cholesterol 30mg; Sodium 115mg; Carbohydrate 51g (Dietary Fiber 2g); Protein 2g
Exchanges: 1 Starch, 1 Fruit, 1 1/2 Other Carbohydrates, 2 Fat
Carbohydrate Choices: 3 1/2

Fudge Brownie Pie

Classic

This great recipe is based on a classic! A Gold Medal advertisement in 1953 introduced the new Chocolate Brownie Pie, which was like a pecan pie and a pan of brownies all in one.

Prep Time: 20 min; **Start to Finish:** 1 hr 15 min

8 servings

Nut Cookie Crust (below)

6 tablespoons butter or margarine

2 oz unsweetened baking chocolate

1 cup sugar

2 tablespoons Gold Medal all-purpose flour

2 tablespoons milk

2 tablespoons light corn syrup

1 teaspoon vanilla

1/4 teaspoon salt

3 eggs

1 quart (4 cups) vanilla ice cream

1 Heat oven to 350°F. Make Nut Cookie Crust.

2 In 2-quart saucepan, melt butter and chocolate over low heat, stirring occasionally; remove from heat. Add remaining ingredients except ice cream to saucepan; stir until smooth and well blended. Pour mixture into baked crust.

3 Bake 20 minutes; place strips of foil over crust to prevent crust from becoming too dark. Bake 20 to 25 minutes longer or until top is crusty and filling is set (do not overbake). Cool on wire rack. Serve slightly warm with ice cream. (If pie has cooled before serving, heat individual pieces of pie in the microwave for about 15 seconds.) Store pie covered in refrigerator.

Nut Cookie Crust

1/2 cup butter or margarine, softened

1/3 cup packed brown sugar

1 1/4 cups Gold Medal all-purpose flour

1/2 cup chopped nuts

1/2 teaspoon vanilla

1/4 teaspoon salt

In large bowl, mix butter and brown sugar. Stir in remaining ingredients just until crumbly. Press mixture against bottom and side of ungreased 9-inch pie plate, building up 1/2-inch edge. Bake 10 to 12 minutes or until crust is light golden.

High Altitude (3500 to 6500 feet): Bake Nut Cookie Crust 12 to 14 minutes. Bake pie 45 to 50 minutes.

1 Serving: Calories 670 (Calories from Fat 340); Fat 38g (Saturated 20g); Cholesterol 165mg; Sodium 370mg; Carbohydrate 73g (Dietary Fiber 3g); Protein 9g **Exchanges:** 3 Starch, 2 Other Carbohydrates, 7 Fat **Carbohydrate Choices:** 5

BAKING FOR TODAY

Two favorites, pecan pie and chocolate, come together for a sensational dessert. The sweet, buttery crust adds a nutty flavor and a bit of crunch—you can use chopped walnuts or almonds or any type of nut you prefer.

FUDGE BROWNIE PIE

Peach-Raspberry Streusel Tart

Prep Time: 35 min; Start to Finish: 3 hr 5 min   8 servings

Tart Crust (below)

1 can (21 oz) peach pie filling

1 cup frozen unsweetened raspberries

1/2 cup quick-cooking oats

1/2 cup Gold Medal all-purpose flour

1/2 cup packed brown sugar

1/4 cup butter or margarine

1/4 cup chopped pecans

1 Heat oven to 400°F. Make Tart Crust; bake as directed.

2 Reduce oven temperature to 350°F. Spread pie filling over baked crust. Top with raspberries. In medium bowl, mix remaining ingredients, using pastry blender or fork, until crumbly; sprinkle over raspberries and pie filling.

3 Bake 20 to 25 minutes or until filling is hot and topping is golden brown. Cool completely, about 1 hour 30 minutes.

Tart Crust

1 cup Gold Medal all-purpose flour

1/2 cup butter or margarine, softened

2 tablespoons packed brown sugar

1 egg yolk

In small bowl, mix all ingredients with spoon or electric mixer on low speed until dough forms. Press dough firmly and evenly against bottom and side of ungreased 9 x 1-inch tart pan with removable bottom. Place crust-filled pan on cookie sheet. Bake 15 to 20 minutes or until light brown. Cool 10 minutes before filling.

BAKING FOR TODAY

Using pie filling saves you the time needed to peel and slice fresh fruit, and combining the filling with frozen fruit adds a fresh taste while still being convenient. You can make this memorable tart with other fruit combinations. Try apple or cherry pie filling in place of the peach.

High Altitude (3500 to 6500 feet): Not recommended.

1 Serving: Calories 415 (Calories from Fat 155); Fat 17g (Saturated 4g); Cholesterol 60mg; Sodium 240mg; Carbohydrate 60g (Dietary Fiber 1g); Protein 6g **Exchanges:** 2 Starch, 1 Fruit, 1 Other Carbohydrates, 3 Fat **Carbohydrate Choices:** 4

PEACH-RASPBERRY STREUSEL TART

LINDY'S CHEESECAKE

Lindy's Cheesecake

Classic

This recipe is also called New York or New York–Style Cheesecake. The famous cheesecakes we associate with urban settings like New York City actually got their start in the country cheese pies and kuchens of immigrants from Western and Central Europe.

Prep Time: 45 min; Start to Finish: 15 hr   16 to 20 servings

1 cup Gold Medal all-purpose flour

1/2 cup butter or margarine, softened

1/4 cup sugar

1 tablespoon grated lemon peel

1 egg yolk

5 packages (8 oz each) cream cheese, softened

1 3/4 cups sugar

3 tablespoons Gold Medal all-purpose flour

1 tablespoon grated orange peel

1 tablespoon grated lemon peel

1/4 teaspoon salt

5 whole eggs

2 egg yolks

1 cup whipping (heavy) cream

1/3 cup slivered almonds, toasted, if desired

1 Heat oven to 400°F. Lightly grease 9-inch springform pan with shortening or spray with cooking spray; remove bottom. In medium bowl, mix 1 cup flour, the butter, 1/4 cup sugar, 1 tablespoon lemon peel and 1 egg yolk with fork until dough forms; gather into a ball. Press 1/3 of the dough evenly on bottom of pan; place on cookie sheet. Bake 8 to 10 minutes or until light golden brown; cool. Assemble bottom and side of pan; secure side. Press remaining dough 2 inches up side of pan.

2 Heat oven to 475°F. In large bowl, beat cream cheese, 1 3/4 cups sugar, 3 tablespoons flour, the orange peel, 1 tablespoon lemon peel and the salt with electric mixer on medium speed about 1 minute or until smooth. Beat in whole eggs, egg yolks and 1/4 cup of the whipping cream on low speed until well blended. Pour into crust.

3 Bake 15 minutes. Reduce oven temperature to 200°F. Bake 1 hour longer. Cheesecake may not appear to be done, but if a small area in the center seems soft, it will become firm as cheesecake cools. (Do not insert a knife to test for doneness because the hole could cause cheesecake to crack.) Turn off oven; leave cheesecake in oven 30 minutes longer. Remove from oven and cool in pan on wire rack away from drafts 30 minutes.

4 Without releasing or removing side of pan, run metal spatula carefully along side of cheesecake to loosen. Refrigerate uncovered about 3 hours or until chilled; cover and continue refrigerating at least 9 hours but no longer than 48 hours.

5 Run metal spatula along side of cheesecake to loosen again. Remove side of pan; leave cheesecake on pan bottom to serve. In chilled small bowl, beat remaining 3/4 cup whipping cream with electric mixer on high speed until stiff. Spread whipped cream over top of cheesecake. Decorate with almonds. Store covered in refrigerator.

High Altitude (3500 to 6500 feet): In step 3, reduce oven temperature to 225°F and bake 1 hour longer.

1 Serving: Calories 515 (Calories from Fat 340); Fat 38g (Saturated 23g); Cholesterol 215mg; Sodium 310mg; Carbohydrate 35g (Dietary Fiber 0g); Protein 9g **Exchanges:** 1 Starch, 1 Other Carbohydrates, 1 High-Fat Meat, 6 Fat **Carbohydrate Choices:** 2

BAKING FOR TODAY

This luscious cheesecake, with its characteristic rich smoothness, is associated with the style of cheesecake popularized in New York. Originating at Lindy's restaurant, it became world famous. You can serve it with any fresh fruit or fruit sauce.

Strawberry Shortcakes
Classic

This recipe is a tried-and-true all-American classic. Another classic—the Betty Crocker Kitchens. Washburn Crosby Company hired its first home economist in 1921. Within a year, the one-person kitchen was expanded to more spacious and better-equipped quarters, staffed by three home economists. Today there are more than twenty-five home economists testing and creating recipes in the Betty Crocker Kitchens.

Prep Time: 1 hr; Start to Finish: 1 hr　　　　　　　　　　　　　　**6 servings**

1 quart (4 cups) strawberries, sliced

1 cup sugar

2 cups Gold Medal all-purpose flour

2 tablespoons sugar

3 teaspoons baking powder

1 teaspoon salt

1/3 cup shortening

3/4 cup milk

2 tablespoons butter or margarine, softened

Sweetened Whipped Cream (page 232)

1 In large bowl, mix strawberries and 1 cup sugar. Let stand 1 hour.

2 Heat oven to 450°F. In medium bowl, mix flour, 2 tablespoons sugar, the baking powder and salt. Cut in shortening, using pastry blender (or pulling 2 table knives through ingredients in opposite directions), until mixture looks like fine crumbs. Stir in milk just until blended.

3 On lightly floured surface, gently smooth dough into a ball. Knead 20 to 25 times. Roll 1/2 inch thick; cut with floured 3-inch cutter. On ungreased cookie sheet, place dough rounds about 1 inch apart.

4 Bake 10 to 12 minutes or until golden brown. Split warm shortcakes in half. Spread with butter; fill and top with Sweetened Whipped Cream and strawberries.

BAKING FOR TODAY

To make Pat-in-the-Pan Shortcakes, grease bottom and side of 8-inch round pan with shortening or spray with cooking spray. After stirring in milk in step 2, pat dough in pan. Bake 15 to 20 minutes. Cut into wedges.

High Altitude (3500 to 6500 feet): Use 2 teaspoons baking powder.

1 Serving: Calories 550 (Calories from Fat 200); Fat 22g (Saturated 9g); Cholesterol 30mg; Sodium 690mg; Carbohydrate 82g (Dietary Fiber 4g); Protein 6g **Exchanges:** 2 Starch, 2 Fruit, 1 1/2 Other Carbohydrates, 4 Fat **Carbohydrate Choices:** 5 1/2

Cinnamon Shortcakes with Warm Blueberry Sauce

2 cups Gold Medal
all-purpose flour

4 teaspoons baking powder

3/4 teaspoon salt

1 tablespoon sugar

1/2 teaspoon ground cinnamon

2 tablespoons firm butter or
margarine

2 tablespoons shortening

1 cup half-and-half

2 tablespoons butter or
margarine, melted

2 teaspoons prepared
cinnamon-sugar

Warm Blueberry Sauce (below)

1 quart (4 cups) vanilla
ice cream

1 Heat oven to 450°F. In large bowl, mix flour, baking powder, salt, sugar and cinnamon. Cut in firm butter and shortening, using pastry blender (or pulling 2 table knives through ingredients in opposite directions), until crumbly. Stir in half-and-half just until moistened.

2 On ungreased cookie sheet, drop dough by rounded 1/4 cupfuls. Brush with melted butter; sprinkle with cinnamon-sugar.

3 Bake 10 to 15 minutes or until golden brown. Meanwhile, make Warm Blueberry Sauce.

4 To serve, split warm shortcakes and place in shallow bowls. Fill and top with ice cream. Spoon warm sauce over ice cream.

Warm Blueberry Sauce

1/2 cup sugar

1 tablespoon cornstarch

1/2 teaspoon ground cinnamon

1/4 cup water

2 tablespoons lemon juice

2 cups fresh or unsweetened frozen
(thawed and drained) blueberries

In 1 1/2-quart saucepan, mix sugar, cornstarch and cinnamon. Stir in water and lemon juice until smooth. Stir in 1 cup of the blueberries. Heat to boiling over medium heat, stirring constantly. Boil and stir 2 minutes or until thickened. Stir in remaining 1 cup blueberries. Serve warm.

BAKING FOR TODAY

Today's version of an American icon! You can try other berries in place of the blueberries in the sauce, if you like—raspberries, strawberries or a combination of several berries, cooked in the same way, make a terrific substitution.

High Altitude (3500 to 6500 feet): Use 2 teaspoons baking powder.

1 Serving: Calories 410 (Calories from Fat 160); Fat 18g (Saturated 10g); Cholesterol 50mg; Sodium 510mg; Carbohydrate 56g (Dietary Fiber 2g); Protein 6g
Exchanges: 2 Starch, 2 Fruit, 2 Fat
Carbohydrate Choices: 4

Apple Dumplings

Classic

The recipe for Apple Dumplings was available free in Gold Medal flour bags, as noted in a 1938 advertisement, and has also been included in many of the company's cookbooks over the years, beginning with the 1904 Christmas Edition of *Gold Medal Flour Cook Book*.

Prep Time: 25 min; Start to Finish: 1 hr 20 min   6 servings

2 cups Gold Medal all-purpose flour or whole wheat flour

1 teaspoon salt

2/3 cup plus 2 tablespoons firm butter or margarine

4 to 5 tablespoons cold water

6 baking apples (about 3-inch diameter), peeled and cored

3 tablespoons raisins

3 tablespoons chopped nuts

2 1/2 cups packed brown sugar

1 1/3 cups water

Sweetened Whipped Cream (page 232), if desired

1 Heat oven to 425°F. In large bowl, mix flour and salt. Cut in butter, using pastry blender (or pulling 2 table knives through ingredients in opposite directions), until particles are size of small peas. Sprinkle with cold water, 1 tablespoon at a time, mixing well with fork until all flour is moistened. Gather dough together; press into a ball. On lightly floured surface, roll 2/3 of dough into 14-inch square; cut into 4 squares. Roll remaining dough into 14 x 7-inch rectangle; cut into 2 squares. Place an apple on each square.

2 In small bowl, mix raisins and nuts. Fill center of each apple with raisin mixture. Moisten corners of each square; bring 2 opposite corners of pastry up over apple and press corners together. Fold in sides of remaining corners; bring corners up over apple and press together.

3 In 13 x 9-inch glass baking dish, place dumplings. In 2-quart saucepan, heat brown sugar and 1 1/3 cups water to boiling; carefully pour around dumplings.

4 Bake about 40 minutes, spooning syrup over apples 2 or 3 times, until crust is browned and apples are tender when pierced with a fork. Serve warm or cold with Sweetened Whipped Cream.

Peach Dumplings: Substitute 6 peaches, peeled, halved and pitted, for the apples and 1/4 cup cranberry relish for the raisins and chopped nuts.

High Altitude (3500 to 6500 feet): For all-purpose or whole wheat flour, bake about 55 minutes.

1 Serving: Calories 840 (Calories from Fat 245); Fat 27g (Saturated 15g); Cholesterol 65mg; Sodium 590mg; Carbohydrate 144g (Dietary Fiber 4g); Protein 5g **Exchanges:** 2 Starch, 2 Fruit, 5 1/2 Other Carbohydrates, 5 Fat **Carbohydrate Choices:** 9 1/2

BAKING FOR TODAY

Wondering which apples are best for baking? The best baking apples are slightly tart. Top choices are Granny Smith, Braeburn, Cortland, Northern Spy and Rome Beauty.

Apple Crisp

Classic

During World War II, many Gold Medal ads featured recipes that made the most of rationed or scarce foods such as butter, eggs and sugar. Apple Crisp was promoted as "easy on shortening and sugar."

Prep Time: 20 min; Start to Finish: 50 min — 6 servings

4 medium tart cooking apples (such as Greening, Rome, Granny Smith), sliced (4 cups)

3/4 cup packed brown sugar

1/2 cup Gold Medal all-purpose flour

1/2 cup quick-cooking or old-fashioned oats

1/3 cup butter or margarine, softened

3/4 teaspoon ground cinnamon

3/4 teaspoon ground nutmeg

Cream or ice cream, if desired

1 Heat oven to 375°F. Grease bottom and sides of 8-inch square pan with shortening or spray with cooking spray. Spread apples in pan.

2 In medium bowl, stir remaining ingredients except cream until well mixed; sprinkle over apples.

3 Bake about 30 minutes or until topping is golden brown and apples are tender when pierced with a fork. Serve warm with cream.

Cherry Crisp: Substitute 1 can (21 oz) cherry pie filling for the apples.

Peach Crisp: Substitute 1 can (29 oz) peach slices, drained, for the apples.

BAKING FOR TODAY

To make this easy recipe even easier, microwave it. Just assemble the apples and topping in an ungreased 2-quart microwavable casserole or 8-inch glass baking dish. Microwave uncovered on High about 12 minutes, rotating the dish every 4 minutes, until the apples are tender.

High Altitude (3500 to 6500 feet): Bake about 40 minutes.

1 Serving: Calories 325 (Calories from Fat 100); Fat 11g (Saturated 7g); Cholesterol 30mg; Sodium 80mg; Carbohydrate 54g (Dietary Fiber 4g); Protein 2g
Exchanges: 1 Starch, 1 1/2 Fruit, 1 Other Carbohydrates, 2 Fat
Carbohydrate Choices: 3 1/2

Chocolate Fudge–Raspberry Crisp

1 can (21 oz) raspberry
pie filling

2 cups fresh or frozen (thawed
and drained) raspberries

1/2 cup packed brown sugar

1/2 cup Gold Medal
all-purpose flour

1/2 cup old-fashioned oats

1/4 cup baking cocoa

1/3 cup butter or margarine,
cut into pieces

1/4 cup miniature semisweet
chocolate chips

Vanilla ice cream, if desired

1 Heat oven to 350°F. In ungreased 8-inch square glass baking dish, place pie filling and raspberries; gently stir together.

2 In medium bowl, mix brown sugar, flour, oats and cocoa. Cut in butter, using pastry blender (or pulling 2 table knives through ingredients in opposite directions), until mixture looks like coarse crumbs. Stir in chocolate chips. Sprinkle over raspberry mixture.

3 Bake 40 to 50 minutes or until juices bubble. Cool 15 minutes. Serve warm topped with ice cream.

BAKING FOR TODAY

If it works with apples and brown sugar, why not with raspberries and chocolate? With the combination of fresh raspberries and chocolate in this updated, unbeatable version of a vintage dessert, how can you lose? Other fruit combinations also work well; try cherry pie filling and fresh raspberries or sliced strawberries.

High Altitude (3500 to 6500 feet): Heat oven to 375°F.

1 Serving: Calories 265 (Calories from Fat 80); Fat 9g (Saturated 5g); Cholesterol 20mg; Sodium 55mg; Carbohydrate 43g (Dietary Fiber 4g); Protein 3g
Exchanges: 1 Starch, 2 Fruit, 1 1/2 Fat
Carbohydrate Choices: 3

Rhubarb Meringue Dessert

Classic

Rhubarb was the earliest "fruit" from the garden in many locations. Originally found in the *Century of Success Cookbook* from 1978, this dessert is still popular now.

Prep Time: 15 min; Start to Finish: 1 hr 20 min   9 servings

1/2 cup butter or margarine, softened

1 cup Gold Medal all-purpose flour

1 tablespoon sugar

3 egg yolks

1 cup sugar

2 tablespoons Gold Medal all-purpose flour

1/4 teaspoon salt

1/2 cup half-and-half

2 1/2 cups cut-up fresh rhubarb

3 egg whites

1/3 cup sugar

1 teaspoon vanilla

1/4 cup flaked coconut

1. Heat oven to 350°F. In small bowl, mix butter, 1 cup flour and 1 tablespoon sugar. On bottom of ungreased 9-inch square pan, press dough evenly. Bake 10 minutes.

2. Meanwhile, in medium bowl, mix egg yolks, 1 cup sugar, 2 tablespoons flour, the salt and cream. Stir in rhubarb. Pour over hot crust. Bake 45 minutes.

3. In medium bowl, beat egg whites with electric mixer on high speed until foamy. Beat in 1/3 cup sugar, 1 tablespoon at a time; continue beating until stiff and glossy (do not underbeat). Beat in vanilla. Spread over hot rhubarb mixture; sprinkle with coconut. Bake about 10 minutes or until light brown.

BAKING FOR TODAY

Because of its intense tartness, rhubarb is usually combined with a fair amount of sugar. If you are not able to find fresh rhubarb in your supermarket, you can use frozen rhubarb in this terrific dessert.

High Altitude (3500 to 6500 feet): In step 1, bake crust 12 minutes.

1 Serving: Calories 335 (Calories from Fat 135); Fat 15g (Saturated 9g); Cholesterol 105mg; Sodium 170mg; Carbohydrate 45g (Dietary Fiber 1g); Protein 5g **Exchanges:** 2 Starch, 1 Fruit, 2 1/2 Fat **Carbohydrate Choices:** 3

RHUBARB MERINGUE DESSERT

Hot Fudge Pudding Cake

Classic

This old-time favorite, like Gold Medal flour, has been around for over a century. In 1905, there was a major change to how flour was packaged. Before then, flour was packed in barrels, each weighing 196 pounds. The new trend was for millers to use large, hand-sewn fabric bags. Next came paper bags, and now you can buy Gold Medal flour in either paper sacks or zip-type plastic bags.

Prep Time: 15 min; Start to Finish: 1 hr 5 min   **9 servings**

1 cup Gold Medal all-purpose flour

3/4 cup granulated sugar

2 tablespoons baking cocoa

2 teaspoons baking powder

1/4 teaspoon salt

1/2 cup milk

2 tablespoons vegetable oil

1 teaspoon vanilla

1 cup chopped nuts, if desired

1 cup packed brown sugar

1/4 cup baking cocoa

1 3/4 cups very hot water

Ice cream, if desired

1 Heat oven to 350°F. In ungreased 9-inch square pan, mix flour, granulated sugar, 2 tablespoons cocoa, the baking powder and salt. Mix in milk, oil and vanilla with fork until smooth. Stir in nuts.

2 Spread batter in pan. Sprinkle with brown sugar and 1/4 cup cocoa. Pour hot water over batter.

3 Bake about 40 minutes or until top is dry. Cool 10 minutes.

4 Spoon warm cake into dessert dishes. Top with ice cream. Spoon sauce from pan onto each serving.

Hot Fudge–Mallow Pudding Cake: Omit nuts; add 1 cup miniature marshmallows.

Hot Fudge–Butterscotch Pudding Cake: Omit nuts; add 1 cup butterscotch-flavored chips. Decrease brown sugar to 1/2 cup; decrease the 1/4 cup cocoa to 2 tablespoons.

Hot Fudge Peanutty Pudding Cake: Omit nuts; stir in 1/2 cup peanut butter and 1/2 cup chopped peanuts.

High Altitude (3500 to 6500 feet): Use 13 x 9-inch pan. Bake 25 minutes.

1 Serving: Calories 265 (Calories from Fat 35); Fat 4g (Saturated 1g); Cholesterol 0mg; Sodium 190mg; Carbohydrate 54g (Dietary Fiber 2g); Protein 3g **Exchanges:** 1 Starch, 2 1/2 Other Carbohydrates, 1 Fat **Carbohydrate Choices:** 3 1/2

BAKING FOR TODAY

You can make this moist cake-with-its-own-sauce dessert in your microwave oven. Just measure the 1 3/4 cups water into a 2-cup glass measuring cup; microwave on High about 4 minutes until boiling. Make the batter in an ungreased 2-quart glass casserole instead of the square pan; pour boiling water over batter in casserole. Microwave uncovered on High 8 to 10 minutes, rotating once after 4 minutes, until cake is no longer doughy. Let stand a few minutes; spoon into dessert dishes.

Streusel In-Between Pumpkin Cake

Prep Time: 25 min; Start to Finish: 3 hr 55 min 16 servings

STREUSEL

1/2 cup packed brown sugar

1 teaspoon ground cinnamon

1/4 teaspoon pumpkin pie spice

2 teaspoons butter or margarine, softened

CAKE

3 cups Gold Medal all-purpose flour

2 teaspoons baking soda

1 tablespoon ground cinnamon

1 teaspoon salt

1 cup butter or margarine, softened

2 cups granulated sugar

4 eggs

1 cup canned pumpkin (not pumpkin pie mix)

1 cup sour cream

1 teaspoon vanilla

Powdered sugar, if desired

1 Heat oven to 350°F. Grease 12-cup fluted tube cake pan with shortening or spray with cooking spray; lighty flour. In small bowl, stir all streusel ingredients until crumbly; set aside.

2 In medium bowl, mix flour, baking soda, cinnamon and salt; set aside. In large bowl, beat butter and granulated sugar with electric mixer on medium speed, scraping bowl occasionally, until creamy. Add eggs, two at a time, beating well after each addition. Beat in pumpkin, sour cream and vanilla. Gradually beat in flour mixture on low speed until blended.

3 Spread half of the batter in pan. Sprinkle Streusel over batter, making sure Streusel does not touch side of pan. Top with remaining batter, making sure batter layer touches side of pan.

4 Bake 55 to 60 minutes or until toothpick inserted in cake comes out clean. Cool 30 minutes; remove from pan to wire rack. Cool completely, about 2 hours. Sprinkle with powdered sugar.

BAKING FOR TODAY

This fantastic dessert twists streusel in a new way by layering it in the middle instead of sprinkling it on top. Serve with vanilla frozen yogurt or ice cream, or for a super-spice hit, with cinnamon ice cream.

High Altitude (3500 to 6500 feet): Use 1 1/2 teaspoons baking soda. Bake 63 to 68 minutes.

1 Serving: Calories 370 (Calories from Fat 150); Fat 16g (Saturated Fat 8g); Cholesterol 95mg; Sodium 410mg; Carbohydrate 52g (Dietary Fiber 1g); Protein 5g **Exchanges:** 1 1/2 Starch, 2 Other Carbohydrates, 3 Fat **Carbohydrate Choices:** 3 1/2

Gingerbread
Classic

A number of recipes using Gold Medal flour that were included in the 1880 *Miss Parloa's New Cook Book* are still favorites today. In addition to Gingerbread, other recipes in that cookbook were Steamed Brown Bread (page 56), Applesauce Jumbles (page 103) and Pound Cake (page 182).

Prep Time: 20 min; Start to Finish: 1 hr 10 min   **9 servings**

2 1/3 cups Gold Medal all-purpose flour

1/3 cup sugar

1 cup molasses

3/4 cup hot water

1/2 cup butter or margarine, softened

1 egg

1 teaspoon baking soda

1 teaspoon ground ginger

1 teaspoon ground cinnamon

3/4 teaspoon salt

Old-Fashioned Lemon Sauce (below), if desired

1 Heat oven to 325°F. Grease bottom and sides of 9-inch square pan with shortening or spray with cooking spray; lightly flour. In large bowl, beat all ingredients except Butterscotch-Pear Sauce with electric mixer on low speed 30 seconds, scraping bowl constantly. Beat on medium speed 3 minutes, scraping bowl occasionally. Pour into pan.

2 Bake about 50 minutes or until toothpick inserted in center comes out clean. Serve warm with Old-Fashioned Lemon Sauce.

Old-Fashioned Lemon Sauce

1 cup sugar

1/2 cup butter or margarine

1/4 cup water

1 egg, well beaten

3/4 teaspoon grated lemon peel

3 tablespoons lemon juice

In 1-quart saucepan, mix all ingredients. Heat to boiling over medium heat, stirring constantly.

Whole Wheat Gingerbread: Substitute 1 cup Gold Medal whole wheat flour for 1 cup of the all-purpose flour. Decrease sugar to 1/4 cup.

BAKING FOR TODAY

Gingerbread is great served warm or cool. To refresh in the microwave, microwave one piece of room-temperature Gingerbread 15 to 20 seconds, two pieces 25 to 30 seconds or four pieces 1 minute 20 seconds to 1 minute 25 seconds. To heat frozen Gingerbread, microwave one piece 30 to 35 seconds, two pieces 50 to 55 seconds or four pieces 1 minute 30 seconds to 1 minute 35 seconds.

High Altitude (3500 to 6500 feet): Heat oven to 350°F. In Gingerbread, use 2 1/2 cups flour, 3/4 cup molasses and 1/3 cup butter.

1 Serving: Calories 345 (Calories from Fat 100); Fat 11g (Saturated 7g); Cholesterol 50mg; Sodium 430mg; Carbohydrate 58g (Dietary Fiber 1g); Protein 4g **Exchanges:** 1 1/2 Starch, 2 1/2 Other Carbohydrates, 1 1/2 Fat **Carbohydrate Choices:** 4

GINGERBREAD

Easy Peach Kuchen

Through the years, Washburn Crosby Company sponsored cooking schools in conjunction with women's clubs and newspapers. Their home economists also provided cooking advice to home economics teachers and 4-H club leaders.

2 cups Gold Medal all-purpose flour

1/4 teaspoon baking powder

1 cup sugar

1/2 cup butter or margarine, melted

3 cups 1/2-inch slices fresh peaches or 1 bag (16 oz) frozen (thawed and drained) peaches

1 teaspoon ground cinnamon

3 eggs

2 containers (6 oz each) vanilla yogurt (2/3 cup)

1/2 teaspoon vanilla

1/2 cup chopped pecans

1 Heat oven to 350°F. In large bowl, mix flour, baking powder and 2 tablespoons of the sugar. Stir in butter until mixture is crumbly. On bottom and 1 1/2 inches up sides of 8-inch square glass baking dish, pat mixture evenly. Top with peaches. In small bowl, mix remaining sugar and the cinnamon; sprinkle over peaches. Bake 15 minutes.

2 Meanwhile, in medium bowl, beat eggs, yogurt and vanilla with wire whisk until smooth. Pour over top of partially baked kuchen. Sprinkle pecans over yogurt mixture.

3 Bake 40 to 50 minutes longer or until knife inserted in center comes out clean. Serve warm.

BAKING FOR TODAY

Kuchen, from German kitchens, is a fruit- or cheese-filled cake often served for breakfast, but it's equally good served as a dessert. You can vary the Kuchen by using different flavors of yogurt each time you make it.

High Altitude (3500 to 6500 feet): Heat oven to 400°F. In step 1, bake 20 minutes. In step 3, bake 45 to 55 minutes.

1 Serving: Calories 425 (Calories from Fat 160); Fat 18g (Saturated 8g); Cholesterol 100mg; Sodium 125mg; Carbohydrate 59g (Dietary Fiber 3g); Protein 8g
Exchanges: 2 Starch, 1 Fruit, 1 Other Carbohydrates, 3 Fat
Carbohydrate Choices: 4

Cherry Cobbler

Classic

Prep Time: 20 min; Start to Finish: 50 min   8 servings

1 cup sugar

3 tablespoons cornstarch

4 cups pitted fresh
red tart cherries

1/4 teaspoon almond extract

1 cup Gold Medal
all-purpose flour

1 tablespoon sugar

1 1/2 teaspoons baking powder

1/2 teaspoon salt

3 tablespoons butter or
margarine, softened

1/2 cup milk

Sweetened Whipped Cream
(page 232), if desired

1 Heat oven to 400°F. In 2-quart saucepan, mix 1 cup sugar and the cornstarch. Stir in cherries and almond extract. Cook over medium heat, stirring constantly, until mixture thickens and boils. Boil and stir 1 minute. Pour into ungreased 2-quart casserole.

2 In small bowl, mix flour, 1 tablespoon sugar, the baking powder and salt. Cut in butter, using pastry blender (or pulling 2 table knives through ingredients in opposite directions), until mixture is size of small peas. Stir in milk.

3 Drop dough by 8 spoonfuls onto hot cherry mixture. Bake 25 to 30 minutes or until topping is golden brown. Serve warm with Sweetened Whipped Cream.

BAKING FOR TODAY

To make a Triple-Berry Cobbler, substitute 1 1/2 cups fresh or frozen blueberries, 1 1/2 cups fresh or frozen raspberries and 1 1/2 cups fresh or frozen blackberries for the cherries.

High Altitude (3500 to 6500 feet): No changes.

1 Serving: Calories 275 (Calories from Fat 45); Fat 5g (Saturated 3g); Cholesterol 15mg; Sodium 280mg; Carbohydrate 54g (Dietary Fiber 2g); Protein 3g **Exchanges:** 1 Starch, 1 Fruit, 1 1/2 Other Carbohydrates, 1 Fat **Carbohydrate Choices:** 3 1/2

Blueberry-Pineapple Buckle

Classic

1 can (8 oz) crushed pineapple in syrup

1 1/4 cups Gold Medal all-purpose flour

1/2 cup sugar

1/4 cup butter or margarine, softened

1/4 cup shortening

1/2 cup milk

1 1/2 teaspoons baking powder

1 teaspoon grated lemon peel, if desired

1/2 teaspoon vanilla

1/4 teaspoon salt

1 egg

1 cup fresh blueberries*

Crumb Topping (below)

Pineapple Sauce (below)

*1 cup frozen blueberries, thawed and well drained, can be substituted for the fresh blueberries.

1 Heat oven to 350°F. Drain pineapple, reserving syrup for Pineapple Sauce. In large bowl, mix flour, sugar, butter, shortening, milk, baking powder, lemon peel, vanilla, salt and egg with spoon. Fold in blueberries and pineapple.

2 In ungreased 8-inch square pan, spread batter. Make Crumb Topping; sprinkle over batter.

3 Bake 45 to 50 minutes or until golden brown and toothpick inserted in center comes out clean. Serve warm with Pineapple Sauce.

Crumb Topping

1/2 cup sugar

1/3 cup Gold Medal all-purpose flour

1/4 cup butter or margarine, softened

1/2 teaspoon ground cinnamon

In small bowl, mix all ingredients with pastry blender or fork until crumbly.

Pineapple Sauce

2 tablespoons packed brown sugar

1 teaspoon cornstarch

Reserved pineapple syrup

1/4 teaspoon lemon juice

In 1-quart saucepan, mix brown sugar and cornstarch. Add enough water to reserved pineapple syrup to measure 2/3 cup; stir into brown sugar mixture. Cook over medium heat, stirring constantly, until mixture boils. Boil and stir 1 minute; remove from heat. Stir in lemon juice. Serve warm.

High Altitude (3500 to 6500 feet): Heat oven to 375°F. Use 1 teaspoon baking powder. Bake 50 to 55 minutes.

1 Serving: Calories 385 (Calories from Fat 155); Fat 17g (Saturated 8g); Cholesterol 50mg; Sodium 230mg; Carbohydrate 54g (Dietary Fiber 1g); Protein 4g **Exchanges:** 1 Starch, 1 1/2 Fruit, 1 Other Carbohydrates, 3 1/2 Fat **Carbohydrate Choices:** 3 1/2

BAKING FOR TODAY

A "buckle" is an old American term for a simple, single layer cake made with blueberries or other berries. This pineapple-blueberry version uses pineapple in the cake and on top, giving it a golden color and lively, fruity taste.

BLUEBERRY-PINEAPPLE BUCKLE

Classic Apple-Blackberry Pandowdy

This pandowdy, a homespun American dessert, combines apples and blackberries for an extra-special dessert. The term *dowdy* refers to the practice of cutting the dough into pieces while the dessert is baking: it's not pretty (in fact it's downright dowdy) but still tastes great!

Prep Time: 20 min; Start to Finish: 1 hr 20 min **8 servings**

4 medium tart cooking apples, peeled and thinly sliced (4 cups)

2 cups fresh blackberries*

1/2 cup sugar

1/2 teaspoon ground cinnamon

1/4 teaspoon salt

1/4 teaspoon ground nutmeg

1/3 cup maple-flavored syrup or mild-flavor molasses

2 tablespoons butter or margarine, melted

Pastry (below)

3 tablespoons butter or margarine, melted

Whipping (heavy) cream or Sweetened Whipped Cream (page 232)

2 cups frozen blackberries, thawed and drained, can be substituted for the fresh blackberries.

High Altitude (3500 to 6500 feet): After baking 60 minutes (steps 3 and 4), remove from oven and stir. Bake about 10 minutes longer or until apples are tender.

1 Serving: Calories 410 (Calories from Fat 180); Fat 20g (Saturated 9g); Cholesterol 35mg; Sodium 220mg; Carbohydrate 54g (Dietary Fiber 4g); Protein 3g **Exchanges:** 1 Starch, 1 1/2 Fruit, 1 Other Carbohydrates, 4 Fat **Carbohydrate Choices:** 3 1/2

1 Heat oven to 350°F. In large bowl, mix apples, blackberries, sugar, cinnamon, salt and nutmeg. In ungreased 2-quart casserole, spread fruit mixture. In small bowl, mix syrup and 2 tablespoons butter; pour over fruit mixture.

2 Make Pastry. Fit pastry over fruit mixture inside rim of casserole. Brush with 3 tablespoons butter.

3 Bake 30 minutes; remove from oven. Cut crust into small pieces with sharp knife, mixing pieces into fruit mixture.

4 Bake about 30 minutes longer or until apples are tender and pieces of crust are golden. Serve warm with whipping cream.

Pastry

1 1/4 cups Gold Medal all-purpose flour

1/4 teaspoon salt

1/3 cup shortening

3 to 4 tablespoons milk

In medium bowl, mix flour and salt. Cut in shortening, using pastry blender (or pulling 2 table knives through ingredients in opposite directions), until particles are size of small peas. Sprinkle with milk, 1 tablespoon at a time, tossing with fork until all flour is moistened and pastry almost cleans side of bowl. Gather pastry into a ball. On lightly floured surface, shape into flattened round. Roll into shape to fit top of casserole. Cut slits near center.

BAKING FOR TODAY

Apples and blackberries make a wonderful fruit combination, but if you'd rather use all apples, peel and slice 6 apples and leave out the blackberries.

Rosemary-Lemon Cake Roll

The current Betty Crocker Kitchens have their roots in the test kitchens of the Washburn Crosby Company. The kitchens were formally named the Betty Crocker Kitchens in 1946 and moved to their current location in 1958.

Prep Time: 30 min; Start to Finish: 1 hr 25 min | **10 servings**

3 eggs

1 cup granulated sugar

1/3 cup water

3/4 cup Gold Medal all-purpose flour

1 teaspoon baking powder

1/4 teaspoon salt

2 1/4 teaspoons chopped fresh or 3/4 teaspoon dried rosemary leaves, crumbled

1 teaspoon grated lemon peel

3 tablespoons powdered sugar

Lemon Cream Filling (below)

1 Heat oven to 375°F. Line 15 x 10 x 1-inch pan with foil; generously grease foil with shortening or spray with cooking spray.

2 In large bowl, beat eggs with electric mixer on high speed about 5 minutes or until thick and lemon colored. Gradually beat in granulated sugar. Beat in water on low speed. Gradually beat in flour, baking powder and salt until smooth. Fold in rosemary and lemon peel. Pour into pan; spread evenly to corners.

3 Bake 12 to 15 minutes or until toothpick inserted in center comes out clean. Immediately loosen cake from edges of pan and turn upside down onto towel generously sprinkled with 2 tablespoons of the powdered sugar. Carefully remove foil. Trim off stiff edges of cake if necessary. While cake is hot, carefully roll cake and towel from narrow end. Cool on wire rack at least 40 minutes. Meanwhile, make Lemon Cream Filling.

4 Unroll cake and remove towel. Spread filling over cake; roll up cake. Sprinkle with remaining 1 tablespoon powdered sugar. Store covered in refrigerator.

Lemon Cream Filling

1 cup whipping (heavy) cream

2 tablespoons powdered sugar

1 teaspoon grated lemon peel

In chilled small bowl, beat whipping cream and powdered sugar with electric mixer on high speed until stiff. Stir in lemon peel.

Old-Fashioned Jelly Roll: Omit lemon peel and rosemary. Bake cake, remove from pan and roll up as directed. Beat 2/3 cup jelly or jam with fork. Unroll cake and spread jelly over cake. Roll up and sprinkle with powdered sugar.

High Altitude (3500 to 6500 feet): No changes.

1 Serving: Calories 220 (Calories from Fat 80); Fat 9g (Saturated 5g); Cholesterol 90mg; Sodium 135mg; Carbohydrate 32g (Dietary Fiber 0g); Protein 3g **Exchanges:** 1 Starch, 1 Other Carbohydrates, 2 Fat **Carbohydrate Choices:** 2

BAKING FOR TODAY

A member of the mint family, the herb rosemary, with its hint of lemon and pine, adds a wonderful note to the lemon flavor in this cake.

Heavenly Chocolate Soufflé Cake

Prep Time: 30 min; Start to Finish: 1 hr 20 min   12 servings

1 2/3 cups semisweet
chocolate chunks

1/2 cup butter or margarine

1/2 cup Gold Medal
all-purpose flour

4 eggs, separated

1/4 teaspoon cream of tartar

1/2 cup sugar

Sweetened Whipped Cream
(below)

Chocolate Sauce (below)

1 Heat oven to 325°F. Grease bottom and side of 9-inch springform pan with shortening or spray with cooking spray. In 2-quart heavy saucepan, melt 1 cup of the chocolate chunks and the butter over medium heat, stirring occasionally. Cool 5 minutes. Stir in flour until smooth. Stir in egg yolks until well blended.

2 In large bowl, beat egg whites and cream of tartar with electric mixer on high speed until foamy. Beat in sugar, 1 tablespoon at a time, until soft peaks form. Fold about one-fourth of the egg whites into chocolate mixture; fold chocolate mixture into egg whites. Spread in pan. Sprinkle remaining 2/3 cup chocolate chunks evenly over top.

3 Bake 35 to 40 minutes or until toothpick inserted in center comes out clean (top will appear dry and cracked). Cool 10 minutes. Remove side of pan; leave cake on pan bottom. Cool completely on wire rack.

4 Place cake on serving plate. Make Sweetened Whipped Cream. Just before serving, make Chocolate Sauce. Top servings of cake with whipped cream; drizzle with sauce.

Sweetened Whipped Cream

1 cup whipping (heavy) cream   2 tablespoons powdered sugar
1/2 teaspoon vanilla

In chilled small bowl, beat all ingredients with electric mixer on high speed until soft peaks form.

Chocolate Sauce

1/3 cup semisweet chocolate chunks   1/4 cup evaporated fat-free milk
3 tablespoons sugar   1/2 teaspoon butter or margarine

In 1-quart saucepan, heat chocolate chunks, sugar and milk over medium heat, stirring constantly, until chocolate is melted and mixture boils. Remove from heat; stir in butter.

High Altitude (3500 to 6500 feet): No changes.

1 Serving: Calories 380 (Calories from Fat 215); Fat 24g (Saturated 14g); Cholesterol 115mg; Sodium 90mg; Carbohydrate 36g (Dietary Fiber 2g); Protein 5g
Exchanges: 1 1/2 Starch, 1 Other Carbohydrates, 4 1/2 Fat
Carbohydrate Choices: 2 1/2

BAKING FOR TODAY

A soufflé is a light, airy mixture that begins with an egg yolk–based sauce lightened by stiffly beaten egg whites. It's natural for this cake to have a characteristic "fallen" or cracked top, giving it a homemade look. This is an excellent dessert to serve during the holidays; sprinkle crushed peppermint candy over the chocolate sauce.

HEAVENLY CHOCOLATE SOUFFLÉ CAKE

Fudge Tart

4 oz bittersweet baking
chocolate, chopped

1/3 cup butter or margarine

1 cup sugar

3/4 cup Gold Medal
all-purpose flour

3 eggs, beaten

Chocolate Glaze (below)

White Chocolate Drizzle
(below)

1 Heat oven to 350°F. Grease 9 x 1-inch tart pan with removable bottom with shortening or spray with cooking spray. Wrap outside bottom and side of pan with foil to prevent leaking. In 1-quart saucepan, melt chocolate and butter over low heat, stirring frequently; cool slightly.

2 In large bowl, mix sugar, flour and eggs with spoon until well blended. Stir in chocolate mixture. Pour into pan. Bake 30 to 35 minutes or until edges are set. Cool completely on wire rack, about 1 hour.

3 Make Chocolate Glaze; spread warm glaze over tart. Make White Chocolate Drizzle; drizzle over warm glaze. Let stand until glaze is set. Remove foil and side of pan before serving.

Chocolate Glaze

1 oz unsweetened baking chocolate

1 teaspoon butter or margarine

1 cup powdered sugar

2 to 3 tablespoons boiling water

In 1-quart saucepan, melt chocolate and butter in 1-quart saucepan over low heat, stirring constantly. Remove from heat. Stir in powdered sugar and 2 tablespoons water until smooth. Stir in additional boiling water, 1/2 teaspoon at a time, until spreadable.

White Chocolate Drizzle

1 oz white baking bar (white chocolate)
(from 6-oz package), chopped

1/2 teaspoon vegetable oil

In small microwavable bowl, microwave white baking bar and oil on Medium (50%) 20 seconds; stir. Microwave 10 to 20 seconds longer if necessary to melt baking bar.

High Altitude (3500 to 6500
feet): No changes.

1 Serving: Calories 340 (Calories
from Fat 125); Fat 14g (Saturated
8g); Cholesterol 80mg; Sodium
65mg; Carbohydrate 49g (Dietary
Fiber 1g); Protein 4g
Exchanges: 1 Starch, 2 Other
Carbohydrates, 3 Fat
Carbohydrate Choices: 3

BAKING FOR TODAY

Chocolate lovers, beware! This has a triple dose of your favorite—bittersweet, unsweetened and white chocolates. This terrific treat, similar to a classic recipe, shows that no food is ever really new—it's either a twist on an old favorite, a new ingredient or perhaps just goes by a different name.

Lemon Tart

Classic

In 1955, General Mills began the Betty Crocker Search for the All-American Homemaker of Tomorrow. When the program ended in 1977, more than 9.5 million high school seniors had taken part, and General Mills had awarded more than $2.1 million in student scholarships. This is a popular recipe for Life Skills or Home Economics classes as it has several very useful teaching components, such as separating eggs, baking a crust and making a filling.

Prep Time: 30 min; Start to Finish: 2 hr 30 min
8 servings

Tart Crust (page 210)
1/2 cup lemon juice
2/3 cup granulated sugar
1/2 cup butter or margarine
2 tablespoons milk
5 egg yolks
3 whole eggs
1 tablespoon finely grated lemon peel
2 tablespoons powdered sugar

1 Heat oven to 400°F. Make Tart Crust; bake as directed.

2 Reduce oven temperature to 350°F. In 2-quart saucepan, heat lemon juice and granulated sugar over medium heat, stirring occasionally, until sugar is dissolved. Cut butter into pieces; stir butter into sugar mixture until melted. Stir in milk.

3 In medium bowl, mix egg yolks and whole eggs. Gradually stir a small amount of the hot mixture into eggs, then stir back into hot mixture in saucepan. Cook over medium heat about 6 minutes, stirring constantly, until slightly thickened and mixture coats a spoon. Stir in lemon peel. Pour mixture into baked crust. Place tart on cookie sheet.

4 Bake 15 to 20 minutes or until just set. Cool completely, about 1 hour 30 minutes. Sprinkle powdered sugar around edge. Store covered in refrigerator.

BAKING FOR TODAY

For a simple yet beautiful look, top this luscious lemon tart with a few fresh raspberries and curls of lemon peel.

High Altitude (3500 to 6500 feet): Bake Tart Crust 18 to 23 minutes. Bake filled tart 20 to 25 minutes.

1 Serving: Calories 475 (Calories from Fat 325); Fat 36g (Saturated 14g); Cholesterol 245mg; Sodium 400mg; Carbohydrate 32g (Dietary Fiber 1g); Protein 6g **Exchanges:** 2 Starch, 7 Fat **Carbohydrate Choices:** 2

Tiramisu Bars

Prep Time: 40 min; Start to Finish: 2 hr 40 min

24 bars

3/4 cup Gold Medal all-purpose flour

1/2 cup butter or margarine, softened

1/4 cup powdered sugar

3 oz semisweet baking chocolate, grated (about 1 1/4 cups)

1 cup granulated sugar

3/4 cup whipping (heavy) cream

1/4 cup butter or margarine, melted

3 tablespoons Gold Medal all-purpose flour

1 tablespoon instant coffee (dry)

1/2 teaspoon vanilla

2 eggs

1 package (3 oz) cream cheese, softened

1/4 cup whipping (heavy) cream

1 Heat oven to 350°F. In medium bowl, beat 3/4 cup flour, 1/2 cup softened butter and the powdered sugar with electric mixer on medium speed until soft dough forms. On bottom of ungreased 8-inch square pan, spread dough evenly. Bake 10 minutes. Sprinkle 1 cup of the grated chocolate over hot baked crust.

2 In medium bowl, beat granulated sugar, 3/4 cup whipping cream, 1/4 cup melted butter, 3 tablespoons flour, the coffee, vanilla and eggs with wire whisk until smooth. Pour over chocolate in pan.

3 Bake 40 to 45 minutes or until golden brown and set. Cool completely in pan on wire rack, about 1 hour 15 minutes.

4 In medium bowl, beat cream cheese and 1/4 cup whipping cream on medium speed about 2 minutes or until fluffy. Spread over cooled bars in pan. Sprinkle with remaining 1/4 cup grated chocolate. For bars, cut into 6 rows by 4 rows. Store covered in refrigerator.

BAKING FOR TODAY

Here's a trendy, "today" dessert made into bars—or you can turn them into mini-desserts! Just cut the bars into bite-size squares, and serve in small paper candy cups to add an extra-special look to any occasion.

High Altitude (3500 to 6500 feet): In step 1, bake crust 12 minutes. In step 3, bake 45 to 50 minutes.

1 Bar: Calories 180 (Calories from Fat 110); Fat 12g (Saturated 7g); Cholesterol 50mg; Sodium 60mg; Carbohydrate 16g (Dietary Fiber 0g); Protein 2g
Exchanges: 1 Starch, 2 Fat
Carbohydrate Choices: 1

TIRAMISU BARS

White Chocolate Mousse–Raspberry Pie

Prep Time: 50 min; Start to Finish: 2 hr 30 min   8 servings

Pastry for 9-Inch One-Crust Pie (page 197) or Easy-Roll Buttermilk Pastry (page 204)

1 teaspoon unflavored gelatin

2 tablespoons orange-flavored liqueur or orange juice

1 1/2 cups whipping (heavy) cream

3 oz white baking bars (white chocolate) (from 6-oz package), chopped

1 pint (2 cups) fresh raspberries

1/4 cup currant jelly

1 Heat oven to 475°F. Make pastry. On lightly floured surface, roll pastry into circle 2 inches larger than upside-down 9-inch glass pie plate with floured rolling pin. Fold pastry into fourths; place in pie plate. Unfold and ease into plate, pressing firmly against bottom and side. Trim overhanging edge of pastry 1 inch from rim of plate. Fold and roll pastry under, even with plate; press with tines of fork or flute if desired. Prick bottom and side of pastry thoroughly with fork. Bake 8 to 10 minutes or until light brown. Cool completely, about 30 minutes.

2 Meanwhile, in 2-quart saucepan, sprinkle gelatin over orange liqueur; let stand 5 minutes to soften. Stir in 3/4 cup of the whipping cream. Heat over low heat, stirring frequently, until gelatin is dissolved. Stir in white chocolate until melted and smooth. Transfer to medium bowl; refrigerate about 30 minutes, stirring occasionally, until cool but not set.

3 In chilled medium bowl, beat remaining 3/4 cup whipping cream with electric mixer on high speed until stiff peaks form. Fold whipped cream into white chocolate mixture. Spoon mixture into baked crust. Refrigerate about 1 hour or until filling begins to set. Arrange raspberries over filling.

4 In small microwavable bowl, microwave currant jelly uncovered on High about 30 seconds or until melted. Brush jelly over raspberries. Refrigerate until serving.

BAKING FOR TODAY

Try this delightful pie with other seasonal berries, such as blueberries, strawberries or blackberries, or a combination of all for a mixed-berry treat.

High Altitude (3500 to 6500 feet): Bake pastry 9 to 11 minutes.

1 Serving: Calories 390 (Calories from Fat 250); Fat 28g (Saturated 13g); Cholesterol 52mg; Sodium 180mg; Carbohydrate 31g (Dietary Fiber 3g); Protein 4g
Exchanges: 1 Starch, 1 Fruit, 5 1/2 Fat
Carbohydrate Choices: 2

WHITE CHOCOLATE MOUSSE-RASPBERRY PIE

Apple Crostata with Caramel Topping

Prep Time: 40 min; **Start to Finish:** 1 hr 20 min   **8 servings**

Crostata Crust (below)

1/4 cup sugar

3 tablespoons Gold Medal
all-purpose flour

4 medium apples, peeled and
thinly sliced (4 cups)

1 tablespoon sugar

1/2 teaspoon ground cinnamon

1/2 cup caramel topping

1 Make Crostata Crust.

2 Heat oven to 400°F. In large bowl, mix 1/4 cup sugar and the flour. Stir in apples. Mound apple mixture on center of dough circle to within 2 inches of edge. Fold edge of dough over apple mixture; crimp edge of dough slightly. In small bowl, mix 1 tablespoon sugar and the cinnamon; sprinkle over apples and dough.

3 Bake 27 to 32 minutes or until crust is golden brown. Cut into wedges. Serve warm drizzled with caramel topping.

Crostata Crust

1 1/4 cups Gold Medal all-purpose flour

2 tablespoons sugar

1/4 teaspoon salt

1/2 cup firm butter or margarine, cut into 1/2-inch pieces

1/4 teaspoon vanilla

3 tablespoons cold water

In medium bowl, mix flour, sugar and salt. Cut in butter, using pastry blender (or pulling 2 table knives through ingredients in opposite directions), until particles are size of small peas. Mix vanilla and water; sprinkle over flour mixture, 1 tablespoon at a time, tossing with fork until all flour is moistened and dough almost cleans side of bowl (up to 1 tablespoon more water can be added if necessary). Gather dough into a ball; shape into flattened 5-inch round. Wrap in plastic wrap and refrigerate about 30 minutes or until firm. On lightly floured surface, roll pastry into 12-inch circle. Place on ungreased large cookie sheet.

High Altitude (3500 to 6500 feet): Bake 30 to 35 minutes.

1 Serving: Calories 325 (Calories from Fat 110); Fat 12g (Saturated 7g); Cholesterol 30mg; Sodium 220mg; Carbohydrate 51g (Dietary Fiber 2g); Protein 3g **Exchanges:** 1 Starch, 1 Fruit, 1 1/2 Other Carbohydrates, 2 Fat **Carbohydrate Choices:** 3 1/2

BAKING FOR TODAY

An updated version of the classic apple pie, this recipe combines two favorite flavors, caramel and apple. Instead of drizzling the caramel sauce over the top, why not serve the crostata on plates drizzled with caramel sauce for a show-stopping dessert?

APPLE CROSTATA WITH CARAMEL TOPPING

The Power of Flour

It all started when Cadwallader C. Washburn and John Crosby won the Gold Medal for the Most Superlative Flour at the Millers Exhibition in 1880. In recognition of that award, they named their flour "Gold Medal." Today, 125 years later, the flour that won the gold medal continues to thrive. A look back at the history of milling reveals that the strong roots of Gold Medal flour, General Mills, Betty Crocker and the Betty Crocker Kitchens run deep and are as interwoven as the streams of water from the waterfalls upon which they were founded:

- **1866:** C.C. Washburn built his first flour mill on the Mississippi River at St. Anthony Falls in Minneapolis, Minnesota.

- **1877:** Washburn, Crosby and Company, the largest predecessor of General Mills, was formed.

- **1880:** The flour milling industry had grown in Minneapolis, called the Mill City. It was perfect for milling because of its waterfalls and the wheat fields of the Midwest nearby, as well as the railroads that were connecting markets from coast to coast. That same year, Washburn Crosby received the esteemed Gold Medal award, and another first, they published *Miss Parloa's Cook Book*. A number of recipes from that cookbook, such as Pound Cake, Jumbles and Gingerbread, are still favorites today.

- **1903:** The first *Gold Medal Cook Book* was printed to help consumers bake their favorite flour recipes.

- **1905:** Flour was first packed in large, hand-sewn cloth bags.

Before this time, it had been packed in 196-pound wooden barrels.

- **1907:** The very successful flour advertising campaign "Eventually—Why Not Now?" was developed and used until the mid-1950s.

- **1915:** Because of World War I, flour was packed in paper bags for the first time as fabric was so scarce. The tying machine was invented to automatically close and tie the paper bags with twine. Flour has remained in paper ever since!

- **1921:** The name Betty Crocker was created to answer consumers' many baking questions and recipe requests. *Betty* was selected because it was a warm, friendly sounding name, and *Crocker* was chosen to honor a popular former director of the company, William G. Crocker. The company also sponsored cooking schools throughout the country and hired its first home economist to carefully test flour recipes for high-quality and consistent results.

- **1923:** In just two years, the consumer demand for baking information, along with the popularity of Betty Crocker, made it necessary to increase the staff of home economists to twenty-one, and the Betty Crocker Kitchens were born.

- **1924:** The Betty Crocker "Cooking School of the Air" was first produced on WCCO radio station in Minneapolis, Minnesota. The station was named for its new owner, the Washburn Crosby Company.

- **1925:** Home economists tested flour in typical baked products and confirmed its quality before it was shipped to grocers. "Kitchen-tested" was first used on Gold Medal flour packages.

- **1928:** General Mills was formed. The new company was composed of several flour mills.

- **1941:** Due to government regulation, flour was enriched to bring the B vitamin content up to the level of the whole wheat grain. Calcium and iron were also added.

- **1943:** Gold Medal flour introduced the one-bowl cake method, which cut mixing time in half and streamlined the cake-baking process.

- **1948:** General Mills created chiffon cake. The cake was described as being "light as angel food, rich as butter cake and easy to make." The mystery ingredient was salad, or cooking, oil.

- **1961:** No-sift flour was introduced. General Mills conducted extensive research to determine how consumers measured flour. It was determined that sifting was not required and more consistent results could be achieved by dipping the measuring cup into the flour and leveling it off.

- **1963:** Wondra quick-mixing flour was developed, a revolutionary new granular form of flour that was particularly useful in making lump-free sauces and gravies because it mixed instantly in cool liquids.

- **1972:** Gold Medal unbleached and whole wheat flours made their way onto grocery store shelves.

- **1980:** Gold Medal turned 100 years old and celebrated by publishing the *Century of Success Cookbook*. The cookbook was a collection of the best Gold Medal recipes of 100 years.

- **1989:** The "spoon and level off" method of measuring flour was introduced. After twenty years of recommending the "dip and level off" method, spooning flour into the measuring cup and leveling it off was found to ensure more accurate measuring by not packing too much flour in the measuring cup.

- **1999:** Gold Medal flour was first packed in resealable plastic bags, in addition to the paper flour bags.

- **2003:** The Mill City Museum in Minneapolis, Minnesota, opened, introducing the history of wheat and flour milling to the world.

- **2005:** The 125th anniversary of Gold Medal flour is proudly celebrated with the publishing of this *Baking for Today* cookbook.

Helpful Nutrition and Cooking Information

Nutrition Guidelines

We provide nutrition information for each recipe that includes calories, fat, cholesterol, sodium, carbohydrate, fiber and protein. Individual food choices can be based on this information.

Recommended intake for a daily diet of 2,000 calories as set by the Food and Drug Administration

Total Fat	Less than 65g
Saturated Fat	Less than 20g
Cholesterol	Less than 300mg
Sodium	Less than 2,400mg
Total Carbohydrate	300g
Dietary Fiber	25g

Criteria Used for Calculating Nutrition Information

- The first ingredient was used wherever a choice is given (such as 1/3 cup sour cream or plain yogurt).
- The first ingredient amount was used wherever a range is given (such as 3- to 3 1/2-pound cut-up broiler-fryer chicken).
- The first serving number was used wherever a range is given (such as 4 to 6 servings).
- "If desired" ingredients and recipe variations were not included (such as sprinkle with brown sugar, if desired).
- Only the amount of a marinade or frying oil that is estimated to be absorbed by the food during preparation or cooking was calculated.

Ingredients Used in Recipe Testing and Nutrition Calculations

- Ingredients used for testing represent those that the majority of consumers use in their homes: large eggs, 2 percent milk, 80 percent–lean ground beef, canned ready-to-use chicken broth and vegetable oil spread containing not less than 65 percent fat.
- Fat-free, low-fat or low-sodium products were not used, unless otherwise indicated.
- Solid vegetable shortening (not butter, margarine, nonstick cooking sprays or vegetable oil spread as they can cause sticking problems) was used to grease pans, unless otherwise indicated.

Equipment Used in Recipe Testing

We use equipmesnt for testing that the majority of consumers use in their homes. If a specific piece of equipment (such as a wire whisk) is necessary for recipe success, it is listed in the recipe.

- Cookware and bakeware without nonstick coatings were used, unless otherwise indicated.
- No dark-colored, black or insulated bakeware was used.
- When a pan is specified in a recipe, a metal pan was used; a baking dish or pie plate means ovenproof glass was used.
- An electric hand mixer was used for mixing only when mixer speeds are specified in the recipe directions. When a mixer speed is not given, a spoon or fork was used.

Cooking Terms Glossary

BEAT: Mix ingredients vigorously with spoon, fork, wire whisk, hand beater or electric mixer until smooth and uniform.

BOIL: Heat liquid until bubbles rise continuously and break on the surface and steam is given off. For rolling boil, the bubbles form rapidly.

CHOP: Cut into coarse or fine irregular pieces with a knife, food chopper, blender or food processor.

CUBE: Cut into squares 1/2 inch or larger.

DICE: Cut into squares smaller than 1/2 inch.

GRATE: Cut into tiny particles using small rough holes of grater (citrus peel or chocolate).

GREASE: Rub the inside surface of a pan with shortening, using pastry brush, piece of waxed paper or paper towel, to prevent food from sticking during baking (as for some casseroles).

JULIENNE: Cut into thin, matchlike strips, using knife or food processor (vegetables, fruits, meats).

MIX: Combine ingredients in any way that distributes them evenly.

SAUTÉ: Cook foods in hot oil or margarine over medium-high heat with frequent tossing and turning motion.

SHRED: Cut into long thin pieces by rubbing food across the holes of a shredder, as for cheese, or by using a knife to slice very thinly, as for cabbage.

SIMMER: Cook in liquid just below the boiling point on top of the stove; usually after reducing heat from a boil. Bubbles will rise slowly and break just below the surface.

STIR: Mix ingredients until uniform consistency. Stir once in a while for stirring occasionally, often for stirring frequently and continuously for stirring constantly.

TOSS: Tumble ingredients (such as green salad) lightly with a lifting motion, usually to coat evenly or mix with another food.

Metric Conversion Guide

Volume

U.S. Units	Canadian Metric	Australian Metric
1/4 teaspoon	1 mL	1 ml
1/2 teaspoon	2 mL	2 ml
1 teaspoon	5 mL	5 ml
1 tablespoon	15 mL	20 ml
1/4 cup	50 mL	60 ml
1/3 cup	75 mL	80 ml
1/2 cup	125 mL	125 ml
2/3 cup	150 mL	170 ml
3/4 cup	175 mL	190 ml
1 cup	250 mL	250 ml
1 quart	1 liter	1 liter
1 1/2 quarts	1.5 liters	1.5 liters
2 quarts	2 liters	2 liters
2 1/2 quarts	2.5 liters	2.5 liters
3 quarts	3 liters	3 liters
4 quarts	4 liters	4 liters

Weight

U.S. Units	Canadian Metric	Australian Metric
1 ounce	30 grams	30 grams
2 ounces	55 grams	60 grams
3 ounces	85 grams	90 grams
4 ounces (1/4 pound)	115 grams	125 grams
8 ounces (1/2 pound)	225 grams	225 grams
16 ounces (1 pound)	455 grams	500 grams
1 pound	455 grams	1/2 kilogram

Measurements

Inches	Centimeters
1	2.5
2	5.0
3	7.5
4	10.0
5	12.5
6	15.0
7	17.5
8	20.5
9	23.0
10	25.5
11	28.0
12	30.5
13	33.0

Temperatures

Fahrenheit	Celsius
32°	0°
212°	100°
250°	120°
275°	140°
300°	150°
325°	160°
350°	180°
375°	190°
400°	200°
425°	220°
450°	230°
475°	240°
500°	260°

Note: The recipes in this cookbook have not been developed or tested using metric measures. When converting recipes to metric, some variations in quality may be noted.

Index

Note: *Italicized* page references indicate photographs.

COMPLETE YOUR COOKBOOK LIBRARY
WITH THESE *Betty Crocker* TITLES

Betty Crocker's Best Bread Machine Cookbook
Betty Crocker's Best Chicken Cookbook
Betty Crocker's Best Christmas Cookbook
Betty Crocker's Best of Baking
Betty Crocker's Best of Healthy and Hearty Cooking
Betty Crocker's Best-Loved Recipes
Betty Crocker's Bisquick® Cookbook
Betty Crocker Bisquick® II Cookbook
Betty Crocker Bisquick® Impossibly Easy Pies
Betty Crocker Celebrate!
Betty Crocker's Complete Thanksgiving Cookbook
Betty Crocker's Cook Book for Boys and Girls
Betty Crocker's Cook It Quick
Betty Crocker's Cookbook, 9th Edition— *The* **BIG RED** *Cookbook* ®
Betty Crocker's Cookbook, Bridal Edition
Betty Crocker's Cookie Book
Betty Crocker's Cooking Basics
Betty Crocker's Cooking for Two
Betty Crocker's Cooky Book, Facsimile Edition
Betty Crocker's Diabetes Cookbook
Betty Crocker Dinner Made Easy with Rotisserie Chicken
Betty Crocker Easy Family Dinners
Betty Crocker's Easy Slow Cooker Dinners
Betty Crocker's Eat and Lose Weight
Betty Crocker's Entertaining Basics
Betty Crocker's Flavors of Home
Betty Crocker 4-Ingredient Dinners
Betty Crocker Grilling Made Easy
Betty Crocker Healthy Heart Cookbook
Betty Crocker's Healthy New Choices
Betty Crocker's Indian Home Cooking
Betty Crocker's Italian Cooking
Betty Crocker's Kids Cook!
Betty Crocker's Kitchen Library
Betty Crocker's Living with Cancer Cookbook
Betty Crocker's Low-Fat, Low-Cholesterol Cooking Today
Betty Crocker More Slow Cooker Recipes
Betty Crocker's New Cake Decorating
Betty Crocker's New Chinese Cookbook
Betty Crocker One-Dish Meals
Betty Crocker's A Passion for Pasta
Betty Crocker's Pasta Favorites
Betty Crocker's Picture Cook Book, Facsimile Edition
Betty Crocker's Quick & Easy Cookbook
Betty Crocker's Slow Cooker Cookbook
Betty Crocker's Ultimate Cake Mix Cookbook
Betty Crocker's Vegetarian Cooking

Share the Fun!

Two Great Cookbooks For You And Your Child.

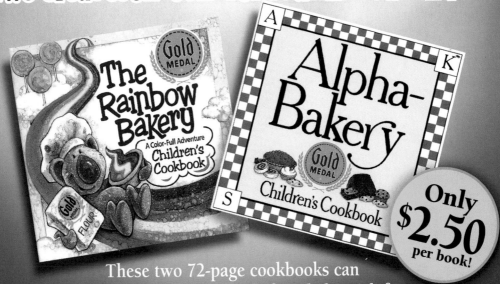

Only $2.50 per book!

These two 72-page cookbooks can
help you teach your little chefs to bake with fun,
easy-to-follow recipes and activities that you can do together!
• Give them as a birthday or holiday gift • Send a copy to school for your child's teacher
• Hand them out as party favors

A55501

Look for the order form in the coupon insert section of this book.

DECORATING TIPS FROM

Gold MEDAL

- Create a custom cake perfect for special occasions. Top with Betty Crocker® Confetti that comes in many different shapes and colors.

- Sprinkle tops of cupcakes with Betty Crocker Colored Sugar, Nonpareils or Sprinkles to create a colorful look, good enough to eat.

- Use Betty Crocker Easy Flow Icing in a can to decorate just like the pros. Use the different tips to make rosettes, decorative borders and flowers on cupcakes or cakes.

- Place drops of Betty Crocker Gels over top of cake. Pull fork or toothpick through gels to make designs that will leave them wondering how you did it.

- To give a special look to your cookies, marble frosting with Betty Crocker Gels. Squeeze gels onto frosted cookies, then swirl the colors using a toothpick to create a marbled effect.